Westchester County
New York's Golden Apple

Westchester County
New York's Golden Apple

By
Paul Votano

Profiles by
Caryn McBride

Featuring the Photography of
Joe Vericker

Produced in cooperation with
The County Chamber
of Commerce, Inc.

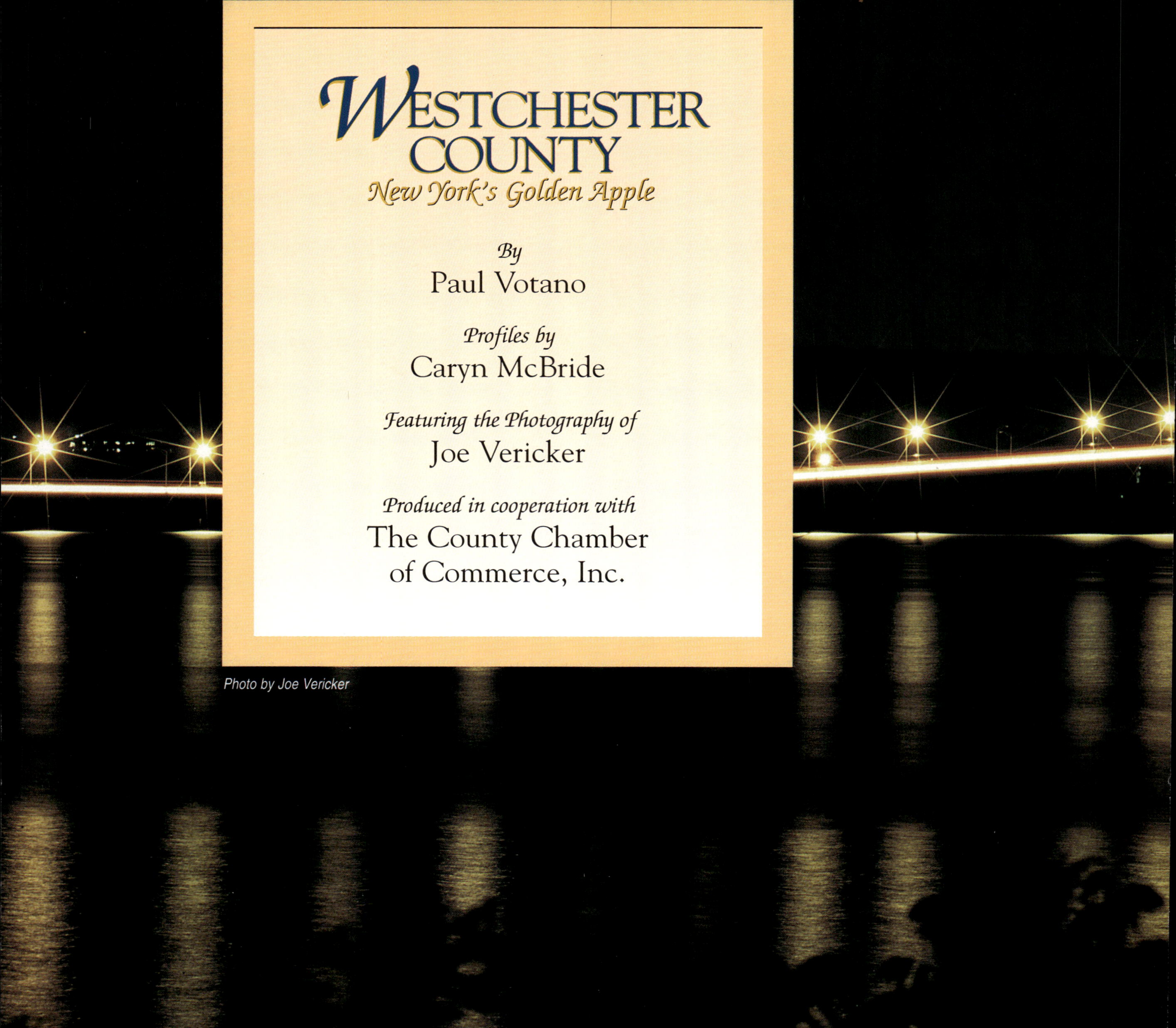

Photo by Joe Vericker

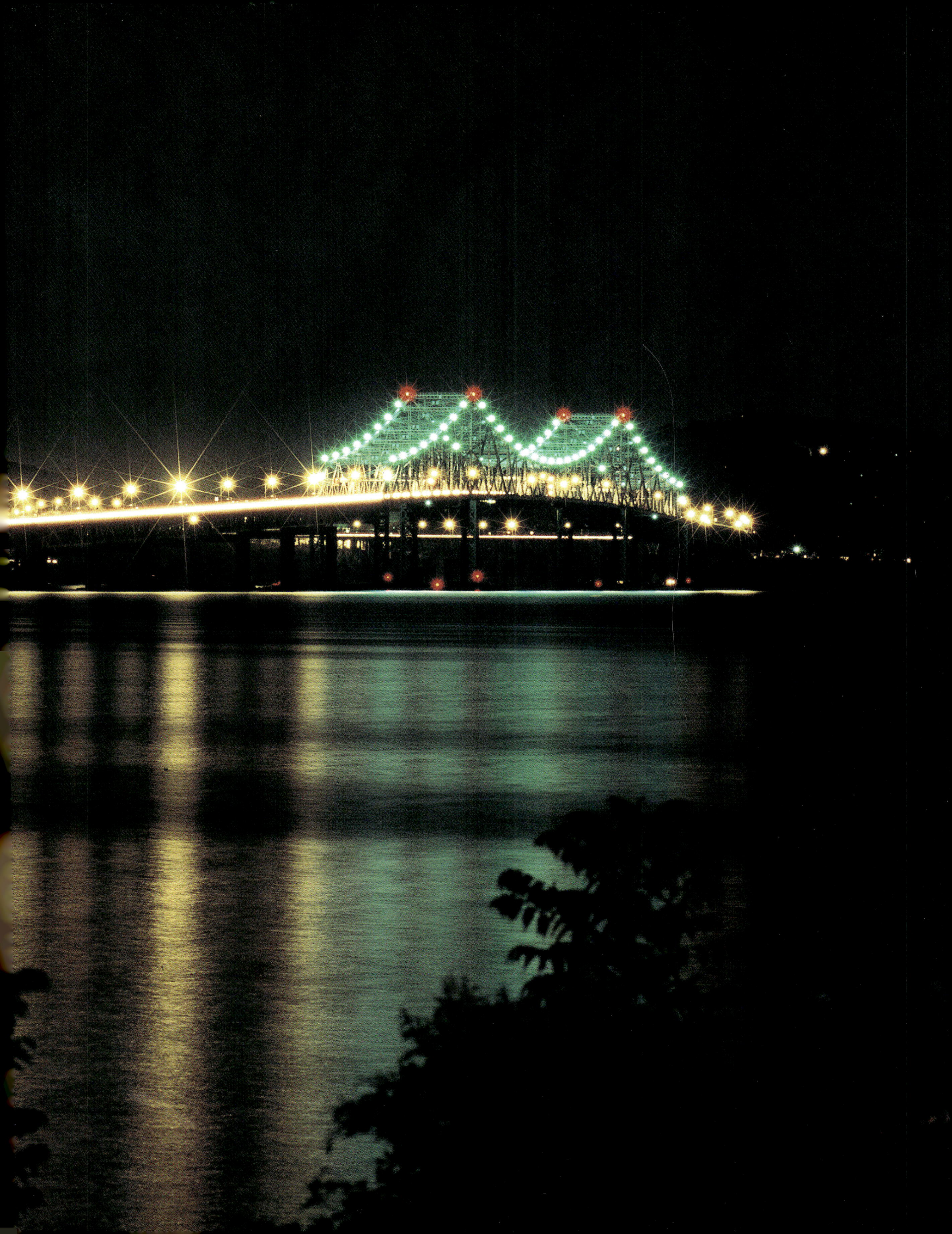

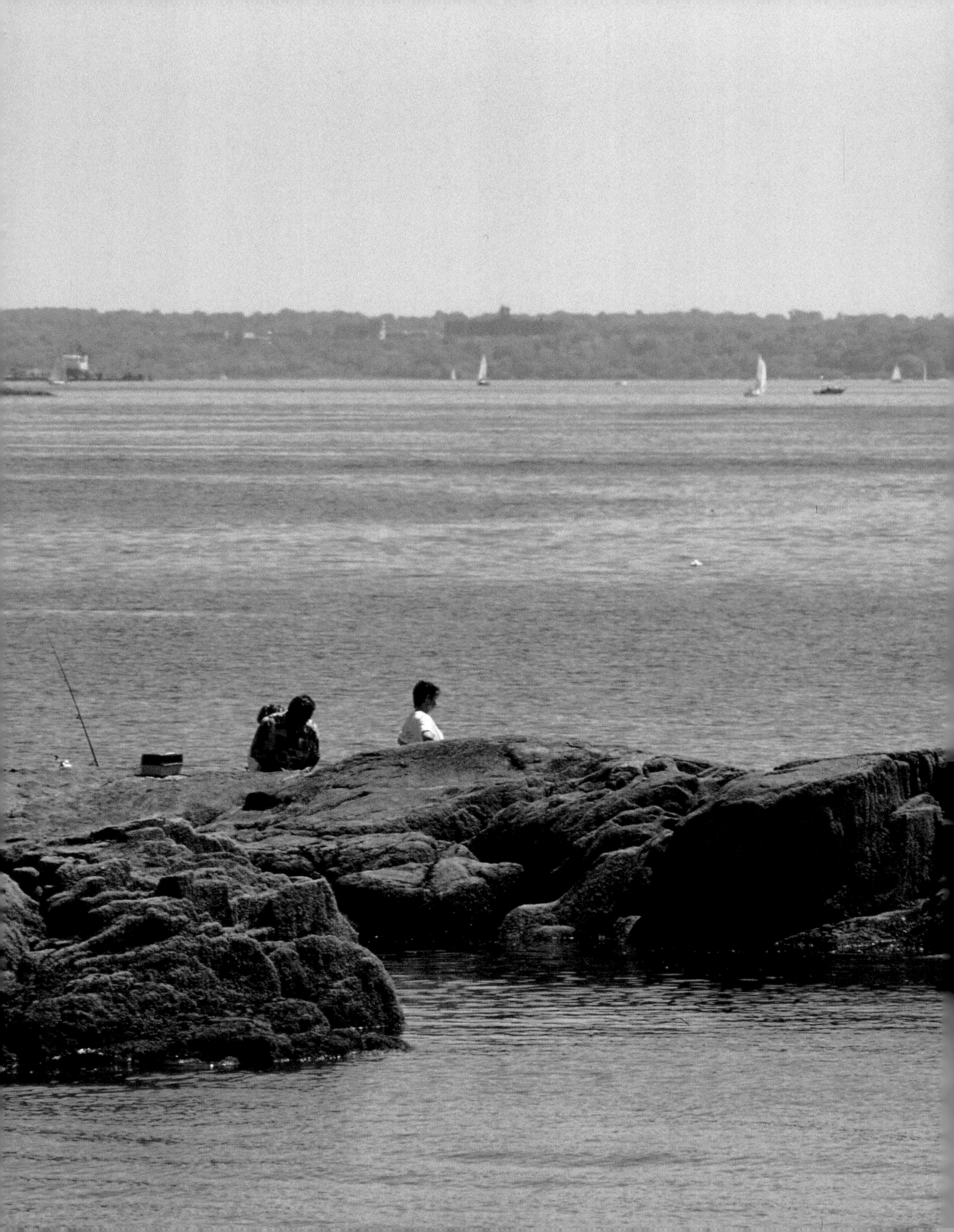

WESTCHESTER COUNTY
New York's Golden Apple

Produced in cooperation with the
The County Chamber of Commerce, Inc.
235 Mamaroneck Avenue
White Plains, New York 10605-1319
(914) 948-2110

Author
Paul Votano

Profile Writer
Caryn McBride

Contributing Profile Writer
Maralyn Steeg

Photographer
Joe Vericker

Community Communications, Inc.
Publishers:
Ronald P. Beers and James E. Turner

Staff for *Westchester County: New York's Golden Apple*
Publisher's Sales Associates:
William S. Koons, Paula T. Haider, and Lynn Ambrosiani
Executive Editor: James E. Turner
Managing Editor: Linda Moeller Pegram
Design Director: Camille Leonard
Designer: Jack Durham
Photo Editors: Linda M. Pegram and Jack Durham
Production Manager: Corrine Cau
Editorial Assistant: Katrina Williams
Sales Assistant: Annette R. Lozier
Proofreader: Wynona B. Hall
Accounting Services: Sara Ann Turner
Printing Production: Frank Rosenberg/GSAmerica

Community Communications, Inc.
Montgomery, Alabama
James E. Turner, Chairman of the Board
Ronald P. Beers, President
Daniel S. Chambliss, Vice President

©1996 Community Communications
All Rights Reserved
Published 1996
Printed in the United States of America
First Edition
Library of Congress Catalog Number: 96-37122
ISBN: 1-885352-42-5

Every effort has been made to ensure the accuracy of the information herein. However, the authors and Community Communications are not responsible for any errors or omissions which might have occurred.

Photo by Joe Vericker

Table of Contents

FOREWORD *Page 8* • PREFACE *Page 10*

Part One

CHAPTER ONE
A REGION THAT HAS IT ALL
Get acquainted with Westchester County, and learn why the county is an ideal place to live, work, or conduct business.
Page 14

CHAPTER TWO
A HISTORY STEEPED IN TRADITION
Journey through the history of Westchester from its earliest days, when Henry Hudson first sailed up the river that would eventually bear his name, through the county's growth to its current stature.
Page 22

CHAPTER THREE
WESTCHESTER MEANS BUSINESS
Discover the reasons why so many Fortune 500 companies have chosen Westchester County as their home base, as well as the factors which contribute to the success of small business here.
Page 34

CHAPTER FOUR
FOR THE GOOD TIMES
Find out how residents and visitors entertain themselves in Westchester County. Discover the county's many attractions, including historical sites, museums, theaters, hotels, restaurants, and conference centers.
Page 50

CHAPTER FIVE
EDUCATION EQUALS EXCELLENCE
Take a tour of Westchester County's public, private, and culture-based primary and secondary schools, as well as its vocational educational training. Examine the more than two dozen colleges and universities.
Page 68

CHAPTER SIX
HEALTH CARE FOR EVERYONE
Westchester County's health care resources are a source of great pride to the local citizenry. Hospitals, specialized care facilities, and growing health maintenance organizations are surveyed in this chapter.
Page 82

CHAPTER SEVEN
A FINE-TUNED TRANSPORTATION NETWORK
Highways, commuter railways, bus transport facilities, and airlines combine to make up Westchester County's efficient transportation network. Take a closer look at the new Westchester County Airport Terminal.
Page 96

CHAPTER EIGHT
AN UNPARALLELED QUALITY OF LIFE
Discover why Westchester County has earned its sterling reputation for a quality of life without equal.
Page 108

TABLE OF CONTENTS

BIBLIOGRAPHY *Page 215* • ENTERPRISES INDEX *Page 218* • INDEX *Page 219*

PART TWO

CHAPTER NINE
NETWORKS

The area's energy, communications, relocation, and transportation firms keep people, information, and power circulating inside and outside the area.

Transamerica Leasing 130; The Reader's Digest Association, Inc. 132; MTA Metro-North Railroad 134; Westchester County Business Journal 136; Gannett Suburban Newspapers 138; New York Power Authority 139; NYNEX Corporation 140; WFAS AM & FM 141; Collins Brothers Moving Corp. 142.

Page 128

CHAPTER TEN
MANUFACTURING, DISTRIBUTION & TECHNOLOGY

Producing and moving goods for individuals and industry, manufacturing, distribution, and technology firms provide employment for many Westchester County residents.

J. F. Jelenko & Company 146; Hitachi Metals America 148; International Paper 150; Philips Research Briarcliff 152; Bally, Inc. 154; IBM Corporation 156; Bayer's Business Group Diagnostics 157; Elmsford Sheet Metal Works, Inc. 158; Tetko Inc 159.

Page 144

CHAPTER ELEVEN
BUSINESS, PROFESSIONS & FINANCE

Westchester County's mix of business talents and resources strengthens the professional community.

The County Chamber of Commerce, Inc. 162; Bleakley Platt & Schmidt 164; Tarrytown House Executive Conference Center 166; Thacher Proffitt & Wood 168; MasterCard International Incorporated 169; Shamberg Marwell Hocherman Davis & Hollis, P.C. 170.

Page 160

CHAPTER TWELVE
EDUCATION & QUALITY OF LIFE

Educational institutions and recreation and leisure-oriented communities all contribute to the high quality of life in Westchester County.

Iona College 174; Mercy College 176; Heritage Hills of Westchester 178; Keio Academy of New York 180; The Ursuline School 182; Iona Preparatory School 183; The Westchester Business Institute 184; The Masters School 185; Monroe College 186.

Page 172

CHAPTER THIRTEEN
HEALTH CARE

The Westchester County area's progressive medical community is shaped by compassionate caring, keen minds, and modern facilities.

Westchester County Medical Center 190; White Plains Hospital Center 194; United Hospital Medical Center 196; Sound Shore Medical Center of Westchester 198; St. John's Riverside Hospital 200; Saint Joseph's Medical Center 200; Yonkers General Hospital 201; Northern Westchester Hospital Center 202; The Bethel Homes 204.

Page 188

CHAPTER FOURTEEN
THE MARKETPLACE

Westchester's hospitality industries vitalize the economic life of the area.

Residence Inn by Marriott 208; Doral Arrowwood 212; Rye Town Hilton 214.

Page 206

Westchester County: New York's Golden Apple / 7

Foreword

The County Chamber of Commerce, Inc., as Westchester's largest, broad-based business organization, often promotes the outstanding quality of life the county offers those who live here, work here, and make business investments in the county. Its scenic beauty, its broad range of residential, educational, and employment choices, and its many cultural, historic, and recreational opportunities make people who reside in Westchester want to stay here, and those who leave want to return.

Those of us who live and work here often take for granted the lifestyle and economic vitality our county possesses. These have truly made Westchester not only New York State's Golden Apple, but among the premier counties in the United States as well. Sometimes overlooked, too, is the fact that many of the country's major national and international corporations make Westchester their home. Their presence and corporate citizenship initiatives have enriched the social and cultural fabric of Westchester's communities while contributing significantly to the county's economic strength.

We at the County Chamber know that Westchester shines in many ways, and as an organization that represents business, the County Chamber is well aware that our business and professional community is first-rate and second to none. From the largest of the giants to the smallest of the entrepreneurs, we are proud of our business community and the contribution it makes to Westchester.

The County Chamber of Commerce, Inc. in Westchester is pleased to present this book to showcase Westchester and its many outstanding qualities. We hope it will offer those who live here a reminder of the outstanding county Westchester is, and those who live elsewhere, a portrait of a community worth visiting and considering as a place to live, work, or grow a business.

Harold E. Vogt
President and CEO
The County Chamber of Commerce, Inc.

Photo by Joe Vericker

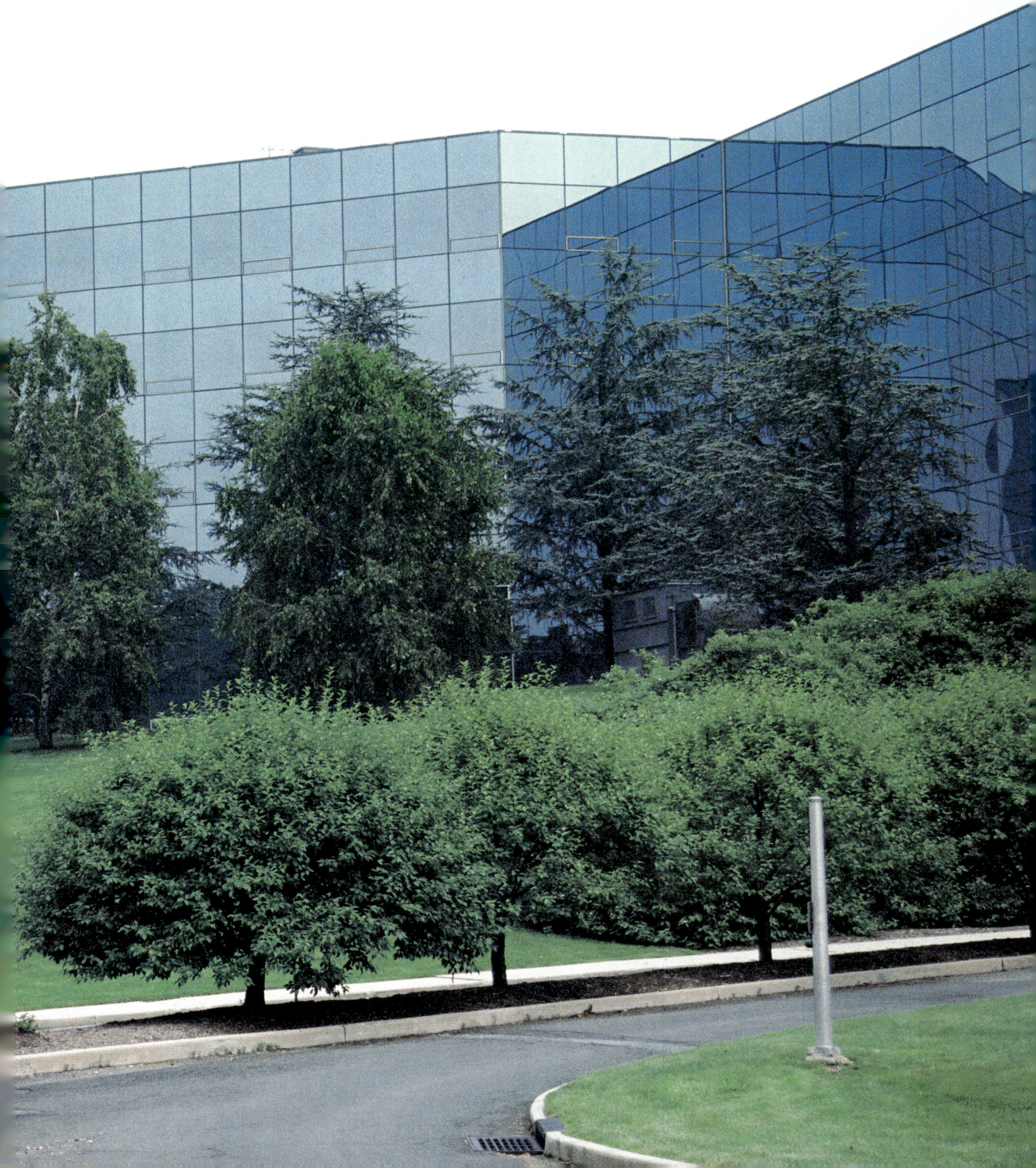

Preface

Several years ago, when for some unknown reason I began to contemplate—somewhat prematurely—where I might live after I retired, I actually considered moving to the Sun Belt. I would either make the break completely with the place where I had spent my entire life—Westchester County—or one of those "six months up here, six months down there" deals. That idea lasted about 15 minutes.

First of all, I decided I would never consider retiring from what I love to do, and that's writing. Oh, I might scale back on my schedule or be more selective on what I choose to write about, but retire? Never!

Secondly, why would I want to leave New York State's Golden Apple? It's just about the most beautiful place in the country in which to live and work, and to raise a family. I've been in 38 states in the good old USA, and while I've found some places I wouldn't mind living in, I have never found another region of this nation that I would choose over Westchester.

As you'll see in this book, Westchester County has it all. In addition to its excellent living and working conditions, it offers a variety of transportation venues from which to get wherever you're going in minutes, not to mention comfort.

Entertainment in the form of outdoor recreation, marvelous restaurants, theaters, museums, and the like truly abounds. And Westchester's proximity to the Big Apple gives it yet another dimension that few other areas can match.

The region has just the right combination of cities, towns, villages, and hamlets that sets it apart from others. It can't be labeled either rural or urban, just a wonderful blend of both in a suburban setting.

As one who has attended both public and private schools here, I can vouch for the high quality educational opportunities that are available in Westchester. And as someone who has had several serious illnesses in my life and been restored to health in the medical and rehabilitation centers here, I believe that the health care in the county is second to none.

If I sound prejudiced on the matter of Westchester County, it's because I am a true believer.

I would be remiss if I did not take this opportunity to thank Harold E. Vogt, the longtime president and chief executive officer of the County Chamber of Commerce, for inviting me to get involved in this project. It has been a labor of love.

Paul A. Votano

Entrance to The Hudson River Museum of Westchester. *Photo: Quesada/Burke.*

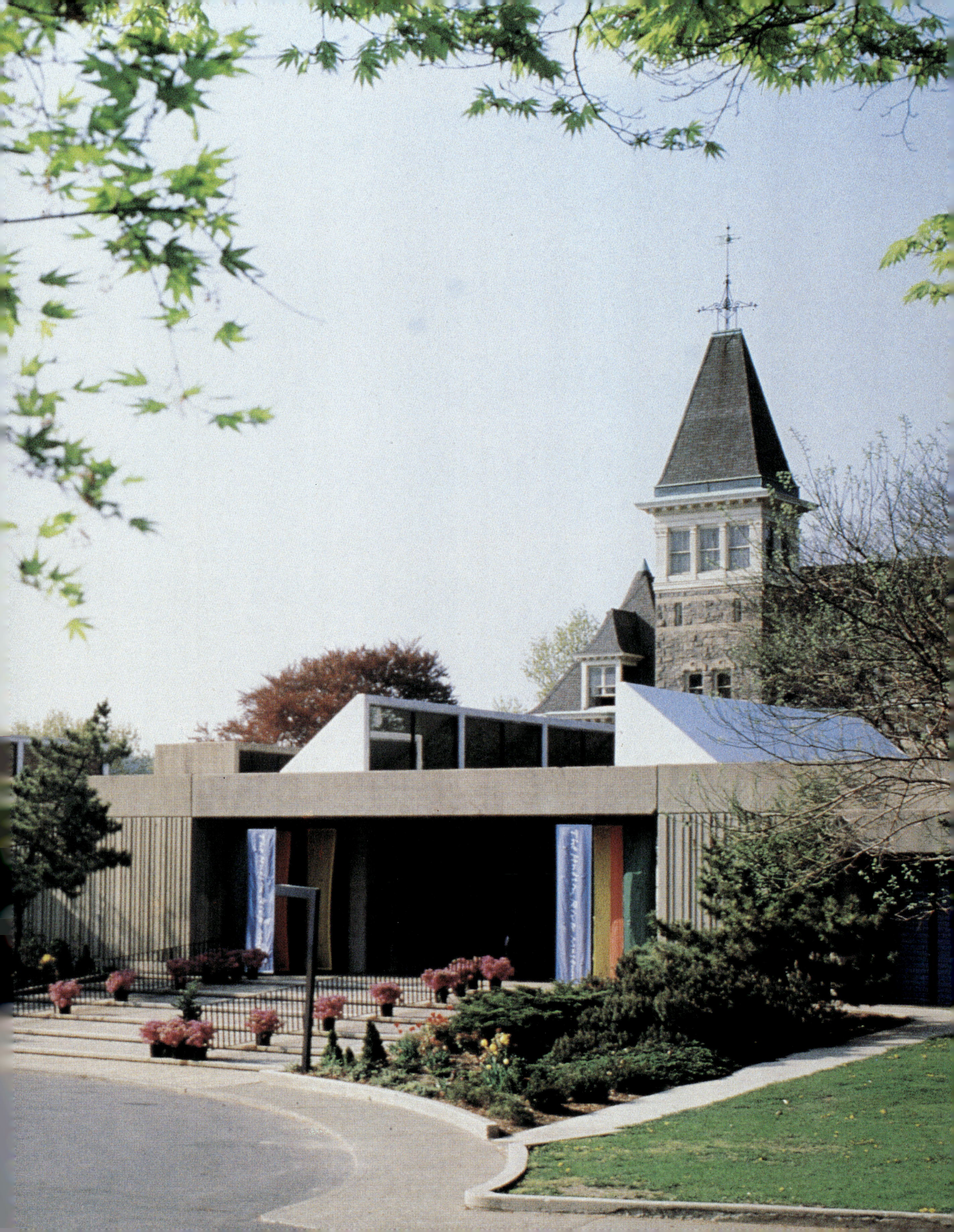

WESTCHESTER COUNTY
New York's Golden Apple

PART ONE

A view of the Hudson River and the Palisades from Kykuit, the Rockefeller House and gardens in North Tarrytown. *Photo: Ted Spiegel/courtesy of Historic Hudson Valley.*

CHAPTER • ONE

A REGION THAT HAS IT ALL

Is it any wonder that Westchester County has earned the title New York's Golden Apple considering its countless and unmatched characteristics? Starting with its ideal location and marvelous quality of life, the 450-square-mile area boasts a skilled and educated workforce to complement its thriving business community. An efficient transportation network speeds the county's traveling public from place to place, while the excellence of its educational institutions and health care industry is second to none.

Photo by Joe Vericker

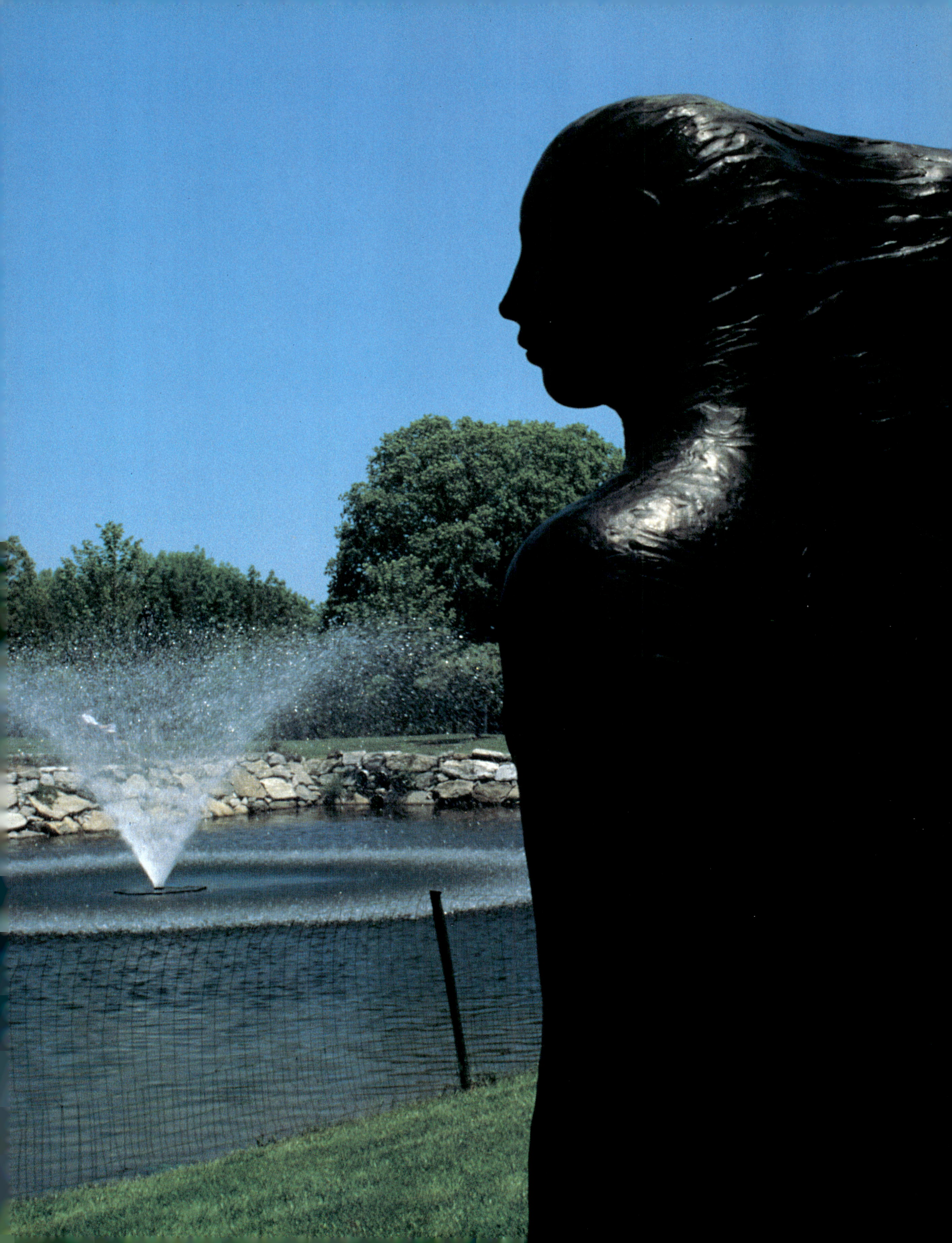

Westchester is justifiably proud of its vast array of cultural and historical sites and its first-rate hospitality facilities. The county's stable, diverse economy affords opportunities for its residents as well as anyone thinking of relocating here.

LOCATION

The area is in the unique position of being located just minutes away from Manhattan, the nation's business and financial capital. Commuters benefit from a reliable mass transit system that speeds them from home to work and back again in comfort. The county's proximity to five major national and international airports permits business travelers and shippers ready access to just about any location in the world in a matter of hours.

And Westchester's roadways provide over 3,200 miles of interstate, state, and local highways to join it with the surrounding areas. To the south of Westchester County is the borough of the Bronx. A body of water known as Long Island Sound is southeast of the county.

Bordering Westchester on the north is Putnam County, while the Hudson River to the west provides the county with access to Rockland County and northern New Jersey via the Tappan Zee Bridge. The Bear Mountain Bridge, also west of the region, leads to such scenic recreation areas as the Catskill Mountains and Bear Mountain State Park, as well as the historic United States Military Academy at West Point.

WORKFORCE

Over 450,000 people make up Westchester County's workforce. They include some of the best skilled, well-educated, and highly motivated individuals found anywhere. Many come into the county daily from New York City, New Jersey, and Connecticut, as well as other counties nearby.

Service industries, retail trade, government agencies, manufacturing, and health services are the leading employers in the county.

Apart from its urban centers, the county is dotted with woods, lakes, rivers, and grass marshlands. **Above,** A father and child enjoy a tranquil moment in Garth Woods along the Bronx River Parkway. *Photo by Joe Vericker.*

16 / Westchester County: New York's Golden Apple

A REGION THAT HAS IT ALL

With the trend in recent years away from manufacturing, the industries attracting the greatest number of workers are service-oriented, and include health care, education, and the public sector. Among the county's largest private sector employers are IBM Corporation, PepsiCo, Texaco, MasterCard International, The Reader's Digest Association, Inc., and Philip Morris International, all of which are headquartered here.

Job opportunities also have increased markedly in the newer, high-technology industries like telecommunications, computers, and the environmental sciences.

QUALITY OF LIFE

Over 870,000 people call Westchester County home, and they reside in one of its 6 cities, 14 towns, or 23 villages. Its largest city—Yonkers, ranked fourth in the state of New York with a population of over 188,000—was judged as the 7th safest city in the country among the top 100. *(Source: Crime in the United States 1993. Uniform Crime Reports)*

Apart from its urban centers, the county is dotted with woods, lakes, rivers, and grass marshlands. It lays claim to some of the nation's best golf courses, and its recreational activities and cultural events are among the finest anywhere. Westchester's combined metropolitan/suburban character provides a marvelous environment in which to live and work.

A setting that has inspired more than one artist—the picturesque view of the Hudson River near the Tappan Zee Bridge. *Photo by Joe Vericker.*

BUSINESS COMMUNITY

Westchester County has long been home to some of America's best-known *Fortune* 500 and 1000 companies. The choice to locate here in the post-World War II era has been facilitated by the area's workforce, lifestyle, transportation network, schools, health care services, and government cooperation. The handsomely designed office buildings in Westchester's cities and corporate parks blend tastefully with the architecture of the various municipalities.

As we approach the twenty-first century, the trend in the county's business community is toward the small- and medium-sized businesses. A rebirth of the entrepreneurial spirit that has long been a part of the Westchester experience has fostered the growth both in the number and the variety of these companies.

TRANSPORTATION

The success of business in Westchester County is due in no small measure to the superior roads, rail, and airlines which provide convenient, dependable transportation for executives and employees alike.

The county's highways make it possible for motorists to reach any of its cities within a 10- to 30-minute time frame. The first parkway in the history of the United States—the

Bronx River Parkway—was built here in 1927.

The Metro-North Railroad offers riders three lines—the Hudson River, Harlem, and New Haven—in a north-south system, which links the western, eastern, and central portions of the county to New York City, neighboring Connecticut, and upstate regions. Travelers can also reach Boston, Buffalo, Philadelphia, and Washington, D.C., via Amtrak from selected Hudson River and New Haven line stations.

The Westchester County Department of Transportation's Bee-Line Bus Service—the fourth largest transit system in the state—was named the foremost system of its size in North America due to its efficiency and effectiveness.

Boasting a brand-new passenger terminal, the Westchester County Airport is a full-service, general-aviation facility, strategically located in the center of the county. Served by nine major carriers, it accommodates some 200,000 flights and 800,000 passengers annually. It is also home base for many corporate and private aircraft owners.

EDUCATION

Forty public school districts and two dozen institutions of higher learning contribute to making Westchester's people among the nation's best-educated.

Not only have county students earned one of the lowest dropout and absentee rates in the state, but 85.8 percent also extend their education after high school. And while the enrollment of primary and secondary schools varies according to the size of their respective communities, the quality of education does not.

An impressive roster of private and parochial elementary and secondary schools, culturally-oriented institutions, and technical and vocational training rounds out the educational facilities available to county students. It all adds up to the development of a highly qualified workforce ready to serve Westchester employers.

HEALTH CARE

Westchester's health care delivery system provides yet another reason to live here. Fourteen general-care hospitals serving every section of the county supply the very best in medical care backed

---

Outdoor recreation in Westchester truly offers something for everyone, from golf to sailing and boating, hiking and cross-country skiing. **Above,** A popular haven for watercraft in the Long Island Sound. Photo by Joe Vericker.

18 / Westchester County: New York's Golden Apple

by state-of-the-art technology. An array of specialized care institutions, wellness programs, and skilled medical personnel offer a wide range of services as well.

The rapid growth of health care maintenance organizations (HMOs) has had a major impact on Westchester County in recent years. Of the 30 HMOs currently operating in New York State, a dozen furnish their services to enrollees in the county.

The Westchester County Medical Center in Valhalla is owned and operated by county government. Over 3,000 employees work there. Within the shadows of the Medical Center is one of the nation's oldest and largest private medical universities, New York Medical College, where some 1,600 students pursue their medical and health-related graduate studies.

LEISURE-TIME ACTIVITIES

Westchester County's history is replete with a number of "firsts": the birthplace of the concept of freedom of the press and also the circus in America; as well as the first-ever public parkway, planned amusement park, shopping center, planned suburban development, and commercial conference center.

Many other sites rich in tradition attract thousands of visitors each year. Some 35 historical sites, 37 parks, and 10 theaters and performing-arts centers are located in Westchester.

And if one's appetite needs whetting, more than 1,400 restaurants, from fast food to the finest cuisine, stand ready to serve you. The county's 19 major hotels, with a total of more than 5,000 rooms, not to mention more than 200,000 square feet of meeting space, offer a wide array of amenities for their guests.

Outdoor recreation in Westchester truly offers something for everyone, from the county's 55 golf courses to sailing and boating, fishing and cross-country skiing, swimming, biking, horseback riding, tennis, and even bird-watching. If a quiet tour of a museum or art gallery is your preference, Westchester provides these enriching, though less strenuous, venues as well.

One of the county's 55 golf courses. *Photo by Joe Vericker.*

HOUSING

Not long after the end of World War II, a massive housing boom exploded in Westchester. Not limited to single-family split level and ranch-style homes, both high-rise and low-rise residential construction proliferated as well.

Affordable housing is available here, proven by the fact that after a recessional slump in 1989, sales of homes began climbing again in 1991 and actually set an all-time county record in 1993.

ECONOMY

The economy of Westchester County is diverse with nearly every economic sector represented: manufacturing, finance, service industries, retailing, and even agriculture to an extent. Recent trends argue well for growth in many sectors, particularly as interest rates remain low. The latter will also assist the housing market, and appreciation of county homes is expected to remain steady.

Westchester's labor market will continue to expand, and it appears that inflation will stay low, which bodes well for employers as labor and energy costs remain on a relatively even keel.

All in all, it looks like growth should continue in an upward direction for Westchester's businesses, bringing with it considerable promise for the future of the county's overall economy. ◆

Westchester County: New York's Golden Apple / 19

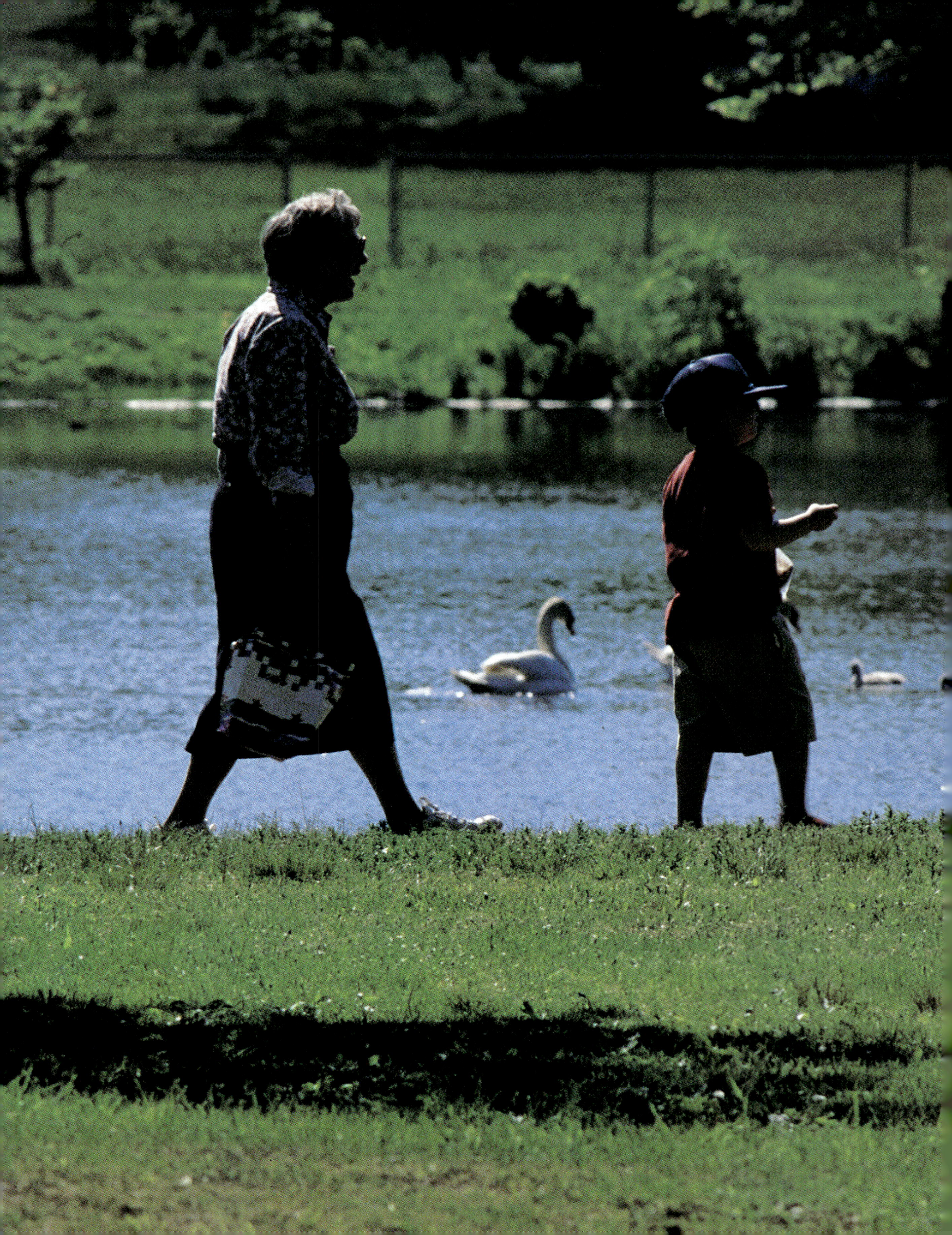

*Photo by
Joe Vericker*

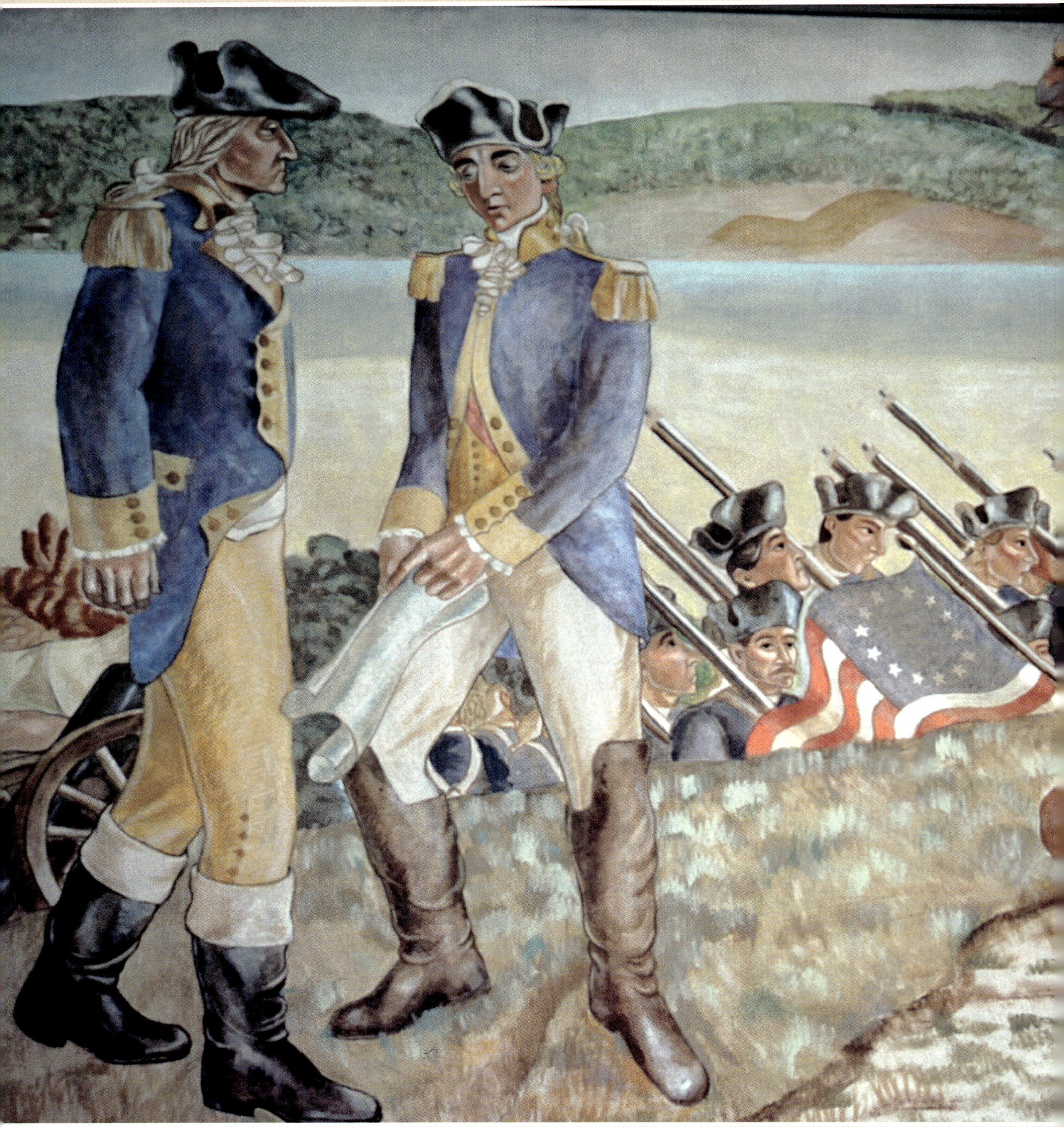

CHAPTER • TWO

A *H*ISTORY STEEPED IN TRADITION

For nearly 400 years, Westchester County has been the scene of some of the most incredible events in the history of the United States. These events—and the people who shaped them—have made an indelible impact upon the development not only of the county itself, but also of the nation as a whole.

This colorful Hudson River scene is part of a mural painted in the 1920s with funding from the Federal Art Project and is located inside Washington Irving Intermediate School in Tarrytown, New York.
Photo by Joe Vericker.

Westchester County: New York's Golden Apple / 23

A History Steeped in Tradition

Philipse Manor Hall, Yonkers, New York, c. 1855, drawn and engraved by James Smillie for Washington Irving's *Life of George Washington*. Around 1781, Frederick Philipse built this fine Georgian-style Manor Hall as the main building of his lower mills. Beginning in 1868, Yonkers' politicians used the venerable structure as the village hall and, from 1872 to 1911, as the first city hall. *Collection of The Hudson River Museum of Westchester.*

THE 1600s

In 1609 when the Englishman Henry Hudson, an employee of the Dutch East India Company, sailed his ship the *Half Moon* up the river now bearing his name, he was very likely the first European to see what is now known as Westchester County. Hudson literally paved the way for Dutch fur traders to profit from their trade with Native Americans. The Native Americans received baubles from the continent in exchange for their valuable mink and beaver pelts. The primary cargo of ships returning to Holland were these and other equally prized pelts. Hudson's goal was to find a new route to the Orient upriver.

However, the newfound fur market led Dutch settlers to forget this trade and instead purchase land from the Native Americans in Manhattan.

Subsequent to Hudson's voyage, Adrien Block became the first European to direct a ship through Long Island Sound, and in the process come upon Rye Beach and the eastern portion of Westchester. Block Island draws its name from this navigator.

The first white man to settle north of the Great Kill (now the Harlem River) was Jonas Bronck, a scholarly Dane who took up 500 acres along the Ahquahung River, later known as Bronck's or the Bronx River. Bronck bought the land from the Native Americans and signed a peace treaty with them in his home in 1642. Westchester was already inhabited by a group of tribes known as the Mohicans. At the time the entire area of the Bronx and Westchester was known as Westchester. It was named after a city in England, having been called that informally by colonists from Connecticut before England took it over in 1664.

As fur growing became scarce in the 1670s, more and more farmers began to move in and settle down. There were some who came to the New World to escape religious persecution, like the Huguenots from La Rochelle, France. With the aid of a German named Jacob Leisler, they founded New Rochelle in 1688. Leisler had purchased the land from Thomas Pell, who earlier had acquired 6,000 acres (including not only New Rochelle, but also Pelham, City Island, and part of Throg's Neck) from the Siwanoy tribe. Three years later, Leisler, for whom a bronze statue was later erected and still stands on the city's North Avenue, was executed as a rebel by the English.

During the last half of the seventeenth century, as communities like Rye, Bedford, White Plains, Scarborough, New Castle, and Mamaroneck were being settled, frenzied land speculation

24 / Westchester County: New York's Golden Apple

Jacob Leisler, of Germany, aided Huguenots fleeing religious persecution from La Rochelle, France, to found the city of New Rochelle, New York, in 1688. Leisler later became governor of New York. This statue stands in commemoration of Leisler on North Avenue in New Rochelle. *Photo by Joe Vericker.*

St. Andrew's Episcopal Church in Hartsdale, New York, is located on property which was originally part of the Philipse estate. *Photo by Joe Vericker.*

A History Steeped in Tradition

Court House, White Plains, from *History of the County of Westchester,* by Robert Bolton Jr., 1848. White Plains and Bedford both had courthouses, since they shared the county seat until 1868. *Collection of The Hudson River Museum of Westchester.*

and boundary disputes were the order of the day. Bribery, slavery, and smuggling were commonplace.

Westchester was finally made a county in 1683. Despite this, the Dutch continued to bequeath huge estates to individuals like Frederick Philipse (Philipsburg Manor) and Stephanus Van Cortlandt (Van Cortlandt Manor), both of which are notable tourist attractions today. Philipse is also credited with building a "castle" known as Sleepy Hollow, another popular landmark in what is now Tarrytown.

THE 1700s

At the turn of the century, Westchester was developing into a heavily agrarian economy. Farmers continued moving into the area to become tenants of aristocratic landowners like Caleb Heathcote, lord of Scarsdale Manor and mayor of New York, who was another of those who had been granted a large estate by the Dutch.

One of the most famous court cases in the history of American jurisprudence took place in 1733 in Mount Vernon, still part of Westchester then. It involved John Peter Zenger, a reporter for the *New York Weekly Gazette,* who covered an important election in which Lewis Morris, former chief justice of the province, was pitted against a candidate supported by the arrogant Royal Governor, William Crosby. Zenger reported on how and why Morris, who was opposed by wealthy landowners, won despite attempts to rig the election. Zenger's story was not printed in his own progovernment paper but did appear in a paper established by Morris and his supporters. Zenger was arrested for libel and defended by Andrew Hamilton at St. Paul's Church, which remains on the corner of South Columbus Avenue in Mount Vernon. His acquittal established freedom of the press in this country and demonstrated the fearlessness of an individual who believed in the justice of his cause.

During the 1700s, cabins and other wood-formed houses were built in Westchester from the county's substantial timber resources. With the building boom came dirt paths and wagon routes for stagecoach travel and mail delivery.

With the acreage to the north cleared by Native Americans now ready for farming and homesteads, and settlements growing where water was plentiful enough to run mills to crush the grain from harvests, the county grew and prospered. Its rocky land produced the stones for walls that separated crops from grazing animals.

In the middle of the eighteenth century, increased taxes and trade restrictions were proving to be extremely hard on the colonists. But King George was waging a war in 1744, and the French and Indian War (1755-63) had to be financed as well. Not only was Westchester being taxed

Westchester County: New York's Golden Apple / 27

The Hudson River Steam Boat *Francis Skiddy,* 1859, by James Bard (1815-97). Oil on canvas, 36 3/8 x 64 1/8". Self-trained New York City artist James Bard specialized in ship portraits. He often used Hudson River scenery as a backdrop. Here, in addition to the Palisades behind the steamboat, Bard also painted a miniature view of the Hudson Highlands on the paddle wheel box. His inscription calls *Francis Skiddy* "the fastest steamer upon the American waters." *Collection of The Hudson River Museum of Westchester.*

to the limit, but it was also providing fathers and sons to help fight the wars, leaving farms at home unattended and losing money.

With the passage of time, loyalty to the Crown was sharply divided in Westchester. In the days just prior to the start of the Revolutionary War, intense public apathy had set in. When the province of New York was to become the state of New York, the Provincial Congress adjourned from New York City to the courthouse in White Plains on June 30, 1776. The state was born at that courthouse on July 4, 1776, when the Provincial Congress received the Declaration of Independence.

All lead, powder, and other military stores were moved to White Plains. Scarcely an acre of Westchester escaped bloodshed or pillaging after the first drop of blood was shed on August 29, 1776, in Mamaroneck. The county was a battleground during the Revolution, including the Battle of White Plains, which Washington fought and lost in only 15 minutes.

Despite its brevity, the action slowed up the superior British forces of General Howe. Washington retreated to North Castle and stayed there for seven months while Howe withdrew to Kingsbridge in the Bronx and picked up Fort Washington and Fort Lee with prisoners and supplies. Westchester was literally a no-man's land between the American lines north of the Croton River and the British, who occupied New York City.

One of the war's most noteworthy espionage stories took place near Tarrytown and is believed to have resulted in the saving of Washington's army. The incident involved three militiamen who captured the notorious British spy Major John Andre on September 22, 1780. Andre was working with the American traitor Benedict Arnold, then commandant of West Point, on a plot that would weaken the fortification and allow the British to cut New York off from New England. The three patriots refused to be bribed by Andre after they intercepted him near North Salem, where they were actually seeking cattle thieves. Washington ordered Andre to be hanged on October 2, 1780.

Several of the county's major historical attractions are tied to the American Revolution. The John Jay Homestead in Katonah contains furnishings from the Federal-style farmhouse built in 1787. The Thomas Paine Cottage and Museum in New Rochelle, built in 1794, was the home of the author of *Common Sense,* the fiery publication that spread throughout the colonies.

By the end of the war, with the land ravaged by a number of scant harvests as well as roving outlaws, Westchester residents set out in earnest to rebuild. With their new freedom from oppression, they ignited a housing boom that first began in the late 1700s when John Jay helped confiscate and seize Loyalist real estate. Large properties were broken up, which effected a greater diffusion of ownership.

Fishing and transportation of farm produce became important occupations. Commerce began to develop on the Hudson River and Long Island Sound. Court-

28 / Westchester County: New York's Golden Apple

A HISTORY STEEPED IN TRADITION

houses and jails were built in Bedford in 1788 for northern Westchester and in White Plains for southern Westchester. In 1795 appropriations of funds from the state specifically aimed at creating a meaningful public school system were approved and implemented. Roads salvaged from the war were repaired and made traversable by stagecoaches traveling to and from Boston and New York. Silver mined in Sing Sing (now Ossining) before the war was replaced by copper after the Revolution. Iron mines started up around Peekskill and Port Chester, while brick industries began at Croton and Verplanck's Point.

The shoemaking industry was thriving in Salem, Bedford, Armonk, Kensico, Unionville, and Pleasantville. Bedford also claimed woolen and linen cloth made on family farms. Before moving to Yonkers early in the nineteenth century, carpet weaving had first been introduced in West Farms in lower Westchester. And silversmiths plied their trade in Salem and Bedford in the late 1700s.

THE 1800s

The nineteenth century introduced what can best be described as modern Westchester. The increasing use of steamboats, the construction of toll roads, and the eventual introduction of the railroad as the primary means of travel and shipping gave rise to a booming economy.

Steamboats were predominant in the early 1800s. Competition grew among makers as to whose vessel was the fastest. Crowds were drawn initially to the ones with the most speed until a few explosions turned patrons away from the reputed quicker boats.

Barges and cargo ships cruised the Hudson, making it a major artery for commercial traffic between New York City and upcounty ports. Manufactured and imported goods were dropped onto Westchester docks while locally produced grain and produce were supplied to city dwellers.

Later Westchester became the major water carrier for New York City when it created the Croton Aqueduct in the 1840s. While toll roads, which were first created in 1809 with the Croton Turnpike, remained viable as transportation routes, it was the railroad which captured the hearts and minds of haulers and passengers alike. The arrival of the Iron Horse was the motivation for many Westchester farmers to move west in search of more land.

A number of wealthy tycoons from New York City began choosing Westchester for their country homes and began acquiring property such as Lyndhurst in Tarrytown, a Gothic Revival mansion first built in 1838, and later bought by financier/rail baron Jay Gould. Author Washington Irving—creator of Rip Van Winkle and Ichabod Crane—obtained Sunnyside, a Dutch Colonial Revival home, in 1835. Also noteworthy is the Elephant Hotel, which was built between 1820 and 1825 by Barnum & Bailey's Hachaliah Bailey, in Somers. The town is known as the birthplace of the American circus.

At first there was great opposition to the railroad by the NIMBYs (Not In My Backyard). However, in 1842 the Harlem Railroad went from New York City to Williamsbridge in the Bronx, and two years later expanded to include the hamlet—"the White Plains." Farmers began to ship their milk by train, and in 1849, when the New York, New Haven, and Hartford line came into existence, passengers from New Rochelle, Pelham, and Mamaroneck started coming aboard. In the following year the New York and Hudson Railroad opened a single track to Manhattan

The Elephant Hotel in Somers, New York, is a historic landmark which now serves as the Somers Town House. In front of the hotel is a tribute to "Old Bet," the first elephant to tour as part of a menagerie in the early 1800s. Old Bet was brought to Somers by Hachaliah Bailey, of Barnum and Bailey fame. *Photo by Joe Vericker.*

A HISTORY STEEPED IN TRADITION

The Hay Sloops of the North River, nineteenth century, from steel plate engraving published by David H. Burn. In the first half of the nineteenth century, Westchester's towns along the Hudson River had busy shipping docks. *Collection of The Hudson River Museum of Westchester.*

and Yonkers. A fourth line, the Putnam Division of the New York Central (formerly the Harlem), was conceived in 1871, and a decade later the New York and Northern Railroad extended travel 56 miles to Brewster.

The railroads followed water routes—the Hudson, Saw Mill, Bronx River Valley, and Long Island Sound. Consequently, along these routes grew cities, hamlets, wealthy developments, and small home areas.

The Civil War had little effect on Westchester, save the tragic losses of families whose loved ones had gone off to war. The period passed with hardly a trace of violence, though the area was clearly a Democratic Party stronghold at the time and voted heavily against Lincoln.

During the 1800s the county drew its greatest strength from the influx of immigrants who began to arrive in increasing numbers, mostly from the tenements of New York City. Originally, the fugitives from the rough, crowded living quarters of the city came to Westchester as servants to the wealthy. Later they drifted into other unskilled occupations, main- ly in the construction field. Italian immigrants were primarily responsible for the backbreaking work that went into the building of the Croton Dam and the marble quarries in Tuckahoe and Mount Pleasant. Marble from these quarries was employed widely in churches, hotels, and homes, including the New York Public Library, the Smithsonian in Washington, D.C., and St. Patrick's Cathedral in New York. For the most part, the immigrants kept to themselves. They built their own communities where they could speak their native languages.

Skilled Irish and Italian artisans apprenticed in their trade for years and eventually started their own businesses, such as carving gravestones and statues and building marvelous stone mansions. Others became wealthy after developing their own contracting and construction companies.

Over nine million immigrated to the United States during the 1880s and 1890s. Among them were Jewish immigrants from eastern Europe and Russia who came to escape religious persecution. Dissatisfied with the cramped tenements of

30 / Westchester County: New York's Golden Apple

A HISTORY STEEPED IN TRADITION

First Engine Crossing McLean Avenue, 1887, photograph by Pach Brothers. The Putnam division of the New York Central was first operated in 1881 as the independent New York City & Northern Railroad. Trains ran from High Bridge to Brewster. Later, as the New York & Northern, the railroad added a three-mile branch to Yonkers' Getty Square. Due to Yonkers' hilly terrain, much of the route of the new section was elevated. This photograph documents a locomotive testing one of the trestles. *Collection of The Hudson River Museum of Westchester.*

New York City, they entered Yonkers and worked for the world's largest carpet maker, Alexander Smith & Sons. Some Jews found their way into New Rochelle, Mamaroneck, White Plains, and Peekskill, where they made their living as tradesmen and skilled craftsmen. Others went further north to Golden's Bridge, Katonah, and Mount Kisco, where they erected temples and began many works of philanthropy which continue even today.

The immigrant population and the southern blacks who made their way north after the Civil War contributed mightily to the success of such companies as Alexander Smith & Sons and Otis Elevator in Yonkers. Other factories went up along the Bronx and Hudson Rivers and on the shores of the Long Island Sound during the latter part of the nineteenth century. An iron industry developed, and with the need of good strong workers, sizable numbers of immigrant laborers from south and central Europe were attracted here.

Carpet Mill Employees, c. 1880. These employees of Alexander Smith & Son's Carpet Co. are posing with Halcyon Skinner *(seated at front right)*, the inventor largely responsible for the success of the factory. He improved the design of the power loom, which reduced the labor and skill necessary in making popular types of carpets. *Collection of The Hudson River Museum of Westchester.*

Westchester County: New York's Golden Apple / 31

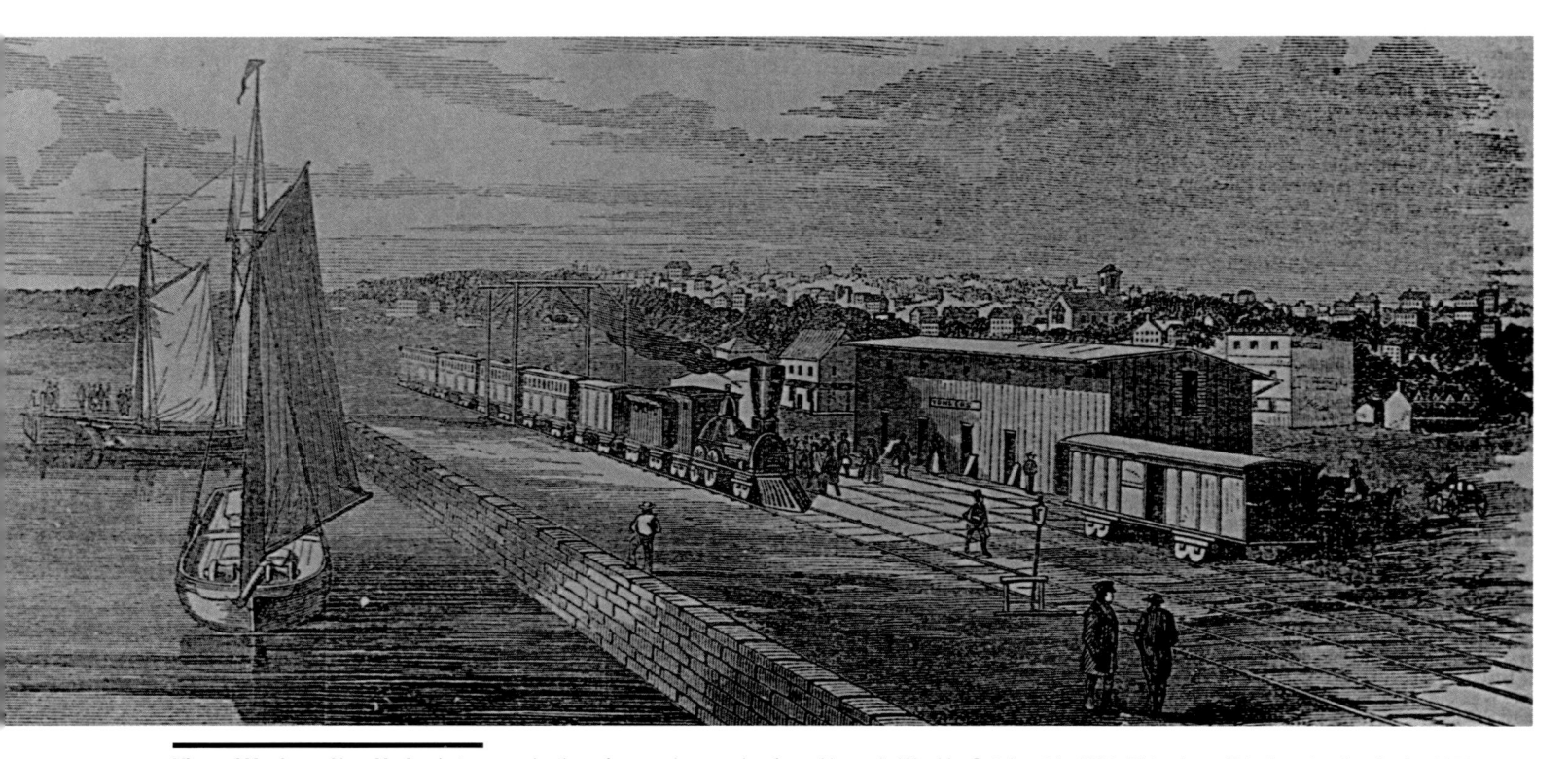

A History Steeped in Tradition

View of Yonkers, New York, photo-reproduction of a wood engraving from *Harper's Weekly*, October 21, 1882. This view of Yonkers landing in the 1850s shows bustling waterfront activity and a locomotive pulling into the town's first Hudson River Railroad station. The humble and homely depot came to be known as the "Rat Pit." By the time *Harper's* published this engraving, Yonkers boasted a fine brick structure on the same site. *Collection of The Hudson River Museum of Westchester.*

THE 1900s

The twentieth century saw Westchester opening its doors to some of the best-known names in American business at the time. With these companies came jobs, new housing, and a period of unparalleled growth for the county.

The Mobile Company of America was producing a steam-driven automobile in Tarrytown early in the new century. And the Chevrolet and Fisher Body Plants were making car parts in the same village, while the Ward Motor Vehicle Company was manufacturing electric trucks in Mount Vernon. Utilities like New York Telephone and the gaslight companies which preceded the electric light companies also took on workers from around the county. Port Chester's P.R. Malloy and Company, Inc. was responsible for the filament which emitted the first, albeit weak, light of the electric bulb early in the century. The Westchester Lighting Company had a gas plant in Pelham, and Yonkers Electric Lighting and Power Company had been in business 15 years before 1900 with the first franchise of its kind in the county.

The movie industry also found Westchester an attractive place in which to do business. Cartoonists like Paul Terry ("Terrytoons") set up shop in New Rochelle, and many scenes from the epic *Birth of a Nation* were shot in the "Queen City."

In 1903 the Sanitas Fabric Wall Covering Company launched its operation in the village of Buchanan and introduced its revolutionary new product coast-to-coast. One of the brightest lights in the Westchester national business scene was Mint Products (later to become the Life Savers Corporation) in Port Chester. In just a few short years the company grew from producing a few thousand rolls of the popular, flavored candies to millions annually. During World War II the company is reputed to have supplied U.S. armed forces personnel with over 250 million rolls of Life Savers.

The county's support of both World Wars in the twentieth century was unwavering. Westchesterites not only served their country in uniform but also bought bonds, did volunteer work as air raid wardens and in hospitals, worked in war plants, and generally assisted the war effort in any way they could.

Fort Slocum in New Rochelle was an embarkation point for troops on their way to Europe in both hostilities. Burroughs Wellcome and Company in Tuckahoe supplied first aid kits for the armed services during World War II and later furnished medicine through the United Nations to recovering countries after the conflict. And barges and tugs built at U.S. Shipbuilding in Yonkers took part in the invasion of Norway and General Douglas MacArthur's Pacific campaigns.

The post-World War II era for Westchester was a period of increased suburbanization with a building boom in both single-family homes and apartments like no other in its history. New jobs and industries and the entrance of huge *Fortune* 500 companies like General Foods, Nestle, IBM, Texaco, PepsiCo, and others created a demand not only for housing but also more schools, shopping outlets, transportation, and all of the other many tangential consequences of an economic and social revolution. ◆

Hudson River View, c. 1915, by Daniel Putnam Brinley (1879-1963), Oil on canvas, 30 1/8 x 31 7/8". Brinley, a student of the American Impressionist John Twachtman, began painting Hudson River views early in his career. This vibrant factory scene at Yonkers, with the Palisades as a backdrop, probably depicts one of the city's two sugar refineries. River and rail transport were vital to the sugar industry in Yonkers, as both still are today. *Collection of The Hudson River Museum of Westchester.*

Abendroth Iron Foundry, Port Chester, from *History of Westchester County,* edited by J. Thomas Scharf, 1886. The Eagle Iron and Stove Works sold furnaces and stoves around the world. William Abendroth established the foundry in the 1840s; by the time of this print, it had grown to be one of the largest on the East Coast. *Collection of The Hudson River Museum of Westchester.*

Captioning for photographs of works from the Collection of The Hudson River Museum of Westchester provided by Laura L. Vookles, the museum's curator of collections.

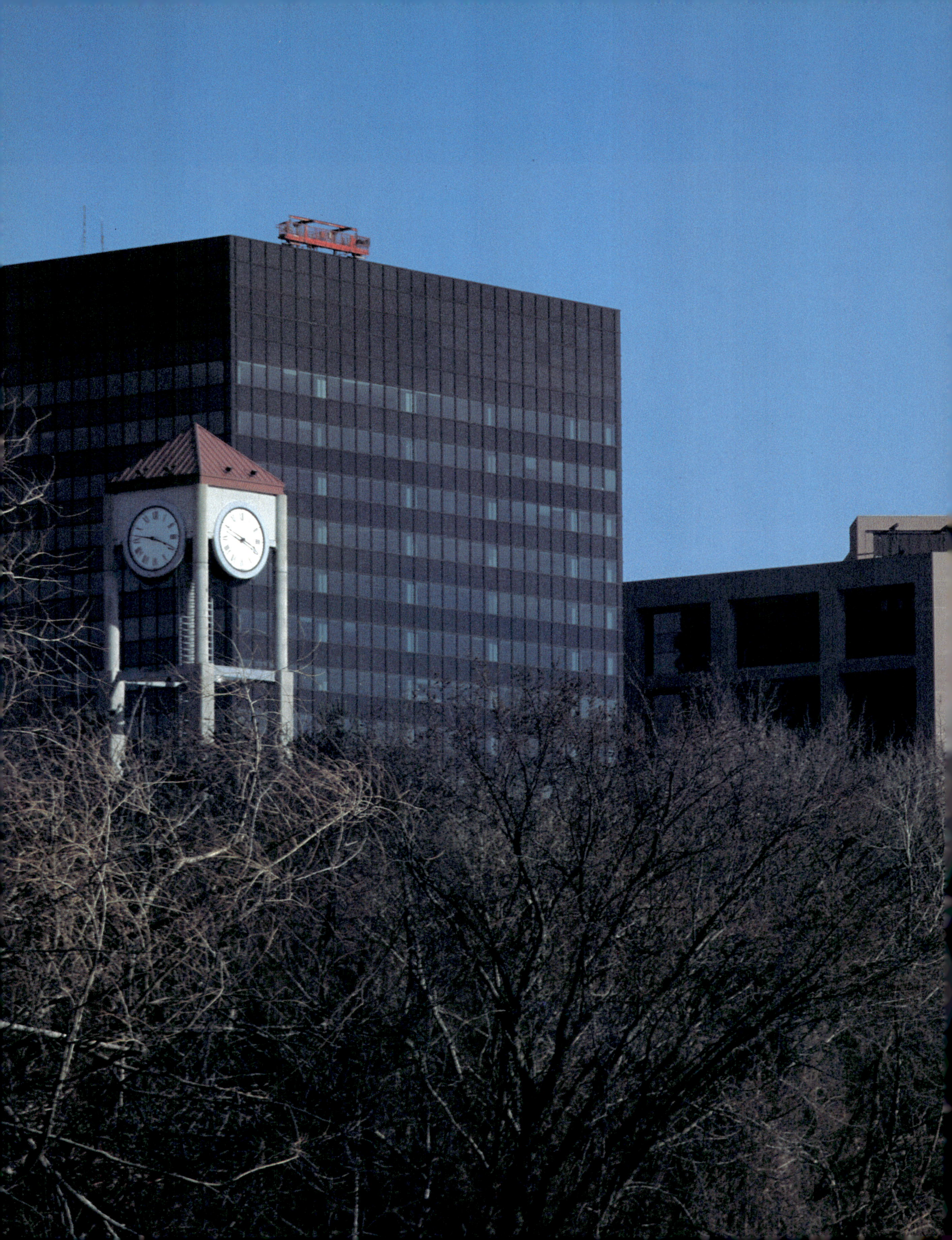

CHAPTER • THREE

Westchester Means Business

A strategic location, a highly skilled workforce, a strong economic support base, and an efficient transportation network—these factors form a dynamic combination of reasons why Westchester County means business.

Photo by Joe Vericker

Westchester County: New York's Golden Apple / 35

WESTCHESTER MEANS BUSINESS

Then, too, the area is blessed with abundant resources: private sector organizations and government agencies eager to help businesses either expand or relocate here; a marvelous environment in which to live and work; all backed by highly desirable commercial real estate, reliable utilities, and excellent business and financial services.

CORPORATE SCENE

The vision exemplified by the founders of *Reader's Digest*, Lila Acheson Wallace and Dewitt Wallace, who started their publishing empire in the 1920s in Pleasantville, reached its peak in the 1950s when *Fortune* 500 companies like General Foods and IBM established their worldwide headquarters in Westchester. Top management of these firms and those that followed, many of whom had resided here for years, reasoned that since the county

Above, Westchester's workforce, of nearly a half million, is one of the most educated and highly skilled found anywhere.

Right, The Reader's Digest Association, Inc. headquarters in Pleasantville, New York. *Photo by Ernest Coppolino/Courtesy of The Reader's Digest Association, Inc.*

36 / Westchester County: New York's Golden Apple

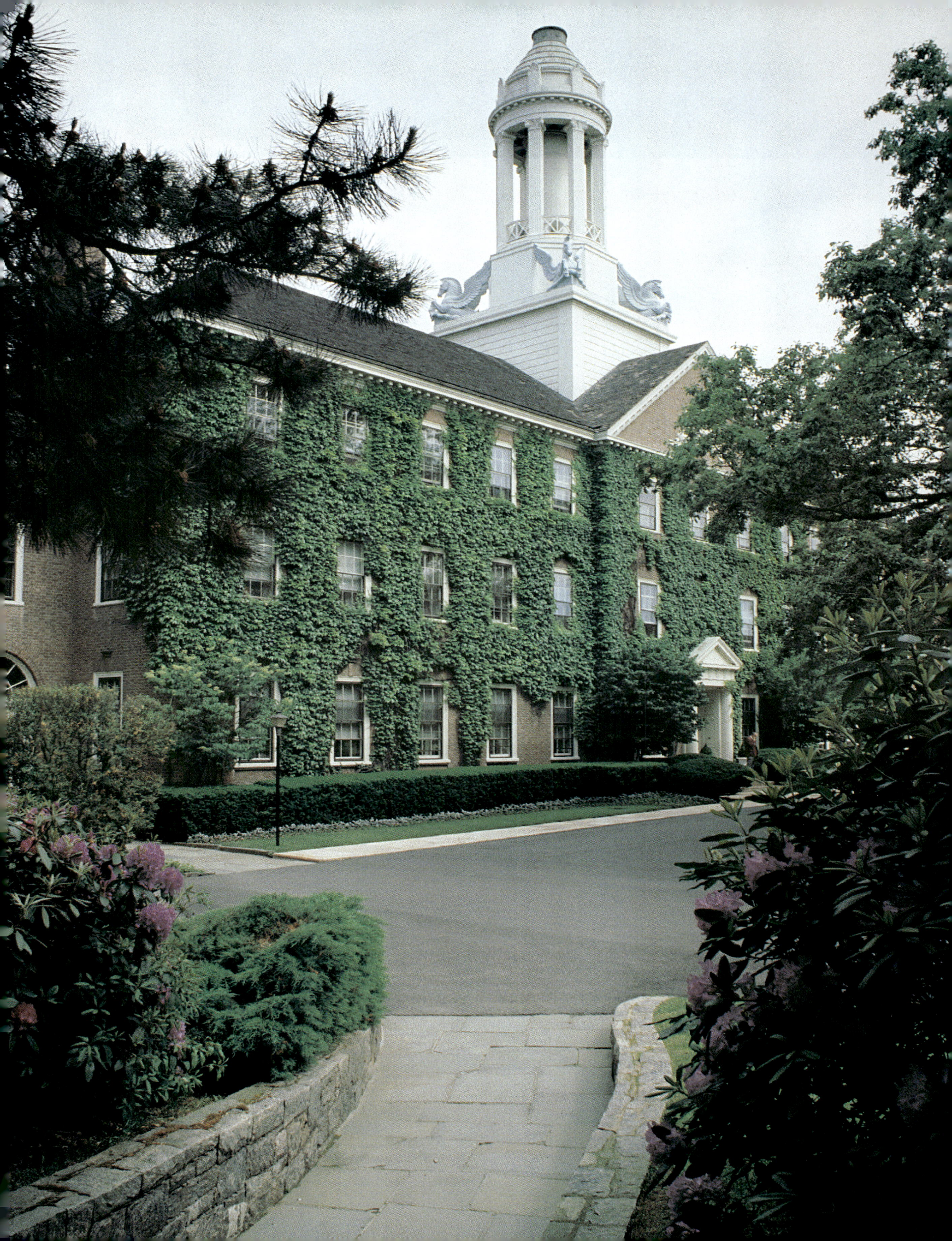

was such a wonderful place in which to live, it would be equally as desirable a location in which to work.

General Foods (now Kraft Foods, a subsidiary of the Philip Morris Companies, Inc.) erected its original home in White Plains and later constructed a magnificent building in Rye Brook. The facility is now occupied by Philip Morris International.

IBM Corporation, at one time the largest employer in Westchester, chose Armonk as its corporate home and has added to its building ownership steadily, particularly in White Plains, and in the mid-1980s in Somers.

PepsiCo, which located and continues in Purchase, also added to the Somers' skyline with a huge complex built at approximately the same time as IBM.

Another leader in its respective field, Texaco has established its corporate presence in White Plains for many years.

Bayer Corp.'s Business Group Diagnostics, a division of the $8-billion research-based Bayer Corp., employs 700 of its 5,000 employees worldwide in Tarrytown.

Bally, Inc., a leading international footwear and leather accessories manufacturer which moved into New

Philip Morris International in Rye Brook, New York. *Photo by Joe Vericker.*

Westchester County: New York's Golden Apple / 39

WESTCHESTER MEANS BUSINESS

Rochelle in 1981, expanded there in 1986 and today has 120 employees on its payroll.

Larchmont-based Collins Brothers Moving Corp., which started with a horse and wagon in 1910, now boasts more than 100 vehicles and 325 employees on its roster.

Tetko Inc, part of a Swiss firm known as the leading manufacturer of precision woven fabrics used in filtration, sifting, shielding, and screen printing applications, maintains a major distribution center in Briarcliff Manor.

The NYNEX Corporation also adds a substantial economic impact with facilities located throughout Westchester.

Other organizations which have long kept either a corporate or regional facility in the county include Loral, Hitachi Metals America, Ltd., Prodigy, Apple Computer, MBIA, Fuji Photo USA, Gannett Suburban Newspapers, International Paper, Combe, Tambrands, and Transamerica. Newcomers to the area in recent years are MasterCard International, Swiss Re, and Heineken USA. All told, some 400 companies chose to relocate to Westchester in the 1990s.

Westchester citizens are grateful for their corporate neighbors who play a major role not only in providing jobs for residents but also in keeping property taxes within reason. Companies here are also very generous when it comes to contributing financially to cultural and charitable activities as well as in assisting local governments and educational institutions.

IBM Corporation is one of many *Fortune* 500 firms who have made Westchester County their choice for business location. *Photo by Joe Vericker.*

40 / Westchester County: New York's Golden Apple

WESTCHESTER MEANS BUSINESS

View of the Platinum Mile in White Plains. *Photo by Joe Vericker.*

STRENGTHS

What is it about Westchester County that is so attractive to business? Well, for one, its workforce of nearly a half million is one of the best educated and most highly skilled to be found anywhere. Its professional, managerial, and technical workers are well-known for their intellectual abilities so necessary to today's high-tech industry requirements.

The location cannot be emphasized strongly enough—30 minutes from midtown Manhattan and the financial capital of the world and within an easy distance of five major airports. A reliable mass transit system and a wide choice of highways permit easy accessibility to those who live and work here, as well as others from neighboring NewJersey, Connecticut, and New York City who provide a substantial portion of Westchester's high-caliber work population.

The county's unparalleled quality of life is well-documented, from its premier golf courses and wealth of other recreational facilities to its wide variety of cultural activities and top-notch health care services.

RETAILING

Long before Westchester introduced the nation to the first shopping center ever built—the Cross County Shopping Center in Yonkers—famous names like

Westchester County: New York's Golden Apple / 41

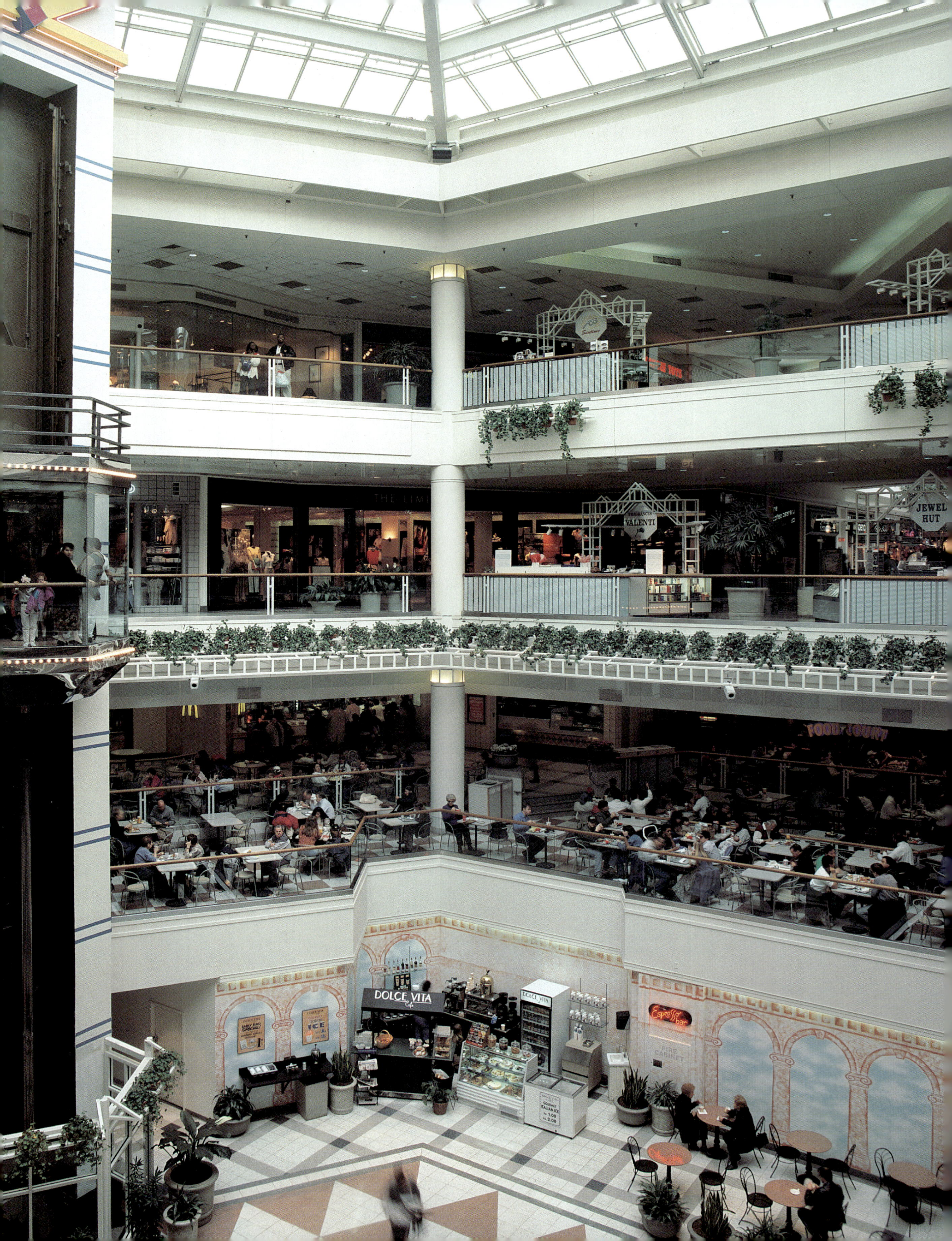
JEWEL HUT
VALENTI
FOOD COURT
DOLCE VITA

WESTCHESTER MEANS BUSINESS

Above, Retailing accounts for more than 20 percent of all business in Westchester County. *Photo by Joe Vericker.*

Four massive shopping malls—the Cross County in Yonkers, the Galleria and The Westchester in White Plains, and the Jefferson Valley Mall in Yorktown Heights—represent a total of nearly five million square feet featuring every type of retail outlet imaginable.
Left, The Galleria in White Plains. *Photo by Joe Vericker.*

Bloomingdale's, Lord & Taylor, Macy's, and Saks Fifth Avenue had dotted the county landscape.

Retailing has always been a healthy part of the economy here. Today it represents better than 20 percent of all the businesses found in Westchester.

The county has been credited with being one of the world's largest regional consumer markets, providing a competitive edge for retailers and others who benefit from ready access to customers.

Shopping centers in Westchester are just about everywhere—over 50 of them with 50,000 square feet or more, with a county total of about 11 million square feet. In fact, the county ranks fourth from the top in New York State in the number of stores and total dollar volume.

Four massive shopping malls—the Cross County in Yonkers, the Galleria and The Westchester, both in White Plains, and the Jefferson Valley Mall in Yorktown Heights—represent a total of nearly five million square feet featuring every type of retail outlet imaginable.

New names that have been added to the Westchester retailing scene in the recent past include Neiman Marcus, Stern's, J.C. Penney, and Nordstrom's. The mix now is augmented by a host of fashionable boutiques and specialty stores as well as a new phenomenon, the warehouse club.

It is estimated that 15 percent of the county's workforce are employed in retailing, which now encompasses over 6,500 outlets with an annual aggregate of $7.5 billion.

Westchester County: New York's Golden Apple / 43

WESTCHESTER MEANS BUSINESS

Westchester County is home to the first commercial conference center in the United States. *Photo courtesy of Tarrytown House Executive Conference Center.*

REAL ESTATE

The development of real estate, particularly in the commercial area, has always been an important piece of the business pie in Westchester. Consider these firsts: the nation's first planned suburban development (Mt. Vernon); the country's first planned amusement park (Playland in Rye); and the first commercial conference center in the United States (Tarrytown House Executive Conference Center in Tarrytown).

And municipalities in the county are always searching for ways to improve. The city of New Rochelle, for example, is in the process of a revitalization effort for its downtown area. This effort is threefold and includes the redevelopment of the New Rochelle Center, a residential market-rate apartment complex development, and a modern state-of-the-art intermodal transportation center.

Today the county boasts over 25 million square feet of office and commercial space, making it the 37th largest office market in the country. Even more important than the county's abundant office space is its stable rental costs. In White Plains, for example, the charges are less in per square foot rental of office space than Boston, Stamford, and northern New Jersey. And without a doubt, office rents are considerably less in Westchester than in neighboring New York City.

Operating costs—that is, energy and taxes—are competitive and often less than those in nearby markets.

44 / Westchester County: New York's Golden Apple

WESTCHESTER MEANS BUSINESS

SUPPORT SERVICES

Business support services abound in the county to assist companies in their sales and marketing goals. Among those which provide first-rate help are advertising and public relations agencies, commercial artists, credit reporters, building-maintenance organizations, legal firms, personnel agencies, equipment leasing companies, computer programmers, accountants, and management counselors.

Businesses considering either expansion or relocation here should know that 12 percent of the county's commerce is represented in the insurance, financial, and real estate fields, with the most rapid growth seen among securities and commodities brokers, nondepository institutions, and insurance carriers.

Five of the 10 largest banks in the nation have branches located throughout Westchester: Citibank, the number one bank in size in the United States; Chase Manhattan, which now includes the former Chemical Bank (merged in 1996); The Bank of New York; Fleet Bank (formerly National Westminster); First Union (formerly First Fidelity Bankcorp). All provide a complete range of services tailored to the business community.

Another key component in the success of commerce in the county is the reliable utility services provided by the Consolidated Edison Company and by New York State Electric and Gas serving northeastern Westchester. The New York

Five of the 10 largest banks in the nation have branches located throughout Westchester County. *Photo by Joe Vericker.*

Westchester County: New York's Golden Apple / 45

WESTCHESTER MEANS BUSINESS

Power Authority operates the Indian Point nuclear plant, the first nuclear plant ever to receive a construction permit in the United States.

SUPPORT GROUPS

The County Chamber and 22 local chambers of commerce are totally committed to the success of business in Westchester and are actively engaged in offering services and programs to their members.

The County Chamber of Commerce, Inc. was founded in 1904 as the White Plains Board of Trade, and is the first and only National Chamber-accredited business organization serving Westchester County. It is the largest broad-based business support group in the county with about 3,000 members from major corporations, small-to-medium-sized businesses, and professional firms and individuals.

The County Chamber offers its members an all-encompassing number of programs aimed at public affairs, area, economic, and business development, and small business issues. It also provides a well-balanced range of programs, information, and services specifically tailored to any size of business.

As a benefit to members and the business community in general, The County Chamber of Commerce, Inc. provides networking opportunities and informational seminars. *Photo courtesy of The County Chamber of Commerce, Inc.*

46 / Westchester County: New York's Golden Apple

WESTCHESTER MEANS BUSINESS

TAXES

One of the major reasons businesses are relocating here is the county's overall tax structure. There is no local corporate income tax and, with the exception of Yonkers, no local personal income tax. Finally, no commercial rent taxes or unincorporated business taxes are levied in Westchester.

New York State does its share to help bring businesses to the county also. For example, the state does not tax business inventory or personal property. With sales double-weighted when interstate income is figured in, this method often results in reduced net taxable income.

New York State permits businesses to carry over net operating losses, which is an advantage for fledgling companies. New organizations are also free of the alternative tax on business for the first two years of their existence.

Now, while Westchester County does not have a personal income tax, New York does have a graduated type. However, the state has actually halved its maximum income tax since 1978, resulting in billions of dollars in savings for taxpayers.

Westchester citizens can appreciate their corporate neighbors for their contributions to the county's quality of life. In addition to providing jobs, they help to keep property taxes within reason. **Above,** Corporate Park Drive at Westchester Avenue. *Photo by Joe Vericker.*

*W*ESTCHESTER MEANS BUSINESS

Photo by Joe Vericker

GOVERNMENT ASSISTANCE

Both Westchester County government and the state of New York are anxious to offer incentive plans and assistance packages to encourage businesses to expand or relocate here.

The Westchester County Industrial Development Agency (WCIDA) is responsible for stimulating economic development by arranging long-term financial assistance at low interest rates. The proceeds of taxable and tax-exempt securities issued by the WCIDA are used to fund the acquisition, construction, reconstruction, and/or equipping of selected manufacturing, commercial, warehousing, industrial, research, pollution-control, and winter recreation projects. The state of New York works closely with the county in furnishing assistance and incentive programs to relocating and expanding companies. This aid includes flexible, low-cost financing for specialized business and industrial development projects as well as site clearance, construction, and reconstruction of infrastructure deficiencies.

The state also offers a mixture of grants, co-funding endeavors, and technical assistance programs for research and development and finances customized, workplace-based training programs for private industry. And it grants tax breaks such as sizable investment tax credits, deferrals, and exclusions for capital investment to new businesses.

WESTCHESTER MEANS BUSINESS

The state of New York works closely with the county in furnishing assistance and incentive programs to relocating and expanding companies. Photo by Joe Vericker.

THE LONG TERM

Executives here look forward to the future with anticipation. It is expected that steadying interest rates will spark increased home construction.

While labor's rate of growth may not match that of the 1980s, productivity is on the rise as a result of corporate downsizing from mergers and reorganizations. This has led many companies to seek the services of outside contractors for work once performed in-house.

As Westchester gradually shifts in the years ahead to a service economy, jobs are expected to become more plentiful once again. Real growth is expected to come from firms specializing in telecommunications and information services, health care, biotechnology, computers and data processing, environmental services, entertainment, and transportation.

Finally, a relatively low rate of inflation should hold wages and energy prices steady, yet another reason for optimism in Westchester County for the twenty-first century. ◆

CHAPTER · FOUR

FOR THE GOOD TIMES

Westchester County, New York State's Golden Apple, shines brightly throughout the year with events and attractions to keep visitors and residents alike occupied with pleasurable things to see and do.

The Donald M. Kendall Sculpture Gardens, PepsiCo at Purchase. Photo by Joe Vericker.

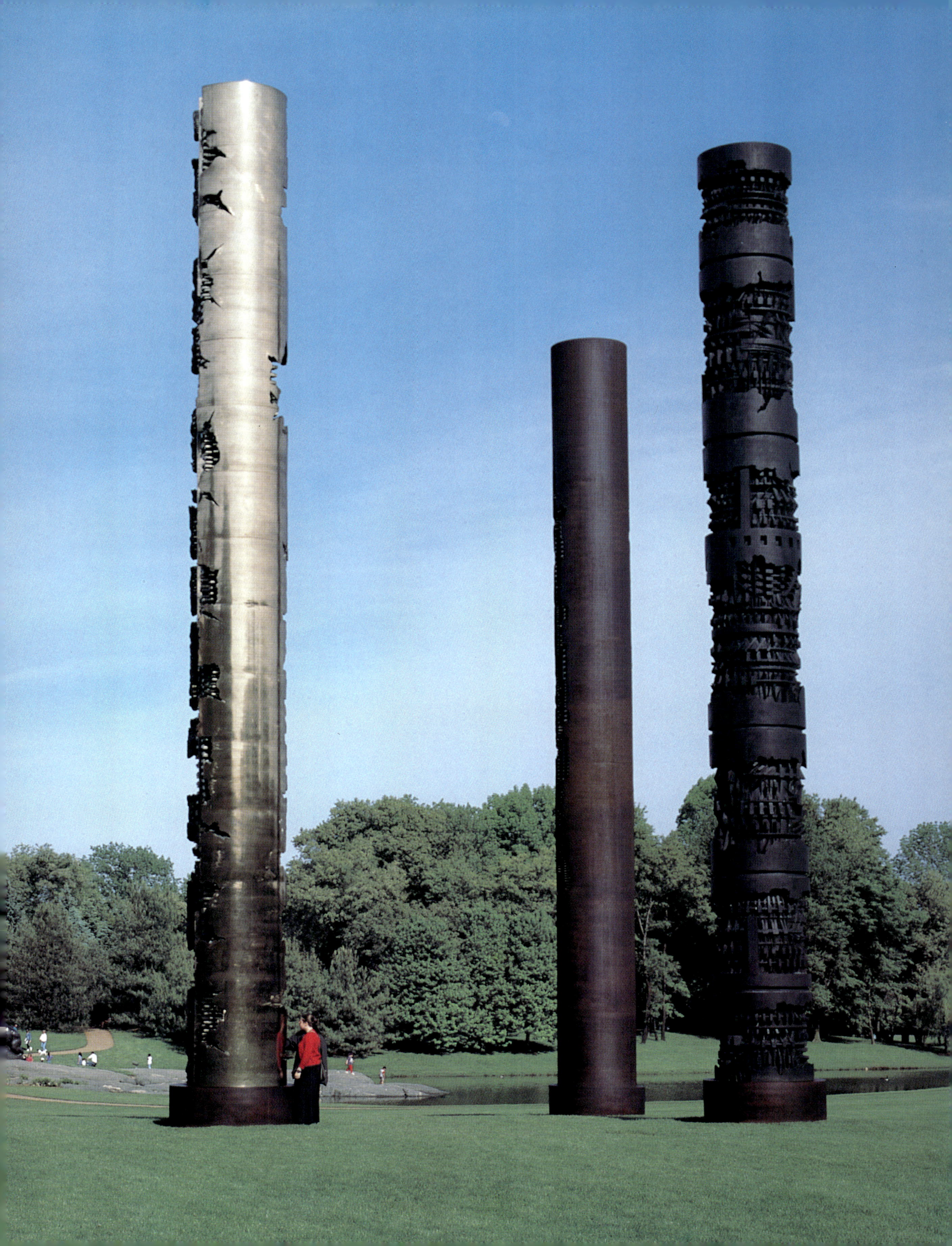

From its majesty views of the Hudson River to the striking landscape of Long Island Sound, Westchester County is as rich and as varied as a small country with historic sites that capture the American spirit. The cultural life here is alive with music, dance, theater, and art exhibitions year round. Leisure activities like water sports, horseback riding, camping, nature trails, golf, and boating are in abundance.

For the shopping aficionado, Westchester offers some of the finest stores north of Manhattan, not to mention scores of quaint antique shops and craft fairs. Also to be discovered here are unique art treasures in the county's many fine museums and galleries.

In short, Westchester has it all. It is a cosmopolitan area rich in country charm and urban sophistication. An ideal setting for a convention, sales meeting, or vacation, the county boasts more than a score of superior hotels and conference centers providing accommodations for even the most discriminating guest.

An aerial view of Kykuit, the Rockefeller House and gardens in North Tarrytown. *Photo: John Hill/courtesy of Historic Hudson Valley.*

52 / Westchester County: New York's Golden Apple

FOR THE *G*OOD TIMES

Philipsburg Manor in North Tarrytown features a water-powered grist mill and farm which are eloquent reminders of Dutch enterprise in colonial America. Restored to represent the early eighteenth century, this farm and trading center, which includes a Dutch Colonial stone manor house, celebrated its 300th anniversary in 1993. *Photo courtesy of Historic Hudson Valley.*

HISTORIC ATTRACTIONS

The John Jay Homestead in Katonah is the restored retirement home of the first Chief Justice of the United States. The home is largely furnished with original items used by five generations of Jays.

St. Paul's Church and Bill of Rights Museum is located in Mount Vernon. It was here that the John Peter Zenger trial and acquittal took place which led to the establishment of freedom of the press and free speech in this country. Exhibits celebrating the trial and the Constitutional freedoms resulting from it are on display.

George Washington's Headquarters in North White Plains is remarkably preserved for a house built in 1738. It served as the General's headquarters for a day and night before the action on Miller Hill which concluded with the Battle of White Plains on November 1, 1776.

Old Dutch Church in North Tarrytown is the oldest church in America. The church was built in 1684, restored in 1787, and is still in use. The adjoining

Westchester County: New York's Golden Apple / 53

Above, Thomas Paine Cottage and Museum in New Rochelle was built in 1794. This restored home of the author of *Common Sense* is now a museum which displays Paine's possessions, including the Franklin stove given to him by Benjamin Franklin himself. *Photo by Joe Vericker.*

Right, The Union Church of Pocantico Hills, with its stained glass windows by modern masters Henri Matisse and Marc Chagall, provides an intense experience of light and color. *Photo: Ted Spiegel/courtesy of Historic Hudson Valley.*

Above, Sunnyside in Tarrytown overlooks the Hudson River. This romantic riverside home was purchased in 1835 by Washington Irving, creator of Ichabod Crane and Rip Van Winkle. *Photo courtesy of Historic Hudson Valley.*

Left, Washington Irving served as warden and vestryman at this location of Christ Church, which was erected in 1837. The ivy growing on the walls was transplanted from cuttings taken from Sunnyside. *Photo by Joe Vericker.*

Westchester County: New York's Golden Apple / 55

cemetery which is featured in Washington Irving's *Legend of Sleepy Hollow* is also where the legendary author is buried.

The Indian Resource Center in Cross River houses a series of permanent and rotating exhibits illustrating the lives and times of the area's earliest settlers.

Kykuit in North Tarrytown was John D. Rockefeller's country villa. This six-story stone house on a hilltop overlooking the Hudson River was first opened to the public in 1994. It is surrounded by landscaped terraces, formal gardens, and an extraordinary collection of modern sculpture.

Lyndhurst in Tarrytown is a magnificent nineteenth-century Gothic mansion representing the finest of the romantic movement in architecture, decorative arts, and landscape design. The home was built in 1838 and subsequently bought by financier/railroad baron Jay Gould.

Philipse Manor Hall in Yonkers was originally constructed in the 1680s and is the oldest house in southern Westchester. Built in Georgian-style architecture, it boasts one of the finest rococo ceilings in the world. It served as the city hall from 1864 to 1908.

Just north of the county, the United States Military Academy in West Point is the home of our country's future generals. The academy boasts a spectacular setting on the banks of the Hudson River. Open every day of the year except June 1 (Graduation Day), it offers daily 50-minute guided bus tours of the grounds every 20 minutes.

Van Cortlandt Manor in Croton-on-Hudson was originally owned by one of New York State's most prominent early families. This magnificently restored home is famed for its elegant gardens and furnishings.
Photo courtesy of Historic Hudson Valley.

56 / WESTCHESTER COUNTY: New York's Golden Apple

FOR THE GOOD TIMES

Left and below, Kykuit in North Tarrytown was John D. Rockefeller's country villa. This six-story stone house on a hilltop overlooking the Hudson River was first opened to the public in 1994. It is surrounded by landscaped terraces, formal gardens, and an unbelievable collection of modern sculpture. *Photos courtesy of Historic Hudson Valley.*

Westchester County: New York's Golden Apple / 57

FOR THE *G*OOD TIMES

MUSEUMS

The Hudson River Museum of Westchester in Yonkers is one of the most fascinating art, history, and science showplaces in the Northeast. The museum, which consists of a modern wing in the enchanting Glenview Mansion built in 1876, has collections of nineteenth-century fine and decorative arts and nineteenth- and twentieth-century paintings. The site is also home to The Andrus Planetarium, the only one of its kind in Westchester.

Katonah Museum of Art in Katonah is a handsome stone structure with spacious interior arenas and large outside exhibit areas. The museum displays a large variety of important paintings and sculpture of national merit. It is home to contemporary as well as classical modern art, making it a "must-see" for avid art lovers as well as the occasional art fancier.

Neuberger Museum of Art at Purchase College is a major visual arts center and vital cultural resource. The facility houses some 5,000 works of art in various media. In addition to the permanent collection, it always offers something new in the evocative, changing exhibitions of twentieth-century art. A regional treasure, the Neuberger Museum combines the scale and excitement of a city museum with the charm of a country setting.

Donald M. Kendall Sculpture Gardens in Purchase is located outdoors at PepsiCo, Inc. world headquarters. This 40-piece collection includes works by Rodin, Alexander Calder, and Henry Moore.

Above, Glenview Mansion. *Photo ©1995 Frederick Charles/The Hudson River Museum.*

Right, The Red Grooms Gift Shop at The Hudson River Museum. *Photo: Quesada/Burke.*

58 / Westchester County: New York's Golden Apple

BOOK STORE
NESTEA INSTANT
HUDSON RIVER VILLAS
THE HUDSON RIVER HIGHLANDS
HUDSON RIVER

FOR THE *G*OOD TIMES

Above and right, Katonah Museum of Art is home to contemporary as well as classical modern art, making it a "must-see" for avid art lovers as well as the occasional art fancier. *Photo by Scott Miles/ courtesy of Katonah Museum of Art.*

60 / Westchester County: New York's Golden Apple

Above, Partial view of the Roy R. Neuberger Collection, an ongoing collection at the Neuberger Museum of Art, Purchase College, State University of New York. The museum combines the scale and excitement of a city museum with the charm of a country setting. *Photo courtesy the Neuberger Museum of Art.*

FOR THE *G*OOD TIMES

DINING AND ENTERTAINMENT

With over 1,400 restaurants of every size and description in Westchester County, the dining industry represents the fastest-growing segment of the economy. Whatever your preference—a 200-year-old inn, gracious mansion, colonial farmhouse, a village pub, or fast-food restaurant—it can be found here.

Dining out in the county is a serious pursuit, and such a demand makes for a rich and varied offering. Restaurant reviews are printed in the columns of half a dozen newspapers, magazines, and special guides or merely proffered by enthusiastic area residents.

Apart from the quality of food and service, Westchester is an international food marketplace where almost every national and regional cuisine is represented. One can feast on Mexican fare in lavish or simple surroundings, savor sushi on a grand scale or at a small neighborhood bar, sample Chinese food from Canton or from Szechuan. Or try a burger at any one of a number of 24-hour diners.

Music and theater lovers are delighted with the number of choices available to them. The Westchester Broadway Theater in Elmsford is the county's only professional dinner theater offering Broadway shows and concerts to theatergoers, matinees and evenings, with special group accommodations. The Para-

Production of *Phantom of the Opera* at the Westchester Broadway Theater in Elmsford. *Photo by John Vecchiolla/Courtesy of the Westchester Broadway Theater.*

FOR THE GOOD TIMES

mount Center for the Arts in Peekskill, the Performing Arts Center at Purchase College, the Music Hall in Tarrytown, the Emelin Theater in Mamaroneck, the Capitol Theater in Port Chester, and Caramoor in Katonah all present top-flight music, dance, films, and plays. And over 70 amateur and equity theater groups perform year round.

Yonkers Raceway offers the excitement of harness racing. Muscoot Farm Park in Somers is a turn-of-the-century interpretive farm featuring original farm buildings and displays of old farm equipment. And Playland Amusement Park in Rye, the nation's first totally planned amusement park, is an Art Deco-style park overlooking Long Island Sound offering 50 rides, a game arcade, picnic area, miniature golf, 1,200-foot beach, Olympic-size outdoor pool, and 80-acre lake with rental boats—open from Memorial Day Weekend through Labor Day.

Above left, World-class violinist Itzhak Perlman rehearses for a concert at Caramoor Center for Music and the Arts in Katonah. *Photo by Joe Vericker.*

Left, Orchestra in concert at Caramoor. *Photo by Joe Vericker.*

Westchester County: New York's Golden Apple / 63

FOR THE *G*OOD TIMES

OUTDOOR ACTIVITIES

If it's the great outdoors one is seeking, opportunities abound in the Golden Apple. Possibly the "golfingest" county in the nation, Westchester has 55 courses. The county hosts the annual PGA Buick Classic and the LPGA/JAL Big Apple Classic. It has also hosted the Men's U.S. Open and the PGA Championship. Yacht clubs and marinas in both the Long Island Sound and Hudson River draw day sailors, cruisers, power squadrons, and ice boaters. The Blue Mountain Reservation in Peekskill, nestled in the northwest portion of the county, offers opportunities for outdoor ice skating during the winter, as does Mountain Lakes Camp in North Salem, Twin Lakes in Eastchester, and Wilson's Woods Park in Mount Vernon. Indoor ice skating is open to the public between the fall and the spring at the beautiful Playland Ice Casino in Rye (where the New

Muscoot Farm Park in Somers is a turn-of-the-century interpretive farm. *Photo by Joe Vericker.*

64 / Westchester County: New York's Golden Apple

FOR THE *G*OOD TIMES

York Rangers work out during their NHL season) and the E. J. Murray Rink in Yonkers.

Cross-country skiing is available at the Cranberry Lake Preserve in North White Plains, a 135-acre unspoiled wetland and hardwoods compound. Then there's the Ward Pound Ridge Reservation in Cross River, Westchester's largest park, covering 4,700 acres at the north end of the county where one can cross-country ski for miles.

Even some area residents may not realize that three quarters of Westchester is forest, featuring over 23,000 acres of parkland. The Westchester County Department of Parks maintains three major trailways: one parallel to the Bronx River Parkway; another on what used to be the right-of-way for the Putnam Division of the old New York Central Railroad; and a third running 12 miles between Briarcliff and Peekskill. A fourth—the old Croton Aqueduct—is maintained by New York State.

And if that isn't enough, Westchester offers many beaches, clubs, horseback riding trails, indoor/outdoor swimming pools, tennis courts, baseball/softball diamonds, snowmobiling and/or sledding, not to mention cricket and polo fields. And, of course, some of the top professional sports teams in the world are just minutes away—the New York Yankees at fabled Yankee Stadium in the Bronx and the New York Mets at Shea Stadium in Queens; the New York Giants, New York Jets, New Jersey Nets, and New Jersey Devils at the Meadowlands in nearby northern New Jersey; the New York Rangers and the New York Knicks at Madison Square Garden in Manhattan; and the New York Islanders at the Nassau County Coliseum in Long Island.

The Buick Classic Golf Tournament, played annually at the Westchester Country Club, provides funding for area charities. *Photo by Joe Vericker.*

Westchester County: New York's Golden Apple / 65

HOTELS AND CONFERENCE CENTERS

Westchester County belongs to that choice group of places in this country both pleasurable to settle in and impressive to visit. Temporary lodgings are almost as remarkable in their variety as permanent ones, and the county is the home of the conference center concept (Tarrytown House Executive Conference Center, which opened in 1964). The growth of hotels and conference centers has followed the pace and paths of growth in commercial office space. Secluded in the Westchester countryside are private conference and training facilities featuring state-of-the-art meeting services.

Nineteen major hotels and two conference centers boast over 5,000 guest rooms and more than 200,000 square feet of meeting space. The county's two largest hotels have facilities that can accommodate over 1,000 people. The properties which make up the Westchester Hotels Association employ 4,000 individuals and contribute over $200 million in revenue to the county's economy.

Whether one is here on business or vacation, Westchester's hotels provide a broad range of services, including concierge and local transportation. Many

The Doral Arrowwood's resort conference center accomodates corporate executives as well as guests looking for a weekend getaway.
Photo courtesy of Doral Arrowwood.

66 / Westchester County: New York's Golden Apple

FOR THE Good TIMES

Rye Town Hilton's Grand Ballroom.
Photo courtesy of Rye Town Hilton.

have Jacuzzis™ and whirlpools as well as complete exercise and fitness gyms. Business travelers can avail themselves of computer business centers, in-room computers, and teleconferencing. Westchester hotels and conference centers can provide groups of any size with accommodations and services equal to those of neighboring New York City, with the added bonus of resort-like amenities in a suburban setting.

Accessibility is a definite plus for Westchester. The county is less than an hour away from southern end to northern tip and can boast of similar access to five major airports. Thanks to Westchester's marvelous array of retail outlets, extensive cultural offerings, and historic attractions, tourism has risen steadily in recent years. The Westchester Convention & Visitors Bureau, Ltd., affiliated with The County Chamber of Commerce, Inc., has also been a major contributor. The Bureau's primary function has been to attract business travelers, tourists, motor coach tours, and other meeting and convention visitors. As the county's designated tourism-promotion agency, it aggressively markets Westchester as a tourist destination to bring tourism and travel revenue to the county. ◆

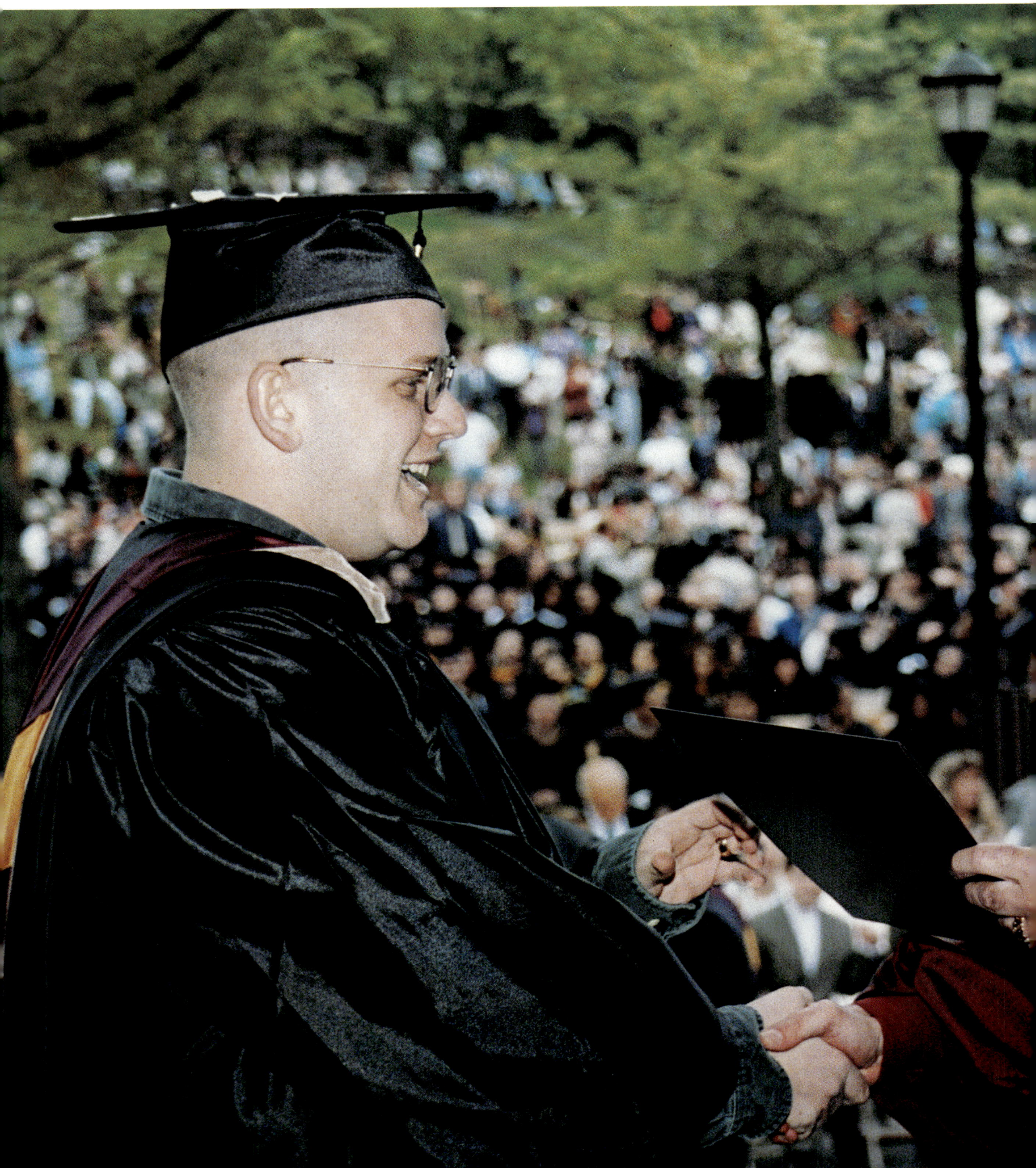

CHAPTER · FIVE

Education Equals Excellence

Education has played a significant role in the development of Westchester as one of the best educated, most affluent counties in the United States. It is a major reason why so many Fortune 500 companies have chosen to relocate here since the end of World War II.

Photo by Joe Vericker

Westchester County: New York's Golden Apple / 69

EDUCATION EQUALS EXCELLENCE

Student track meet in progress at White Plains High School. *Photo by Joe Vericker.*

An article in the October 1995 issue of *American Demographics* titled "America's Most Educated Places" lists 5 Westchester communities among the country's 101 best-educated based on the percentage of adults aged 25 and older who have graduated with a bachelor's degree or higher, according to the 1990 census.

Nationally, only 20 percent of adults have attained a bachelor's degree. The article points out that the most educated communities fall into two categories—college towns like Stanford, California, which topped the list, and affluent suburbs of big cities. However, since college towns typically consist of lesser-paid students and professors, it is suburban areas like Westchester with its proximity to New York City where the connection between affluence and higher education is most apparent. Scarsdale, for example, is listed as number 18 on the magazine's roster of the 20 most affluent places among the best-educated areas. Its 1994 average household income was $160,747, and New Castle, Bronxville, and Larchmont all had incomes of over $100,000 compared to the Westchester County average of $78,281 overall. It all adds up to a willingness on the part of county residents to spend money for education.

Marymount College, in Tarrytown, is an independent liberal arts college for women. *Photo courtesy of Marymount College.*

PUBLIC SCHOOLS

Forty school districts varying considerably in size make up Westchester's primary and secondary educational institutions. In 1994 Yonkers, with nearly 22,000 students, led the way. The Yonkers school district's student population was larger than the next two combined, that of Mount Vernon and New Rochelle. A community like Pocantico Hills, on the other hand, had only 322 students enrolled in the same year. In fact, eight other school districts had student populations of less than a thousand.

Westchester spares no expense in providing a quality education to its public school students. Each pupil's median annual expenditure in county public schools stands at $10,210. Class size is also a factor; the teacher-to-student ratio is only 11 to 1.

The county is well-known for its advanced curricula. Magnet schools, such as those throughout the Yonkers school district, were adopted here long before many other communities in this country. The same holds true for parent and alternative-choice programs. Specially designed programs are available for such diverse groups as theater or creative arts students, the gifted and talented, and students with special needs.

County students excel in classroom academics. As a group, they scored an average

Westchester County: New York's Golden Apple / 71

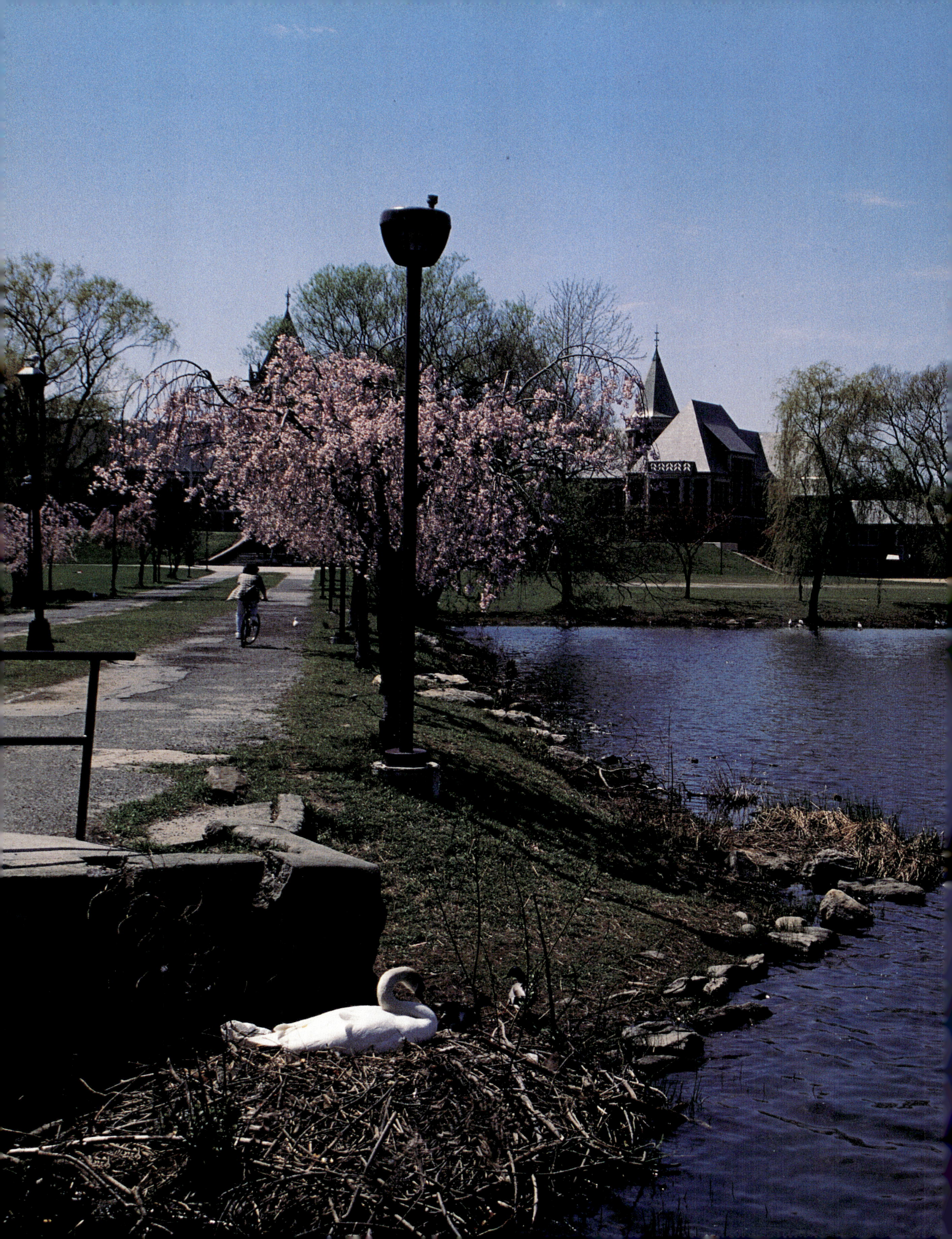

of 898 on the standardized Student Assessment Tests (SATs), or some 16 points higher than the average statewide and much better than the average nationally. Pupils here also score extremely well in the New York State Regents Examinations, well-known for being among the most difficult anywhere for high school students. An examination of the dropout rate here reveals that in this county the percentage of dropouts is 2.3 percent, less than half of the statewide figure and over four times less than the New York City average.

A further illustration of the level of excellence produced by county high schools is the number of graduates who go on to college. An average of 82 percent countywide advanced to institutions of higher learning in 1990. And more than a few districts had almost 100 percent move up the educational ladder. In recent years 30 Westchester schools have been cited by the U.S. Department of Education as National Schools of Excellence.

PRIVATE AND PAROCHIAL SCHOOLS

Private schools have been in existence in Westchester County since the 1800s. They include some of the finest and best-known in the nation.

Westchester spares no expense in providing a quality education to its public school students. Pictured in the background, the campus of New Rochelle High School. *Photo by Joe Vericker.*

73

EDUCATION EQUALS EXCELLENCE

The Hackley School in Tarrytown, which was founded in 1899, is a picturesque 113-acre campus overlooking the Hudson River. A coeducational institution, the school includes kindergarten through grade 12, with boarding available for boys and girls in grades 7 to 12.

Rye Country Day School's campus is located in Rye on 25 acres. The school is coeducational and serves prekindergarten through grade 12.

The Masters School in Dobbs Ferry provides parallel middle schools for young men and women, and a coeducational high school. The high school's students come from all over the world, and most of them board. Its 96-acre campus is adjacent to the Hudson River.

The Harvey School in Katonah boards most of its predominantly male enrollment on a five-day-a-week basis. The 100-acre campus features an indoor skating rink. Grades 6 through 12 are accommodated with a pupil-to-teacher ratio of 7 to 1.

No less than nine parochial high schools, many of them operated by the Archdiocese of New York, are spread throughout the county. All-male schools include Iona Prep in New Rochelle, Archbishop Stepinac in White Plains, and Salesian in New Rochelle. All-female institutions number the Ursuline School in New Rochelle, Good Counsel Academy in White Plains, Maria Regina in Hartsdale, and Holy Child in Rye. Blessed Sacrament in New Rochelle and John F. Kennedy in Somers are coeducational.

Photo courtesy of The Masters School

74 / WESTCHESTER COUNTY: New York's Golden Apple

Above, The United States Department of Education has twice recognized the Ursuline School as a Blue Ribbon School and cited it for "excellence in private education." *Photo by Joe Vericker.*

Left, Iona Prep, founded by the Christian Brothers, is a private Catholic school for young men, grades 9 through 12. Iona is fully accredited by the New York State Board of Regents and the Middle States Association for Secondary Schools and Colleges. *Photo by Joe Vericker.*

EDUCATION EQUALS EXCELLENCE

Photo courtesy of Keio Academy

CULTURALLY ORIENTED SCHOOLS

The composition of Westchester County's population has fostered a need for schools that fulfill specific cultural requirements not typically found in private and public schools.

One such school is Keio Academy in Purchase, which is patterned after Keio University of Japan. Many of the latter's educational methods have been utilized for the children of the county's substantial Japanese community. Students are accepted from any country in the world regardless of national origin.

Among the most significant of the Jewish day schools to be found here is the Solomon Schecter Day School in White Plains, where the scholarship and traditions of Judaism provide a focal point. Other schools with obvious strong cultural roots are the French-American School of New York in Larchmont and the German School in White Plains.

VOCATIONAL SCHOOLS

Because not everyone's plans will include college, some students choose to acquire skills that can be applied in the workforce directly upon graduation from high school. School districts like Yonkers, with its Saunders Trades High School, fill this need.

The Southern Westchester and Putnam/Northern Westchester Board of Cooperative Educational Services (BOCES) provides services for students from kindergarten through grade 12 in

76 / Westchester County: New York's Golden Apple

Photo courtesy of SUNY-Westchester Community College

some 53 districts. In addition, it supplies career training, counseling, and even job placement for many adults. BOCES also provides 20 career-training programs for high school students in such diverse areas as cosmetology, TV and video production, health services, graphic arts, computer repair, travel and tourism, and automobile servicing.

Other programs and services involve occupational education for students with special needs, nighttime vocational education courses for adults, and a free Adult Learning Center for students who need help in basic skills, preparing for the high school equivalency examination, improving their vocabulary in English, or obtaining career guidance.

COLLEGES AND UNIVERSITIES

Few counties in the United States can match Westchester when it comes to its number and variety of institutions of higher learning. Over two dozen degree-granting educational facilities are located here. A single community—the city of New Rochelle—boasts three colleges: Iona, Monroe, and the College of New Rochelle.

Iona College was founded in 1940 by the Christian Brothers of Ireland (now simply the Christian Brothers) as a male-only institution. The school has long been coed and is now the largest—some 9,000 full- and part-time students—four-year college in the county. It offers master's, bachelor's and associate degrees. Among its more

Westchester County: New York's Golden Apple / 77

EDUCATION EQUALS EXCELLENCE

Iona College's state-of-the-art Murphy Science and Technology Center. *Photo by Joe Vericker.*

noteworthy departments are the Hagan School of Business—recognized as one of the finest in the Northeast—as well as computer science, telecommunications, education, pastoral, and family counseling.

The College of New Rochelle, once known as the largest Catholic women's college in the United States, has also been coeducational for some time. Founded in 1904 by the Ursuline Order, it has grown from one school with 12 students on one campus to four schools with seven campuses and a student population of over 6,800. The Graduate School was established in 1969, the School of New Resources for adult learners in 1972, and the School of Nursing in 1976. Only the School of Arts and Sciences continues the tradition of enrolling only women.

Monroe College offers associate degrees in accounting, business administration, computer science, office technologies, and hospitality management, as well as a bachelor of science degree in business management and information systems. A Business Resource Center works closely with area businesses to teach the latest in software packages and hardware functions in customized programs both on campus and at the employer's workplace.

Sarah Lawrence College in Bronxville, founded in 1926, is a selective, coeducational liberal arts school offering undergraduate programs spanning the creative and performing arts, the humanities, the social sciences, mathematics, and the natural sciences. It is renowned for its seminar classes with private, biweekly tutorials and independent projects. The college also provides graduate programs in teaching, child development, dance, human genetics, health advocacy, theater, technical theater design, women's history, and writing.

78 / Westchester County: New York's Golden Apple

New York Medical College in Valhalla, the region's leading academic biomedical research center with $24 million in active research, is committed to working with biomedical companies to advance the development of new products. *Photo courtesy of New York Medical College.*

Also located in Bronxville is Concordia College, another four-year liberal arts college with programs leading to bachelor of arts and bachelor of science degrees in major fields ranging from business to social work, in addition to several two-year associate degree programs. Education is the largest major, with state certification offered in both elementary and secondary education. Premed, prelaw, music, social work, and some business administration options are also available.

The New York Medical College in Valhalla, with more than 1,600 students and 1,000 full-time faculty, is the county's only school of medicine and one of the oldest of its kind in the state. In addition, the graduate school of Basic Medical Sciences awards master's and Ph.D. degrees, while its graduate school of Health Sciences offers master of public health and master of science degrees.

Originally established as the Polytechnic Institute of Brooklyn in 1854, Polytechnic University's Westchester Center in Hawthorne provides graduate programs serving scientists, engineers, and managers employed in the high-technology companies of the region. The Center fulfills students' educational needs by providing part-time graduate degree programs and specialized continuing education programs. Programs are offered in electrical engineering, computer science, metallurgy and materials science, chemistry, management, manufacturing engineering, telecommunications and computing management, and information-systems engineering.

Undergraduates at Mercy College in Dobbs Ferry can choose programs in preprofessional and professional studies and liberal arts and sciences leading to bachelor of arts, bachelor of science, and associate in arts or science degrees. The school's varied preprofessional programs are in law, podiatry, osteopathy, dentistry, medicine, pharmacy, chiropractics, and optometry. It also provides teacher certification programs and master's degrees in science, nursing, learning technology, and human resource management.

Pace University is a comprehensive, independent institution with campuses in Westchester County and New York City. The University offers a wide variety of undergraduate and graduate degree programs in business, the arts and sciences, com-

Westchester County: New York's Golden Apple / 79

Photo courtesy of Pace University School of Law

puter science and information systems, education, and nursing on both the Pleasantville/Briarcliff and Manhattan campuses. The School of Law and the Lubin Graduate Center are located in White Plains. The University's Cooperative Education program, one of the largest in the region, enables students to work while they learn.

During its 50 years SUNY-Westchester Community College in Valhalla during has grown from a small technical institute with 226 students and four curricula to more than 11,000 credit students enrolled in associate degree and certificate programs in more than 40 academic areas. An additional 8,000 students take continuing education, noncredit courses for career enhancement or personal enrichment. SUNY-WCC is the only resource in the county for college-level engineering technologies programs and for programs in the allied health sciences such as respiratory care, radiological technology, and medical laboratory technology. Other programs include extensive liberal arts curricula, human services, criminal justice, travel and tourism, business management and international business, computer science, fine and performing arts, communications, and food services administration.

Manhattanville College in Purchase, founded in 1841, grants bachelor of arts, bachelor of music, and bachelor of fine arts degrees as well as a bachelor of science degree in organizational management, and a master's degree in leadership and strategic management to its more than 800 undergraduates in over 30 academic majors.

Seven hundred graduate students pursue master's degrees in human resource development, teaching, liberal studies, organizational management, leadership and strategic management, and writing. Post-master's teacher certification programs are also available. Some undergraduate and graduate degree programs, including business administration, nursing, law, engineering, and dentistry, are held jointly with other institutions.

Marymount College in Tarrytown, an independent liberal arts college for women with over 30 majors,

80 / Westchester County: New York's Golden Apple

EDUCATION EQUALS EXCELLENCE

grants bachelor of arts and bachelor of science degrees in art business, life science, education, English, fashion, foods and nutrition, history, information systems, foreign languages, prelaw, and premed. The Continuing Education Department offers certificates in human resources, publishing, fundraising, and interior design. In 1975 Marymount College opened its Weekend College (the first of its kind in Westchester), which offers adult men and women the opportunity to pursue a bachelor's degree by attending classes exclusively on weekends. Since then over 1,000 have graduated from the Weekend College.

Since 1975, Fordham University has offered its MBA degree program on the Marymount campus. Marketing, accounting, information and communications systems, education, social services, and finance and management systems are among the courses provided.

Another prominent New York metropolitan area college with a Westchester campus is Long Island University. Also established in 1975, LIU's Westchester Graduate Center, with an enrollment of around 1,000 students, is located on the campus of Mercy College. Master's programs in education and counseling, health, business and public administration, and arts and sciences may be pursued.

Purchase College, the State University of New York, is a major institution of higher education comprising performing, visual, and liberal arts divisions as well as a division of continuing education. The performing and visual arts divisions provide professional conservatory training in dance, theater arts, film, music, and visual arts.

The liberal arts division provides a curriculum in the humanities, natural sciences, and social sciences, while the division of continuing education provides a broad scope of educational opportunities for the entire community.

The Westchester Business Institute in White Plains, a fully accredited private two-year business college, offers full-and part-time programs leading to associate degrees and diplomas. Founded in 1915, it recently introduced courses in entrepreneurship and starting a business in response to a growing demand on the part of prospective students for such instruction.

Berkeley College, also located in White Plains, is another well-regarded institution offering associate degrees in computer programming and accounting. ◆

Westchester Business Institute is meeting the requirements of today's business environment by providing students with a host of multilevel, business career-oriented programs. *Photo by Joe Vericker.*

Westchester County: New York's Golden Apple / 81

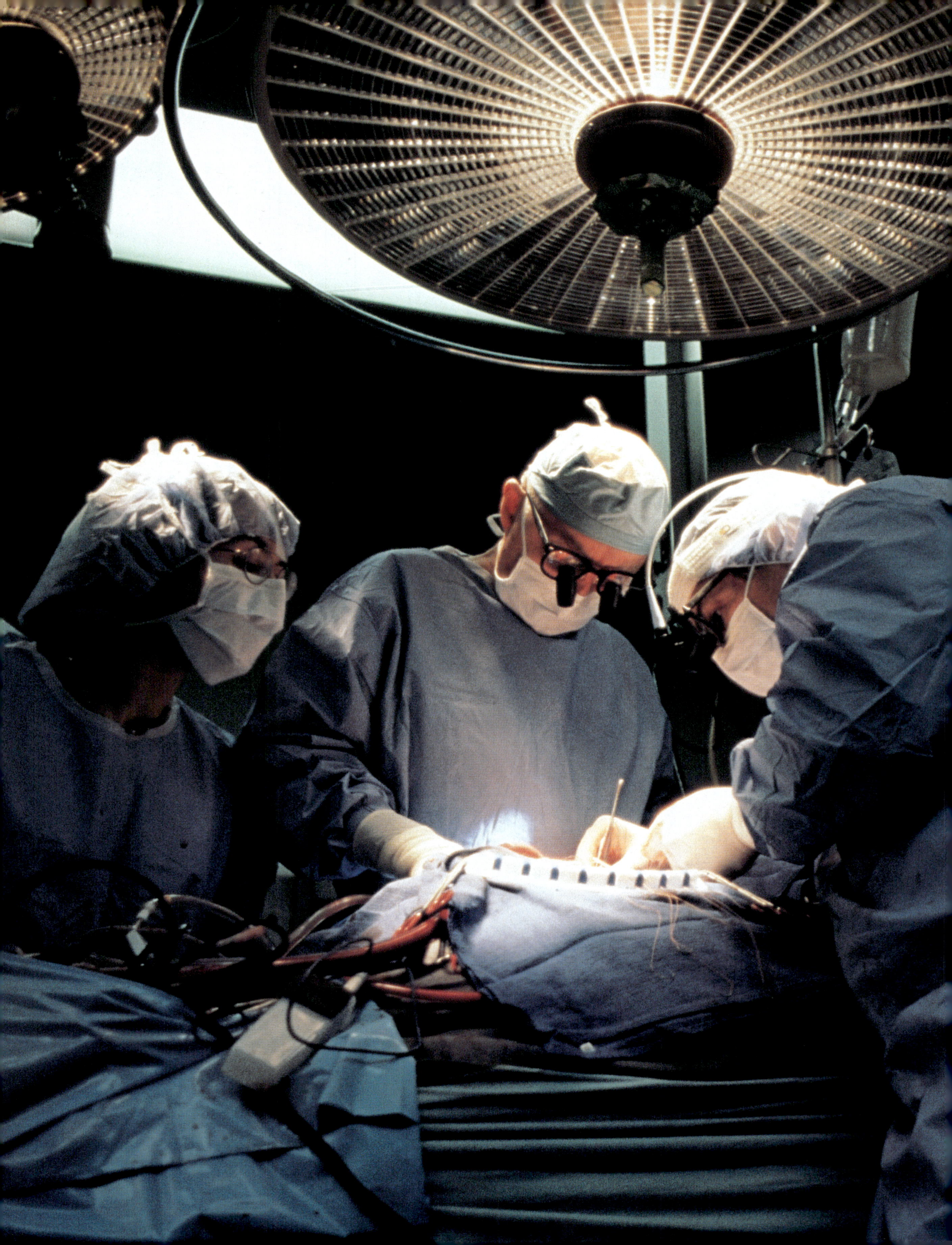

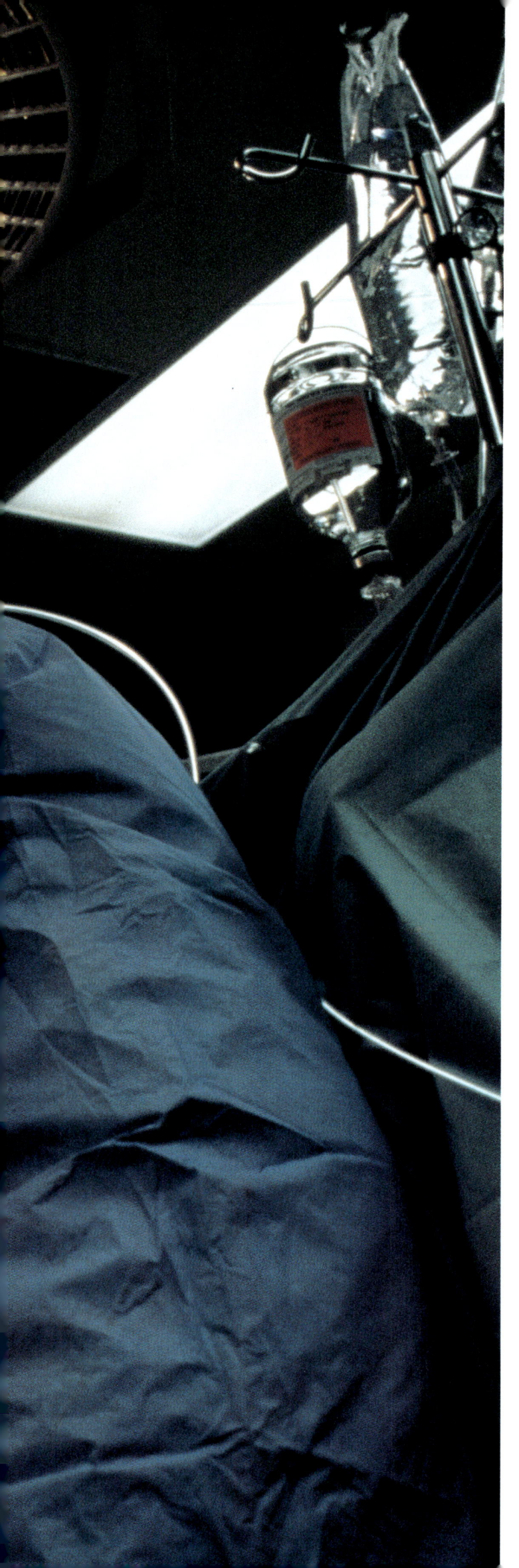

CHAPTER · SIX

HEALTH CARE FOR EVERYONE

The county of Westchester offers a broad range of health care services administered by a highly trained and dedicated cadre of medical professionals. Westchester's 14 hospitals are staffed by talented individuals who are drawn here for the standards of excellence as well as the working enivironment.

Photo courtesy of Westchester County Medical Center

Westchester County: New York's Golden Apple / 83

Augmented by burgeoning health maintenance organizations (HMOs), specialized health care facilities, and wellness programs, the county stands out as a leader in providing a complete array of medical services at reasonable costs. It all adds up to another advantage for businesses choosing New York's Golden Apple.

HOSPITALS

By far the largest single medical facility in the area, the Valhalla-based Westchester County Medical Center is the tertiary care and Level 1 Trauma Center for a region of more than 3.5 million people. Second only to IBM in the number of employees in Westchester, the medical center has more than 1,100 beds in its four facilities: Main Hospital, Behavioral Health Center, Ruth Taylor Geriatric Institute, and Institute for Human Development. With care spanning every medical specialty in existence, the medical center's six Centers of Excellence—Heart, Children's Hospital, Trauma and Burn, Transplant, Neurosciences, and Cancer Institute—offer the finest physicians and highest level of care to the most severely ill and injured infants, children, and adults from the region and beyond.

St. John's Riverside in Yonkers is the county's first hospital (1869) and is still one of its finest and largest with nearly 1,000 employees. Its Cochran School of Nursing (one of only two hospital-based nursing programs in Westchester) offers a two-year accredited R.N. program to qualified candidates. Apart from its renowned emergency care facility,

This trauma team is ready at a moment's notice to render care and treatment to the most critically injured people throughout the county. *Photo courtesy of Westchester County Medical Center.*

84 / Westchester County: New York's Golden Apple

HEALTH CARE FOR EVERYONE

Above, Medical residents listen intently to instruction at Sound Shore Medical Center in New Rochelle. *Photo courtesy of Sound Shore Medical Center.*

Right, Within minutes, STAT Flight helicopters and mobile intensive care units can be dispatched to any location in the 5,000-square-mile region. *Photo courtesy of Westchester County Medical Center.*

Health Care for Everyone

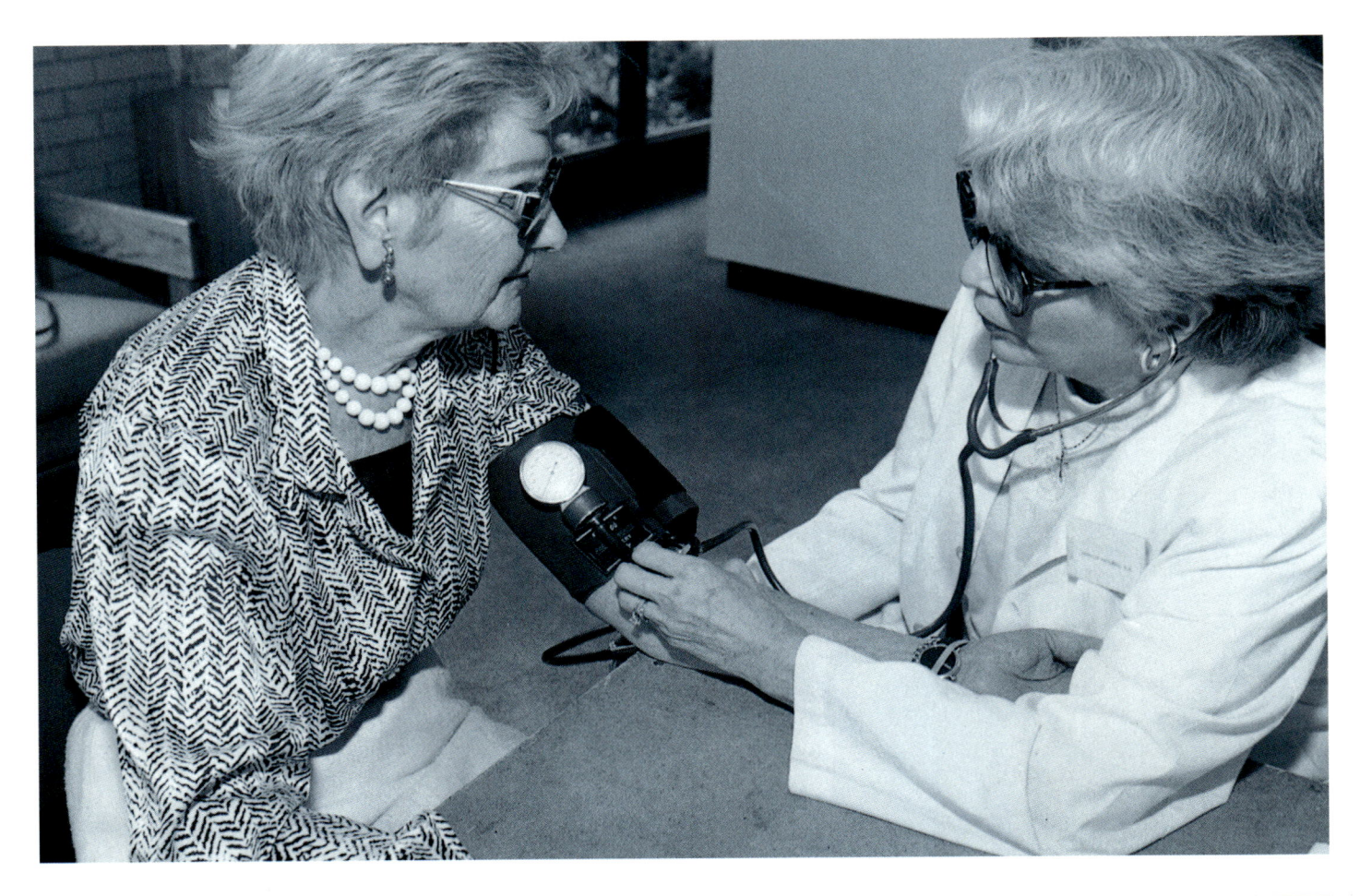

the 270-bed hospital features cardiac rehabilitation, laser surgery, a wound care center, and the only hospital-based maternity care services in the city of Yonkers. The hospital is also noted for its leadership in state-of-the-art vascular surgery and breast cancer detection programs.

Founded in 1893, White Plains Hospital Center has been attending to the health care needs of the greater White Plains community for over 100 years. The hospital has intensified its efforts in serving the needy, especially children. A program called "Healthy Beginnings," started in 1993, furnishes free health care to children in conjunction with the White Plains School District's Prekindergarten Program. Parents and their offspring receive complete medical care from the doctor's office to the hospital, if necessary, at no charge.

Sound Shore Medical Center's 465-bed facility opened in 1892 as New Rochelle Hospital Medical Center. Affiliated with the New York Medical College, it is the second largest hospital in the county, although its annual operating budget is the biggest among the private hospitals. Like most of the health care facilities in Westchester, it offers a comprehensive array of services but is widely known for its geriatric care, laparoscopic surgery, obstetric, and pediatric services.

Mount Vernon Hospital is located outside St. John's Riverside in Yonkers. This facility provides the only other hospital-based school of nursing. Begun in 1890, it offers the complete range of health care services but provides many special treatment programs that others do not. Among these programs are a poison control center, noninvasive vascular and pulmonary function laboratories, an advanced life-support hospital trauma center, a diabetes clinic, and an ambulatory surgical unit. The hospital is also unique in the number and variety of specialty clinics it houses, including those for the treatment of mental health and chronic wounds as well as methadone maintenance. A little-known

Community health screenings provide a vital service to county residents. *Photo courtesy of White Plains Hospital Center.*

HEALTH CARE FOR EVERYONE

United Hospital Medical Center's affiliation with the New York Hospital/Cornell Medical Center enhances the quality of patient care by bringing the outstanding resources of that renowned institution to the local community. As a result, patients at United benefit from the highest levels of medicine and technology close to home. *Photo by Joe Vericker.*

fact about the hospital is that it is the largest employer in the community.

Established in 1889, United Hospital Medical Center serves the Sound Shore with a 311-bed facility and over 900 employees. Among the five private hospitals in Westchester with a psychiatric unit, United's is the biggest. It counts among its specialties a home health care department, a family life center, a full range of inpatient and outpatient diagnostic and treatment services, and a skilled nursing pavilion.

Bronxville's Lawrence Hospital is a 280-bed facility which attends to the acute-care needs of south central Westchester. The hospital is served by 350 doctors, and two-thirds of its approximately 800 employees are nurses. Among its specialized services are sports medicine, emergency services, family-focused maternity care, rehabilitation services, and ambulatory surgery. The

Westchester County: New York's Golden Apple / 87

Health Care for Everyone

St. Agnes Hospital in White Plains. *Photo by Joe Vericker.*

Lawrence Immediate Myocardial Infarction Treatment Program— also known as LIMIT—prides itself on its rapid response to heart attack victims.

The Hudson Valley Hospital Center in Peekskill serves not only northern Westchester but also Rockland, Putnam, and Dutchess Counties. In 1994 it opened the only free-standing birth cottage in the tristate area. The 120-bed facility provides specialized cardiac fitness, methadone maintenance, physical therapy, obstetrics, and ambulatory surgery. The Leonard Wagner Pavilion, a recent 60,000-square-foot addition, includes four surgical suites, a new emergency department, and several laboratories.

The 184-bed St. Agnes Hospital in White Plains includes a Children's Rehabilitation Center, a chemical dependency unit, a diabetic treatment center, an Early Childhood Direction Center, and a vascular unit among its capabilities. The hospital, which is affiliated with the New York Medical College, also offers an oncology unit that provides autologous bone marrow transplants as well as a treatment center for multiple sclerosis patients. St. Agnes is noted for its role in preparing the disabled for their return to life away from a hospital environment.

88 / Westchester County: New York's Golden Apple

HEALTH CARE FOR EVERYONE

Westchester residents expect and receive the most modern diagnostic imaging techniques, including MRI testing. *Photo courtesy of Northern Westchester Hospital Center.*

North Tarrytown-based Phelps Memorial Hospital Center is a full-service community hospital in Westchester. Founded in 1956, the 235-bed facility has more than 1,100 employees on its staff. In recent years it has created a major mental health center with nine satellites dispersed about its immediate environs. The hospital has also established a rehabilitation center with both in- and outpatient capabilities. It is also proud of its radiation oncology department served by physicians from the prestigious Memorial Sloan-Kettering Cancer Center.

Yonkers General Hospital's 190-bed unit was incorporated in 1896 as the Homeopathic Home and Maternity. This facility began as a hospital dedicated to providing maternity and sick infant care because no such treatment was available at the time. Over 25 years ago it was one of the first hospitals in the country to provide cobalt therapy in the treatment of cancer. It now offers a complete oncology program among its wide range of modern patient services, which also includes the largest alcohol and drug detoxification program in Westchester County.

Northern Westchester Hospital Center in Mt. Kisco contains 259 beds and has been serving central and northern Westchester since 1916. Well-known for its maternity care, it opened a state-of-the-art labor and delivery unit in 1993. There

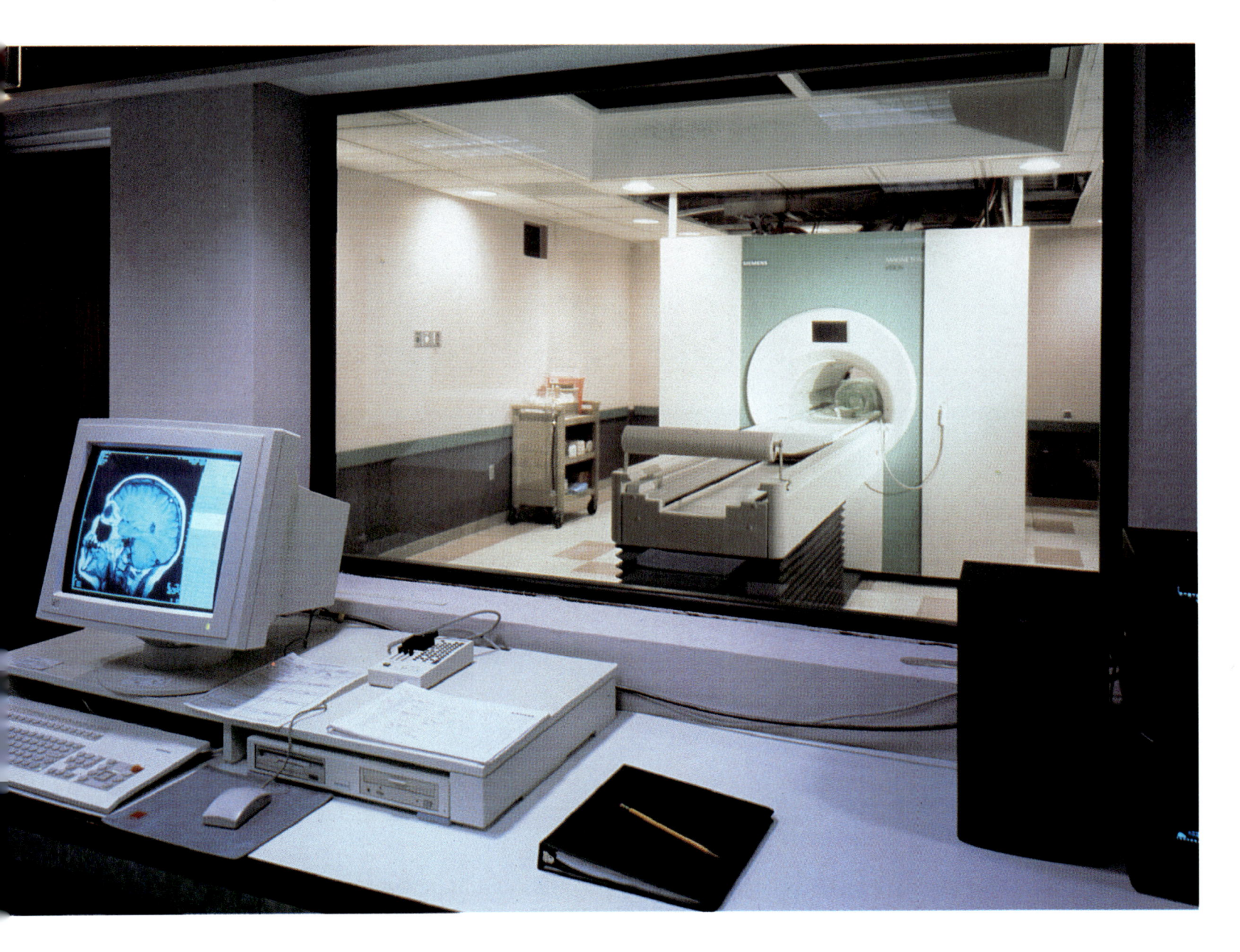

Westchester County: New York's Golden Apple / 89

HEALTH CARE FOR EVERYONE

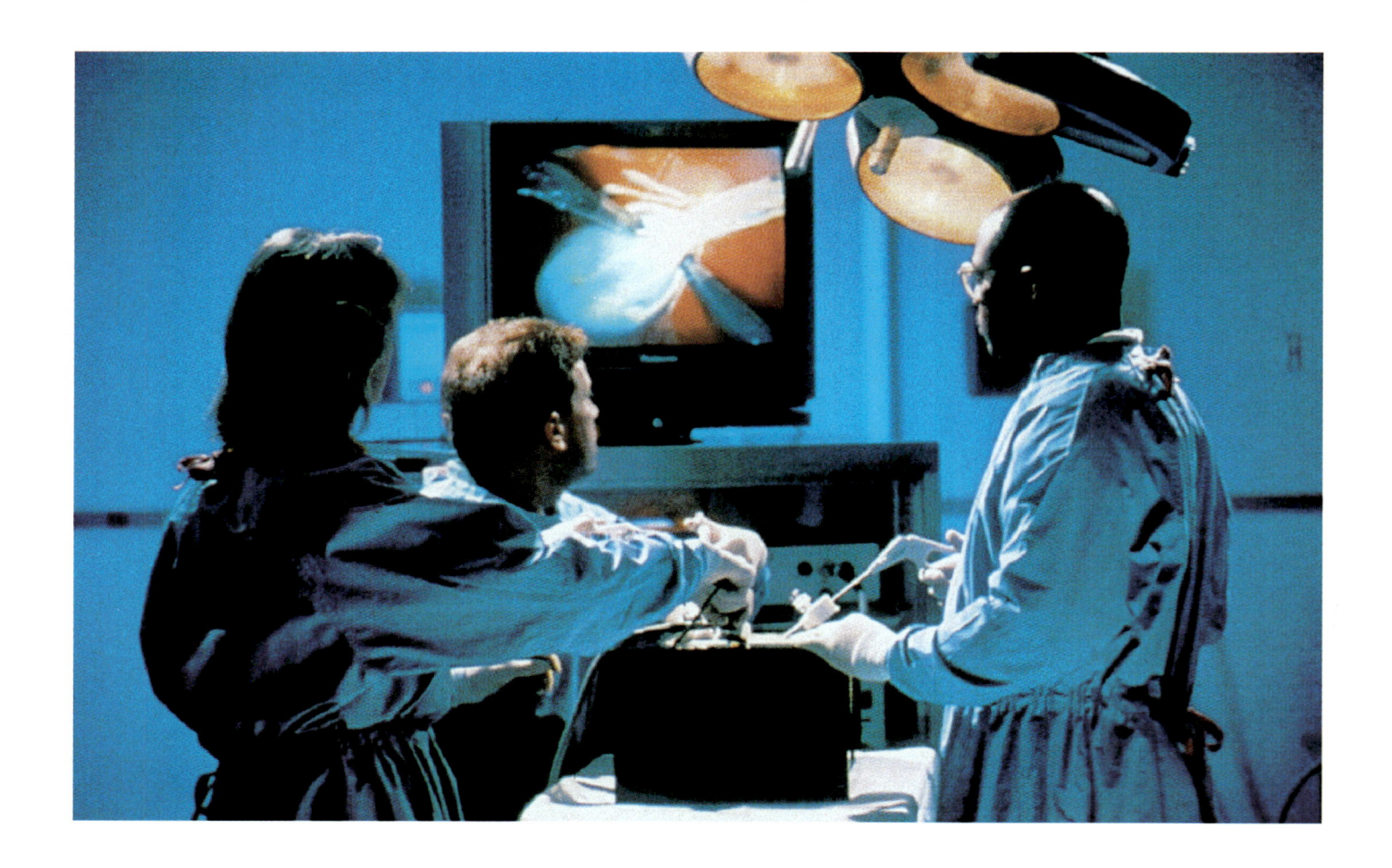

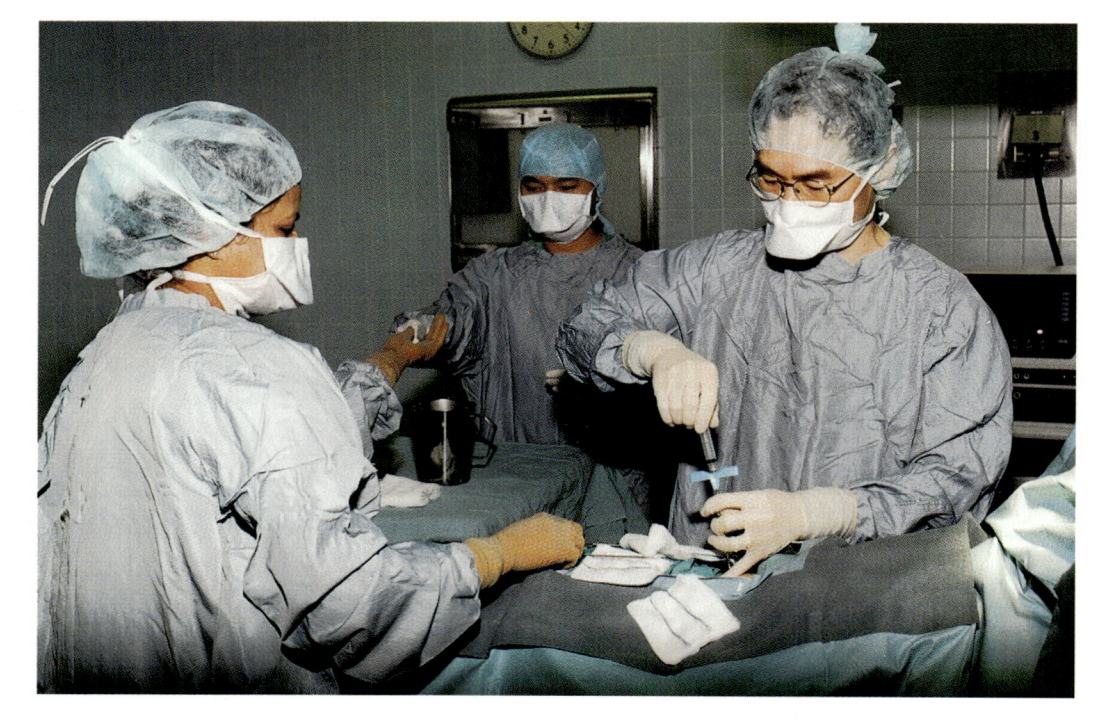

Above, Photo courtesy of St. John's Riverside Hospital

Left, The Hudson Valley Bone Marrow Transplant Center at Saint Joseph's Medical Center in Yonkers is the only one serving southern Westchester. *Photo courtesy of Saint Joseph's Medical Center.*

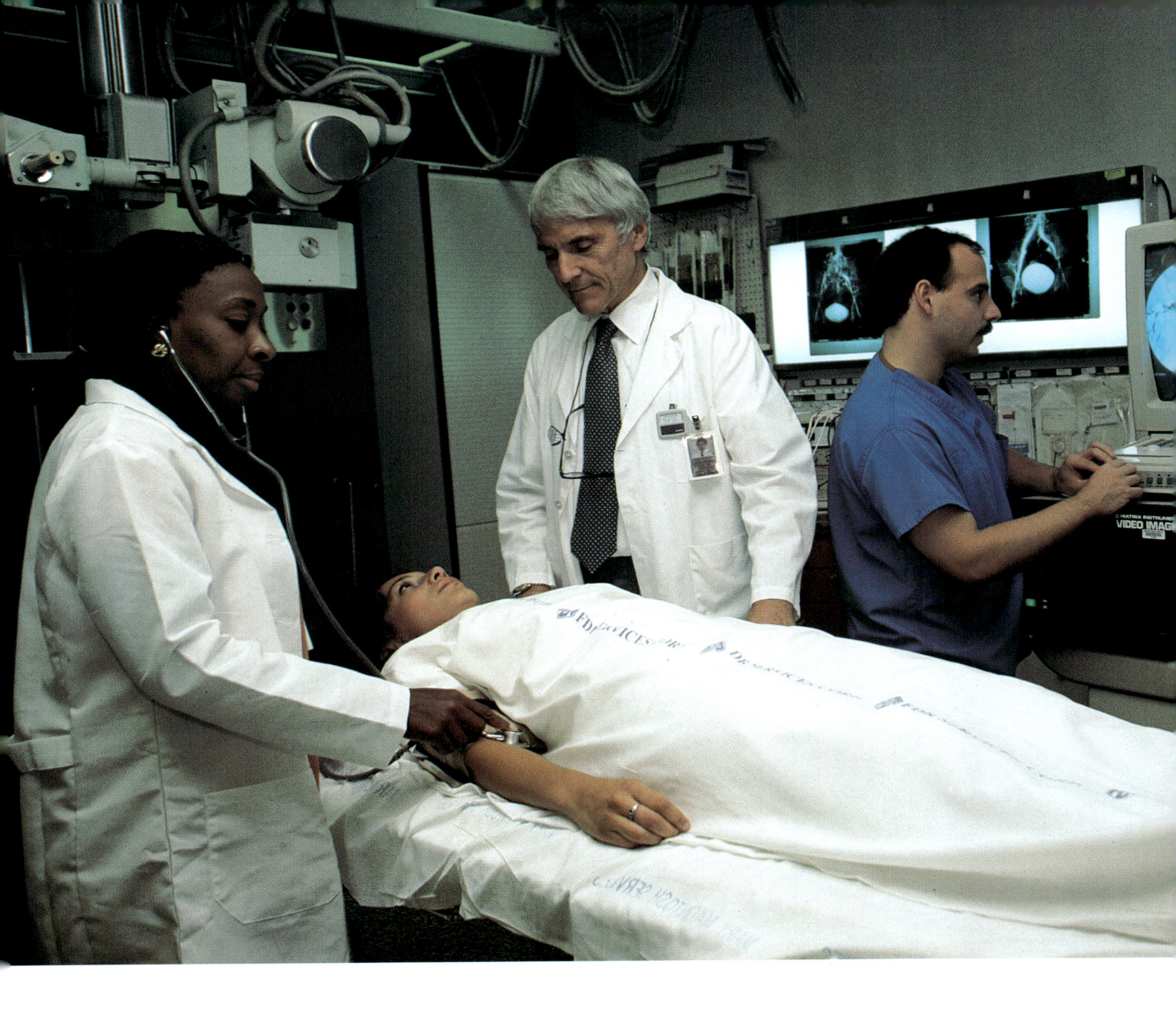

Radiology Department at Yonkers General Hospital. *Photo by Joe Vericker.*

is nothing a mother would lack here, from its 6 labor, delivery, and recovery rooms with an adjacent operating suite to a nursery, 27 post-partum rooms, a neonatal Level II special care nursery staffed by full-time neonatologists, and a Breast-feeding Resource Center supported by lactation consultants.

Founded in 1888 by the Sisters of Charity, Saint Joseph's Medical Center in Yonkers is comprised of a 194-bed acute care hospital, 200-bed nursing home, and numerous outpatient programs. The hospital's 24-hour emergency room, one of the busiest in the county, was completely renovated in 1991, and is the designated Medical Control Hospital and EMS training coordinator for the city of Yonkers. Saint Joseph's also offers such specialized services as laser, laparoscopic and microneuro-surgery, bone marrow transplants, renal dialysis, a sophisticated cardiology department and intensive-care units, psychiatry, and comprehensive programs for the elderly, as well as the full services of a modern health care facility.

Founded in 1893, Community Hospital at Dobbs Ferry is a 50-bed facility serving the western part of Westchester. Particularly noteworthy is the hospital's pacemaker program for coronary-care patients.

Westchester County: New York's Golden Apple / 91

HEALTH CARE FOR SPECIAL NEEDS

When specialized health care is called for, Westchester County can fulfill most requirements. The facilities here are in the forefront of their respective fields, as evidenced by the reputations they have earned over the years.

One of the best known is the Burke Rehabilitation Hospital in White Plains, world-renowned for its excellent multidisciplinary physical rehabilitation for patients recovering from disabling injuries and illnesses. Located on a picturesque 60-acre campus, the facility treats those who have experienced spinal cord injuries, strokes, arthritis and rheumatoid joint diseases, head trauma, limb amputations, and cardiac and pulmonary diseases.

Also located on the grounds at Burke is the Will Rogers Institute, established in 1936 by the motion picture industry in upstate New York to treat entertainers stricken with tuberculosis. It relocated here in 1977 and today is involved with research, fellowships, and laboratories studying AIDS,

World-renowned Burke Rehabilitation Hospital in White Plains. *Photo by Joe Vericker.*

92 / Westchester County: New York's Golden Apple

HEALTH CARE FOR EVERYONE

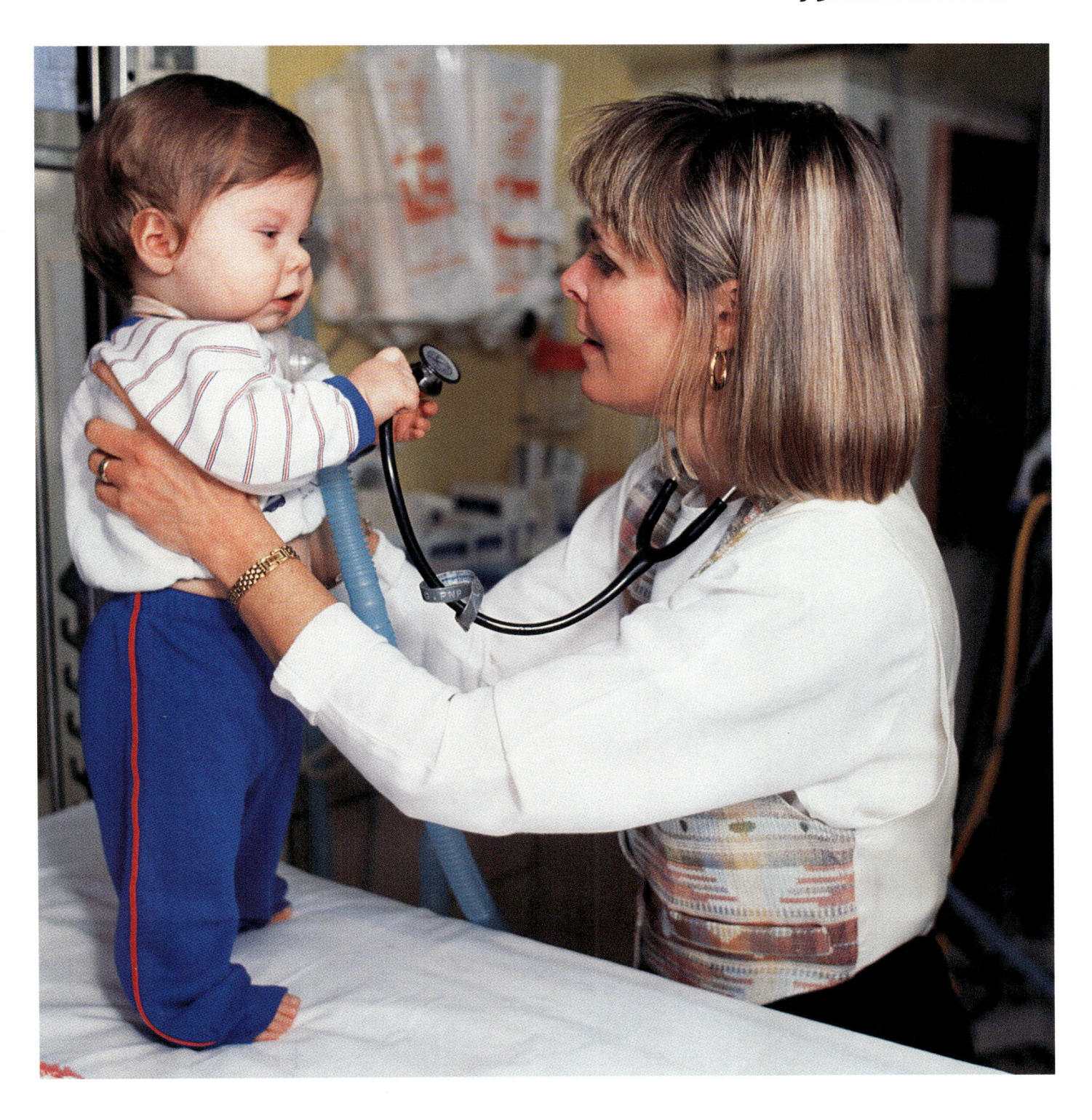

Photo by Smith-Baer/courtesy of Blythedale Children's Hospital

Alzheimer's, and pulmonary diseases. It also continues to treat show business personnel with pulmonary diseases.

Also in White Plains is The Lighthouse, Inc., recognized as the world leader in sight rehabilitation. It provides both individual and group programs that are held at its own facility, at schools, or at patients' homes or job sites to help them better cope with their afflictions. Special optical devices are made available for those who have at least partial use of sight.

Another White Plains-based specialized health care facility is the widely respected New York Hospital/Cornell Medical Center. It is not only the county's largest psychiatric care operation but is also famed for its treatment methodology.

A noteworthy psychiatric hospital in the area since 1879 is St. Vincent's Hospital, located in nearby Harrison. Another facility founded by the Sisters of Charity, St. Vincent's currently accommodates 133 inpatients. Affiliated with the Archdiocese of New York, it also conducts a series of helpful programs for outpatients.

Westchester County: New York's Golden Apple / 93

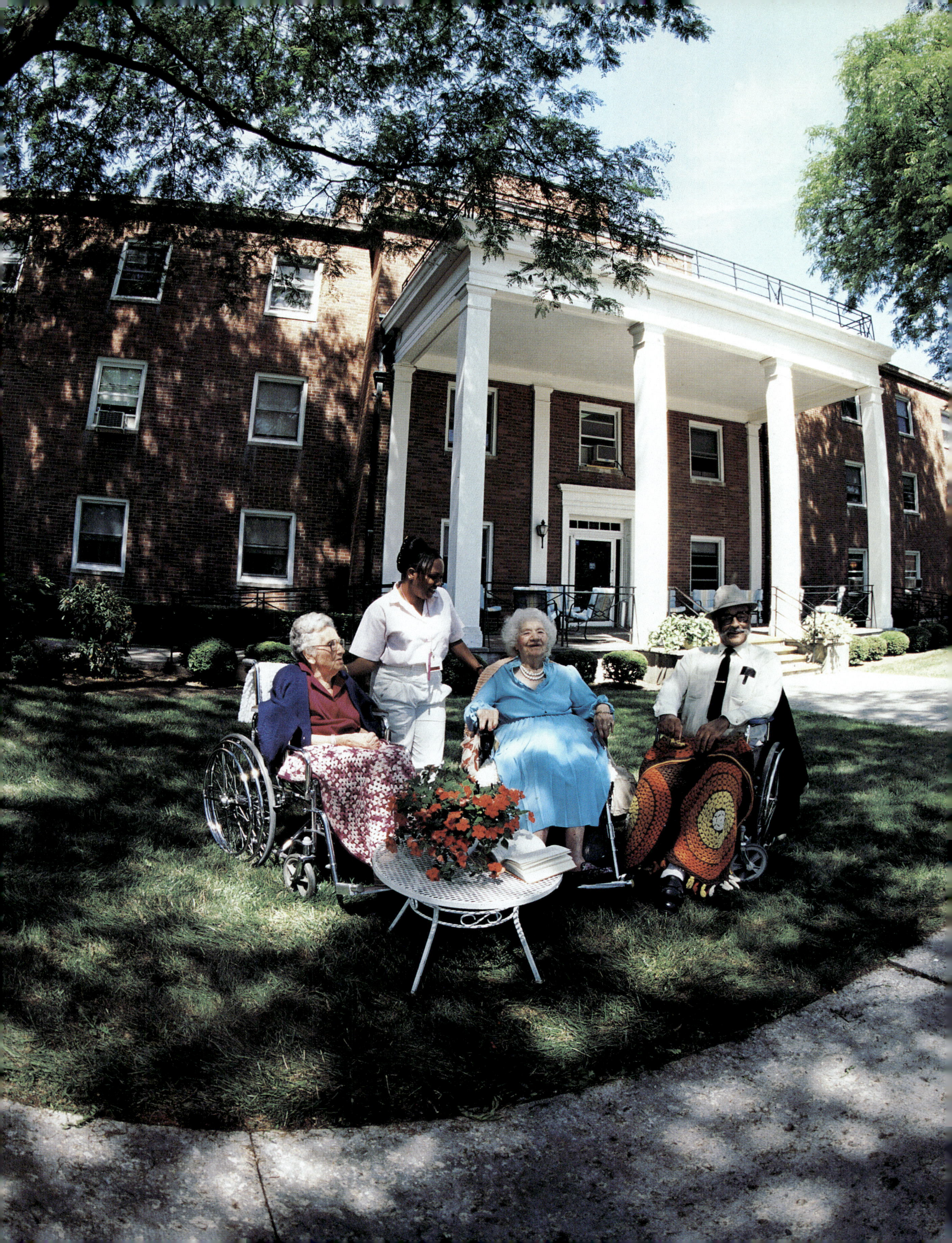

HEALTH CARE FOR EVERYONE

Left, Photo by Whitney Lane/ Courtesy of Bethel Homes

Below, Photo by Joe Vericker

Founded by Methodists, Bethel Homes relocated from Brooklyn to Ossining in 1920. This nonprofit, nonsectarian organization now provides quality care for the elderly in its homes in Ossining and Croton-On-Hudson.

And for over a century now, the Blythedale Children's Hospital in Valhalla has been attending to the rehabilitation therapy needs of youngsters.

Indeed, these specialized facilities form an ideal partnership with the area's general care hospitals to ensure that Westchester County's total health care needs are served.

HEALTH MAINTENANCE ORGANIZATIONS

Health maintenance organizations (HMOs), growing steadily nationwide, have found their niche in both New York State and Westchester. The county represents over a third of all HMOs in the state and leads the nation in enrollees.

HMOs offer approximately the same services as other health care groups such as doctors' visits and hospital confinement. Costs are based upon the plan(s)—called models—selected.

In a Staff Model, the health facilities are owned and operated by the HMO, while a Group Model has physicians practice in their own facilities and contract with an HMO to treat enrolled patients. Still another choice, the Independent Practice Association allows doctors to perform services in their own facilities and serve both HMO enrollees and their own private patients. ◆

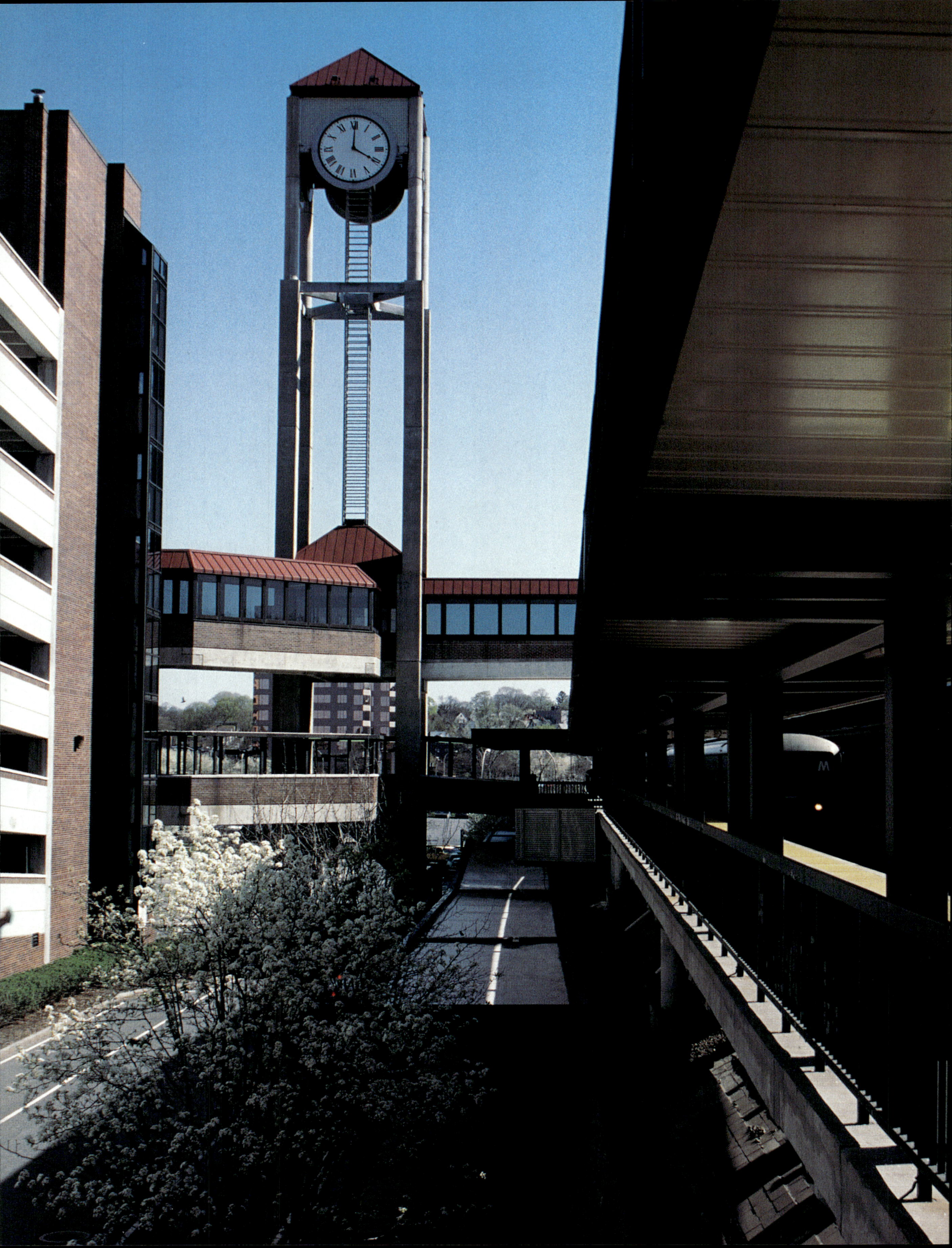
M

CHAPTER · SEVEN

A FINE-TUNED TRANSPORTATION NETWORK

Westchester County combines the strengths of its many transportation systems to help the Golden Apple of New York retain its lofty position as an outstanding area in which to live and work.

Photo by Joe Vericker

Interstate 95 joins Westchester County with the states to the north and New York City and Long Island to the south. It is the major north-to-south highway on the East Coast, extending all the way from Maine to Florida. *Photo by Joe Vericker.*

The county's roadways, rail system, and bus service form a network that makes any of Westchester's major cities reachable within 10 to 30 minutes.

The county's centrally located and vastly improved airport facility, complete with a state-of-the-art passenger terminal, has ushered in a new era for today's county residents and business travelers.

ROADWAYS

If you happen to be one of the thousands of drivers who travel Westchester's roadways each day, you might not give much thought to the value of being able to arrive at work on time and in a proper frame of mind. However, the careful planning by the various governments—federal, state, county, and local—to ensure that privilege is undeniable.

The New York State Department of Transportation has been doing its part to help the county by initiating a number of road improvements in recent years to help make travel both safe and efficient.

Interstate 87 (New York Thruway) runs from New York and New Jersey to southwest Westchester and then west across the Tappan Zee Bridge, parallel to the Hudson River, into Rockland County and then

98 / WESTCHESTER COUNTY: New York's Golden Apple

A FINE-TUNED *T*RANSPORTATION NETWORK

Metro-North, an operating agency of the Metropolitan Transportation Authority (MTA), is the second largest commuter rail operation in the United States. *Photo by Joe Vericker.*

upstate to Albany and Buffalo as far as Montreal.

Interstate 95 (New England Thruway) on the east side of Westchester joins the county with the states to the north and New York City and Long Island to the south, reigning as the major north-to-south highway on the East Coast.

Interstate 287 (Cross Westchester Expressway) is the primary east-to-west artery linking the Tappan Zee Bridge with I-95, crossing into White Plains and along the "Platinum Mile," where many top corporations reside, and then into Rye on the Long Island Sound.

Interstate 684 wends its way north through White Plains and into the county's northern and central suburbs up to Putnam County, some 30 miles to the north.

The Bronx River Parkway, constructed in 1927, is the oldest parkway in the United States. It begins at Westchester's southern border, runs along the river bearing its name to White Plains, and connects at the Kensico Reservoir with the Taconic State Parkway, which then proceeds as far north as Albany between the Hudson River and the Massachusetts border.

The Saw Mill River Parkway begins in Yonkers and travels in a northeasterly direction before merging

Westchester County: New York's Golden Apple / 99

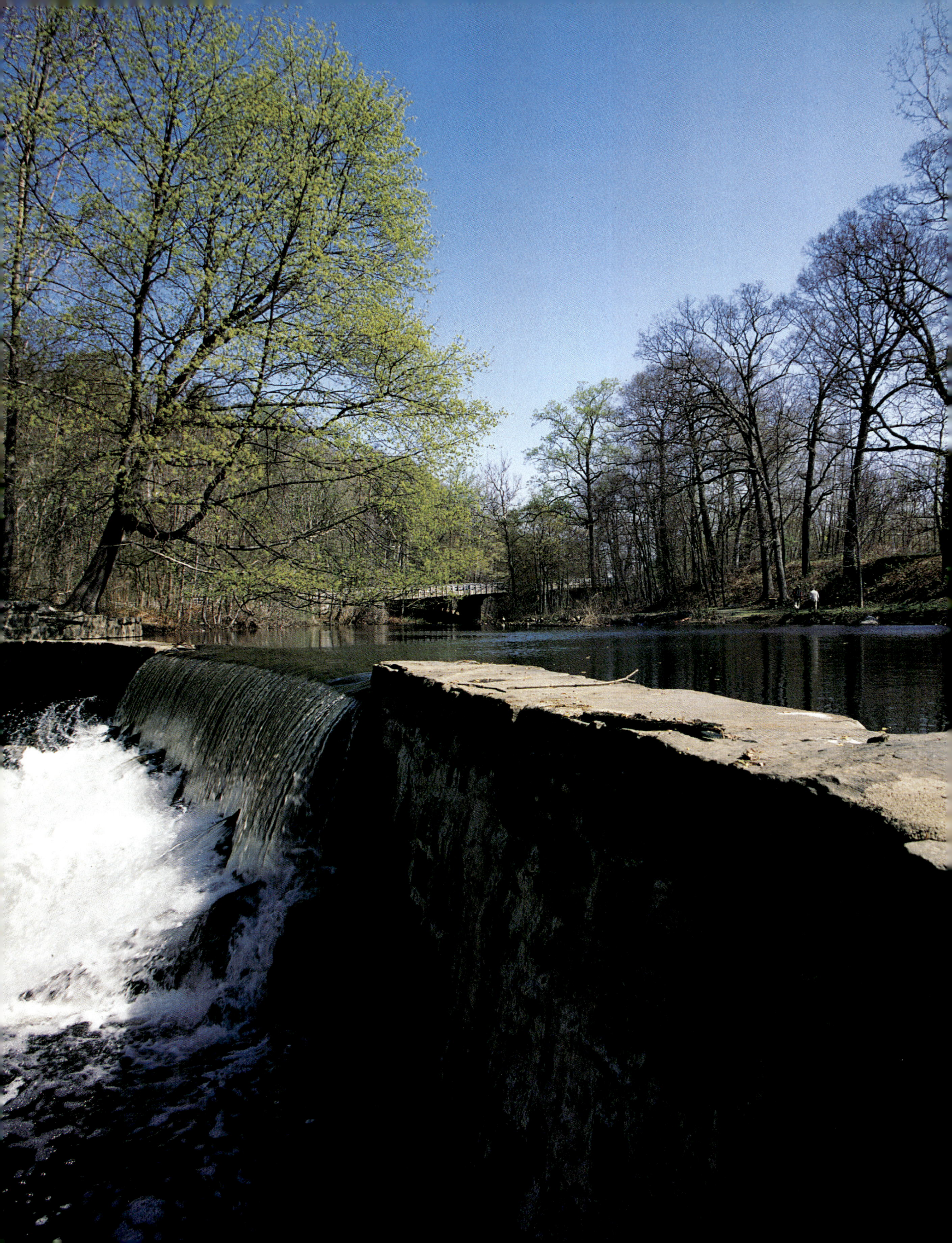

A FINE-TUNED *T*RANSPORTATION NETWORK

Above, Interstate 87 runs from New York and New Jersey to southwest Westchester and then west over the famed Tappan Zee Bridge and the Hudson River. *Photo by Joe Vericker.*

Left, This refreshing vista in Scarsdale is just one of a variety found along the the Bronx River Parkway, the oldest parkway in the United States. *Photo by Joe Vericker.*

with I-684 while paralleling I-95 and eventually reaching the Merritt Parkway into Connecticut.

The Cross County Parkway to the south joins the Henry Hudson Parkway in New York City and links the Saw Mill with the Hutchinson River Parkway. The latter is key to reaching both LaGuardia and Kennedy Airports as well as Westchester County Airport.

RAIL SYSTEM

A recent survey of chief executive officers of companies headquartered in Westchester ranked the county's public transit system as one of the primary reasons for being in business here. High on that list of public transportation is the county's rail system—the Metro-North Railroad—as administered by the Metropolitan Transit Authority (MTA).

Of the 119 station stops served by Metro-North, 44 are located in Westchester. The railroad's Harlem Line serves Fleetwood (Mt. Vernon), Bronxville, Tuckahoe, Crestwood/Eastchester, Scarsdale, Hartsdale, White Plains, and upcounty. To the east, the New Haven Line has stations in Mt. Vernon, Pelham, New Rochelle, Larchmont, Mamaroneck, Rye, and Port Chester. And the Hudson Line in the

Westchester County: New York's Golden Apple / 101

A FINE-TUNED *T*RANSPORTATION NETWORK

western part of the county stretches from Yonkers to Peekskill, running along the famous river northward.

Commuters, as well as those traveling into Manhattan for entertainment, can do so in 35 minutes or less, depending upon the hour of the day. Conversely, Manhattanites working in Westchester can do their "reverse" commute in no less time than it takes to read either their morning or evening newspaper. With trains running at speeds of 90 miles per hour during rush hours and with intervals between departures as little as 15 minutes, rail passengers can travel to and from home in a relaxed, efficient fashion.

The MTA is continually trying to improve conditions for its 225,000 daily riders. In recent years, it has successfully completed an ambitious renovation program. The result has been improved platform and station facilities, new equipment, and more parking space. Metro-North is also working with various regional planning and business groups to help make the county even more accessible. Among the areas being studied are schedule adjustments to satisfy the needs of commuters.

The railroad was honored recently for its overall effectiveness by the American Public Transit Association, which presented Metro-

Waving their goodbyes, children watch an Amtrak train leave the station in New Rochelle on its way to Washington, D.C., from Boston. *Photo by Joe Vericker.*

102 / Westchester County: New York's Golden Apple

A FINE-TUNED TRANSPORTATION NETWORK

North with its prestigious Outstanding Achievement Award.

Amtrak serves Westchester County as well. New Rochelle on the New Haven Line offers connections to Amtrak's Boston-to-Washington Northeast Corridor service, while the Hudson Line's Croton-Harmon station is used as a link for service upstate and to Montreal as well as to Chicago and points farther west.

BUS SERVICE

The county's Bee-Line bus service, which was cited by the American Public Transit Association as the most outstanding transit agency in North America for its size in 1991, is run by the Westchester County Department of Transportation. Ridership has grown continually to the point where its 325 buses now carry 55,000 passengers every weekday.

The line's 54 different routes join Westchester with Manhattan, the Bronx, and Putnam County. A shuttle service started in 1993 which connects Metro-North's White Plains station with a number of corporate parks along the Cross Westchester Expressway (I-287) has been gaining steady popularity. The shuttle gets people to their jobs faster while helping to reduce traffic and pollution at the same time.

A Bee-Line bus whisks passengers home before an impending late-afternoon summer thunderstorm. *Photo by Joe Vericker.*

Westchester County: New York's Golden Apple / 103

Westchester County Airport.
Photo by Joe Vericker.

In 1995 the county added 50 new wheelchair-accessible buses to their fleet at a cost of $222,000 per vehicle to serve five different routes. In addition, Bee-Line's Para-Transit van service has been designated to provide curb pickup from an individual's home provided he or she cannot use the line's regular buses.

AIRPORT

Conveniently located in the town of Harrison just off I-684 and five miles from White Plains, the Westchester County Airport is owned and operated by the county. A full-service facility offering regularly scheduled flights by major airlines and smaller carriers, it also provides charter services as well as corporate and general aviation flying. In addition, over 400 aircraft are based at the airport.

In the fall of 1995 a modern passenger terminal four times the size of the previous 50-year-old "temporary" terminal building was opened to the public. It contains 41,000 square feet of space on three levels and is marked by a sense of spaciousness and light.

An 1,100-car parking garage is linked to the terminal by enclosed walkways on every level so passengers do not have to step outside.

Terminal ticket counters accommodate any size baggage. The walls are trimmed attractively with slate and the floors are carpeted. Escalators are strategically placed to maximize the efficiency of passenger flow.

Every day 85 to 90 commercial flights and 550 corporate flights are recorded. Fourteen hangars at the 700-acre airport and two of the three runways are continually in use.

Airlines currently serving the airport include American, Allegheny Commuter, Northwest, United Express,

104 / WESTCHESTER COUNTY: New York's Golden Apple

A FINE-TUNED *Transportation* NETWORK

The new three-level, 41,000-square-foot passenger terminal of the Westchester County Airport is marked by a sense of spaciousness and light. *Photo by Joe Vericker.*

USAir, USAir Express, Downeast Express, Business Express, and Commute Air, the last two being Delta connections. Their destinations are Chicago, Philadelphia, Boston, Nantucket, Fort Lauderdale, Detroit, Washington, D.C., Buffalo, Pittsburgh, Baltimore, Portland, Maine, and Cincinnati.

Among the services available at the new terminal is a new flight information system with numerous monitors providing information on 24 hours of flights. Curbside check-in, as well as taxis, limousines, and courtesy telephones for hotel reservations, are all available.

There is a newsstand/gift shop and a coffee bar on the first floor; a 70-seat coffee shop on the second floor opens at 5:30 A.M. and closes only after the last flight; and an adjacent 100-seat Skytop Restaurant serves continental cuisine for lunch and dinner from 11 A.M. to 11 P.M.

A business center with fax and computer hookups is accessible to business travelers, including a conference room with a VCR available for rental, and an automatic teller machine. The second floor also houses administrative offices, the noise abatement office, and an outdoor observation deck.

FREIGHT TRANSPORT

Just about every air cargo company and overnight courier service is available to serve clients of not only Westchester County Airport but also the other nearby facilities—LaGuardia, Kennedy, and Stewart in neighboring Orange County. Add that to the fact that almost every major air passenger carrier provides cargo service—businesses here need not worry about getting an important parcel to a critical destination.

Rail freight service offers another valuable method of freight transport. Conrail and a solid group of other ser-

Westchester County: New York's Golden Apple / 105

vices give the New York area 14,000 miles of rail lines to connect it with cities such as Boston and Chicago, and south into Virginia.

In addition to ground transport, Westchester commerce has the ability to take advantage of the New York Port Authority's ocean freight ports to make shipments overseas.

Many businesses make use of the Hudson River when making bulk shipments both in the United States and abroad. Tugboats docked along the Hudson are widely employed for these purposes.

Westchester is proving to be an ideal location for corporations seeking commercial and industrial transportation services, particularly as requirements for nationwide and overseas shipping points increase. ◆

Above, The majestic Tappan Zee Bridge, as viewed from the Tarrytown shoreline. *Photo by Joe Vericker.*

Right, A New York Waterway scenic cruise boards in the shadow of the Tappan Zee Bridge. *Photo by Joe Vericker.*

Westchester County: New York's Golden Apple / 107

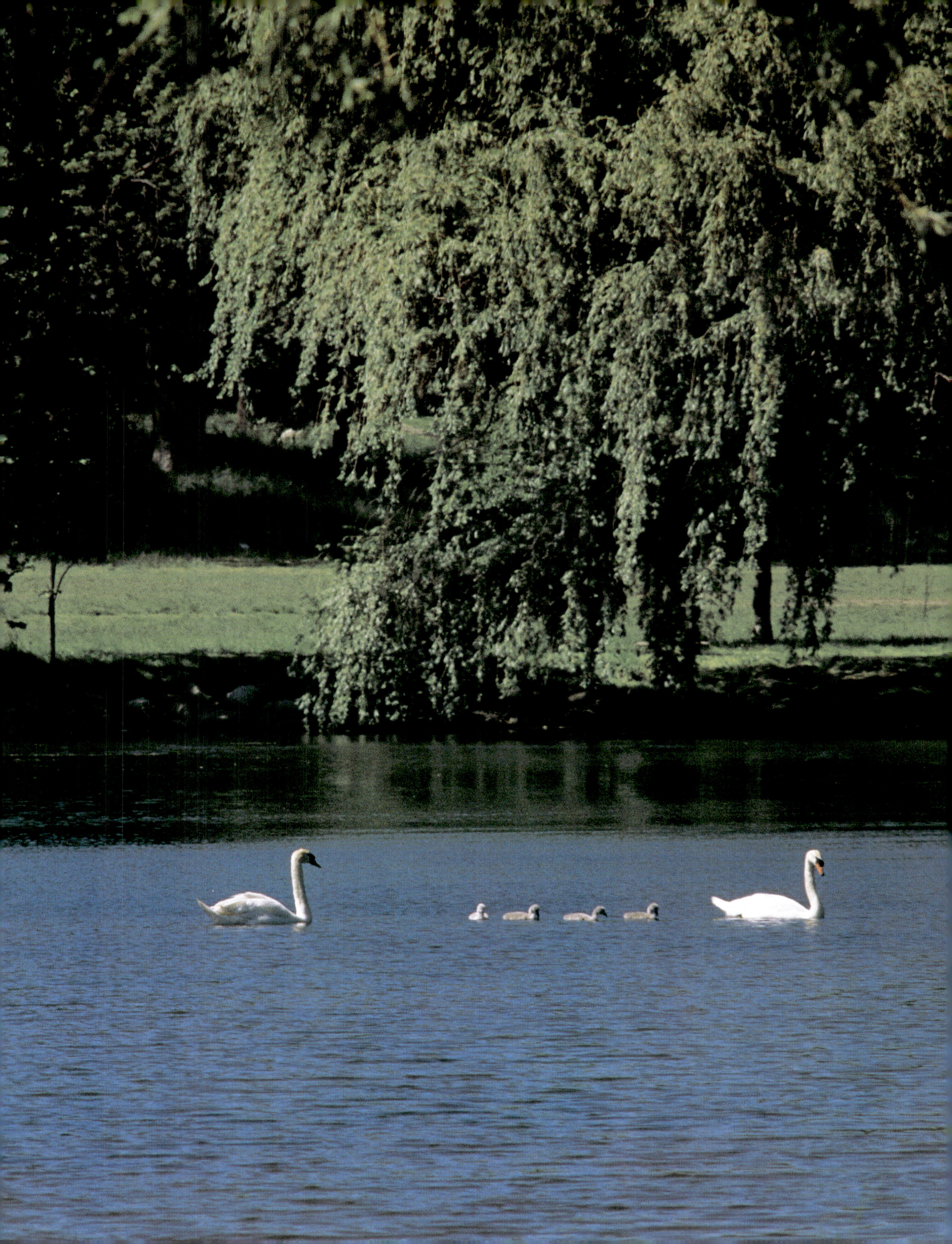

CHAPTER · EIGHT

AN UNPARALLELED QUALITY OF LIFE

It's not surprising that so many individuals and businesses choose to relocate to Westchester. Reasonable zoning ordinances made possible by the cooperation of local governments help to provide the county with an outstanding lifestyle. Then, too, residents here take a keen interest in preserving their environment. These factors, combined with the availability of the widest possible variety of activities, make the decision to locate here a natural.

Photo by Joe Vericker

AN UNPARALLELED Quality OF LIFE

Lifelong residents, as well as many who have lived here for shorter periods, take pride in the traditions that the county has fostered throughout its history. This pride translates into a respect for community, which, in turn, is demonstrated by the care and attention that residents impart to their families, homes, and workplaces.

WHY WESTCHESTER?

Location and property values are probably the two major reasons why people elect to live and work in Westchester County. These days, commuting time can be a prime consideration, and when you realize that you can get to work in a matter of minutes as opposed to an hour or more, Westchester County becomes the logical choice. Coupled with the fact that property values are higher here when compared to similar markets, the proposition becomes even more attractive.

Finally, when one considers the excellent housing found in Westchester, combined with its top-notch schools, a stable and responsible county and local government structure, as well as its commercial ventures which help keep taxes down, the

Above, Residents of Westchester County take an active role in preserving the high quality of life found in their communities. *Photo by Joe Vericker.*

Right, Taking time out to enjoy a stroll in New Rochelle's Glen Island Park. *Photo by Joe Vericker.*

110 / WESTCHESTER COUNTY: New York's Golden Apple

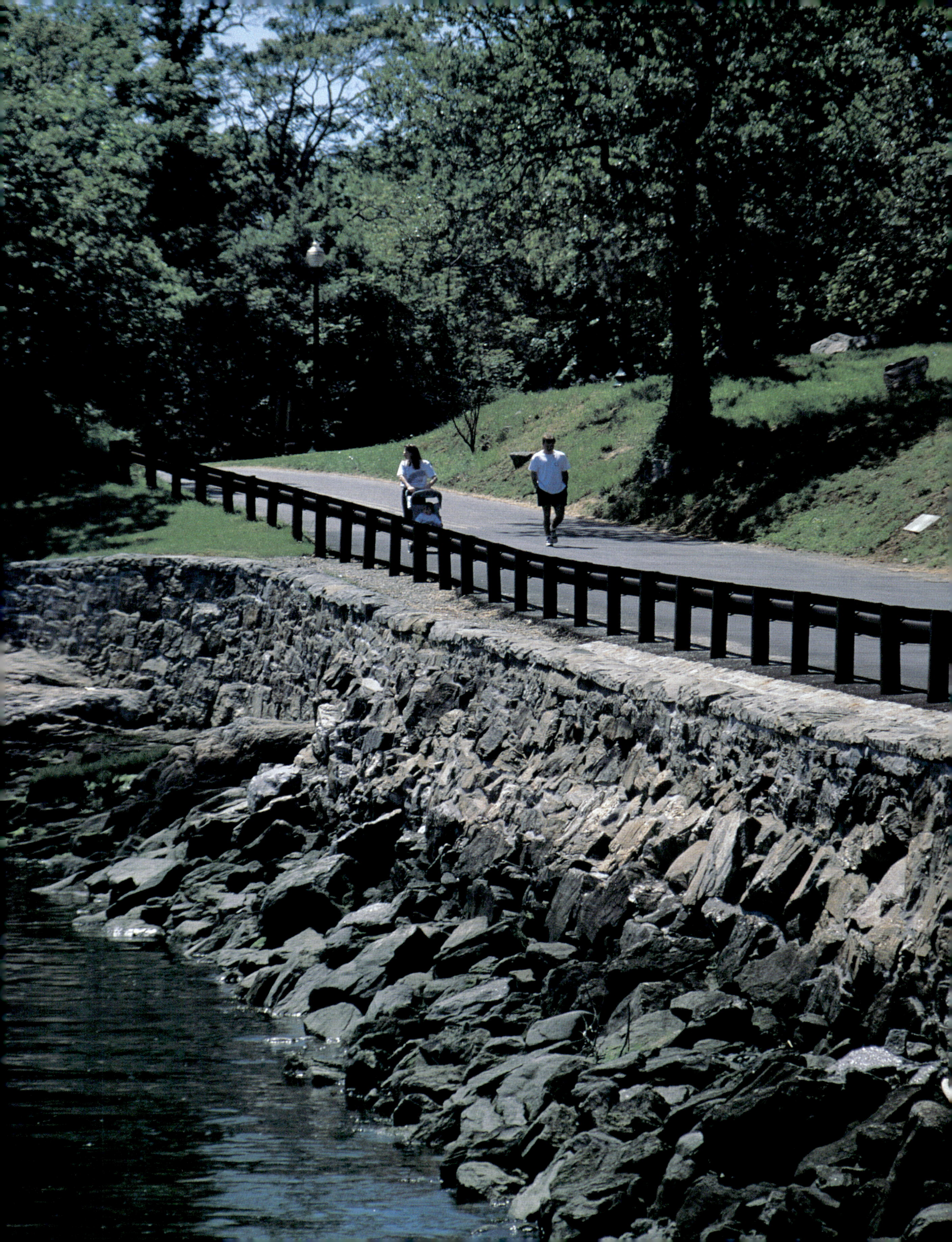

Children of all ages enjoy sleigh-riding at Lake Isle Park in Eastchester. *Photo by Joe Vericker.*

question becomes not "Why Westchester?" but rather "Why not Westchester?"

Visitors to the county are often impressed with the variety of homes available. And a drive of any distance will reveal the ever-forward direction of road improvements in the area.

For those interested in finding a place to nurture their faith, Westchester provides churches of virtually every denomination, along with scores of synagogues and mosques. In addition to providing a place of worship, many of these have become vibrant centers of community activities.

The county is built on its neighborhoods. The Crestwood section of Yonkers, Fleetwood in Mt. Vernon, and Ridgeway in White Plains are just a sampling of dozens of such subcommunities within the county that give Westchester its distinctive character.

HOUSING

Contrary to a popular misconception, Westchester County is affordable to prospective homeowners. True, the area may have a greater proportion than most regions of stately mansions and estates, but it is also adequately represented by homes and apartments affordable to most budgets.

According to the Westchester-Putnam Multiple Listing Service, Inc., in the second quarter of 1996, the

Above, When it comes to recreational activities, Westchester offers incomparable variety. *Photo by Joe Vericker.*

Left, Little League opening-day march down Brook Street in Eastchester. *Photo by Joe Vericker.*

Westchester County: New York's Golden Apple / 113

AN UNPARALLELED *Q*UALITY OF LIFE

median price of single-family homes here stood at $297,000. Condominiums, on the other hand, were valued at $157,000, and a co-operative apartment's median cost was a modest $61,000. That same quarter the dollar volume of closed transactions of $597.7 million actually surpassed that of 1994 by about $10 million to become the highest second quarter volume on record with the multiple listing service.

A growing segment of Westchester County's population chooses to reside in townhouses. Many prefer the planned-community approach to living with its tennis courts, community rooms, and swimming pools, places to meet and interact socially. The popularity of a "maintenance-free" lifestyle is increasing steadily among diverse population groups, as evidenced by successful communities like Heritage Hills in Somers.

RECREATION

When it comes to both indoor and outdoor recreational activities, Westchester offers incomparable variety. Every municipality here has either a recreational commission or department which plans and implements year-long schedules of events. Tennis, swimming, softball, baseball—you name it—are available to one and all.

Literally thousands of youngsters participate in the

Above, Photo by Joe Vericker

Right, The co-op apartment lifestyle appeals to many in the Westchester housing market.
Photo by Joe Vericker.

114 / Westchester County: New York's Golden Apple

Thornycroft
209

Above, Weekend sailors take to the water on Long Island Sound. *Photo by Joe Vericker.*

Left, Walter's Hot Dog Stand in Mamaroneck, a county landmark since 1926. *Photo by Joe Vericker.*

116 / Westchester County: New York's Golden Apple

Left, A lovely sunset view rewards guests dining at one of the county's many fine restaurants. *Photo by Joe Vericker.*

Westchester County: New York's Golden Apple / 117

teams and leagues of Little League baseball, basketball, football, soccer, ice hockey, and the latest-growing sport, lacrosse. Yorktown High School has produced a remarkable number of state championship teams in lacrosse over the years. And Eastchester's Little League field has been the site of championship regional games.

There are approximately 16 recreational park acres per resident in Westchester County, an astounding number which ranks the county among the highest of the 61 counties in New York State.

Golfing and sailing have been two of the biggest sports in Westchester for generations. The first golf club ever built in this country, St. Andrew's in Hastings-on-Hudson, is a familiar landmark even today, and the Buick Open, which draws the greatest players on the pro tour, is an annual event. Another major highlight of Westchester summers is the Larchmont Race, a sailboat regatta without equal.

With its vast natural resources, it makes sense that people will continue to bring their families to where the action is—Westchester County.

Eastchester's Little League field has been the site of championship regional games. *Photo by Joe Vericker.*

118 / WESTCHESTER COUNTY: New York's Golden Apple

AN UNPARALLELED QUALITY OF LIFE

Above, Tennis enthusiasts will find many opportunities to perfect their game at courts located throughout the county. *Photo by Joe Vericker.*

Right, Golfing has long been one of Westchester's most popular sports. *Photo by Joe Vericker.*

Westchester County: New York's Golden Apple / 119

Above, New Rochelle's Huguenot Park, one of many parks found in the family-oriented communities located throughout Westchester. *Photo by Joe Vericker.*

Left, Policemen of the Metro-North Railroad take part in a decoration-day service at Hartsdale Pet Cemetery in honor of hero dogs. *Photo by Joe Vericker.*

Right, Sailing on Long Island Sound is a popular pastime for area residents. *Photo by Joe Vericker.*

120 / Westchester County: New York's Golden Apple

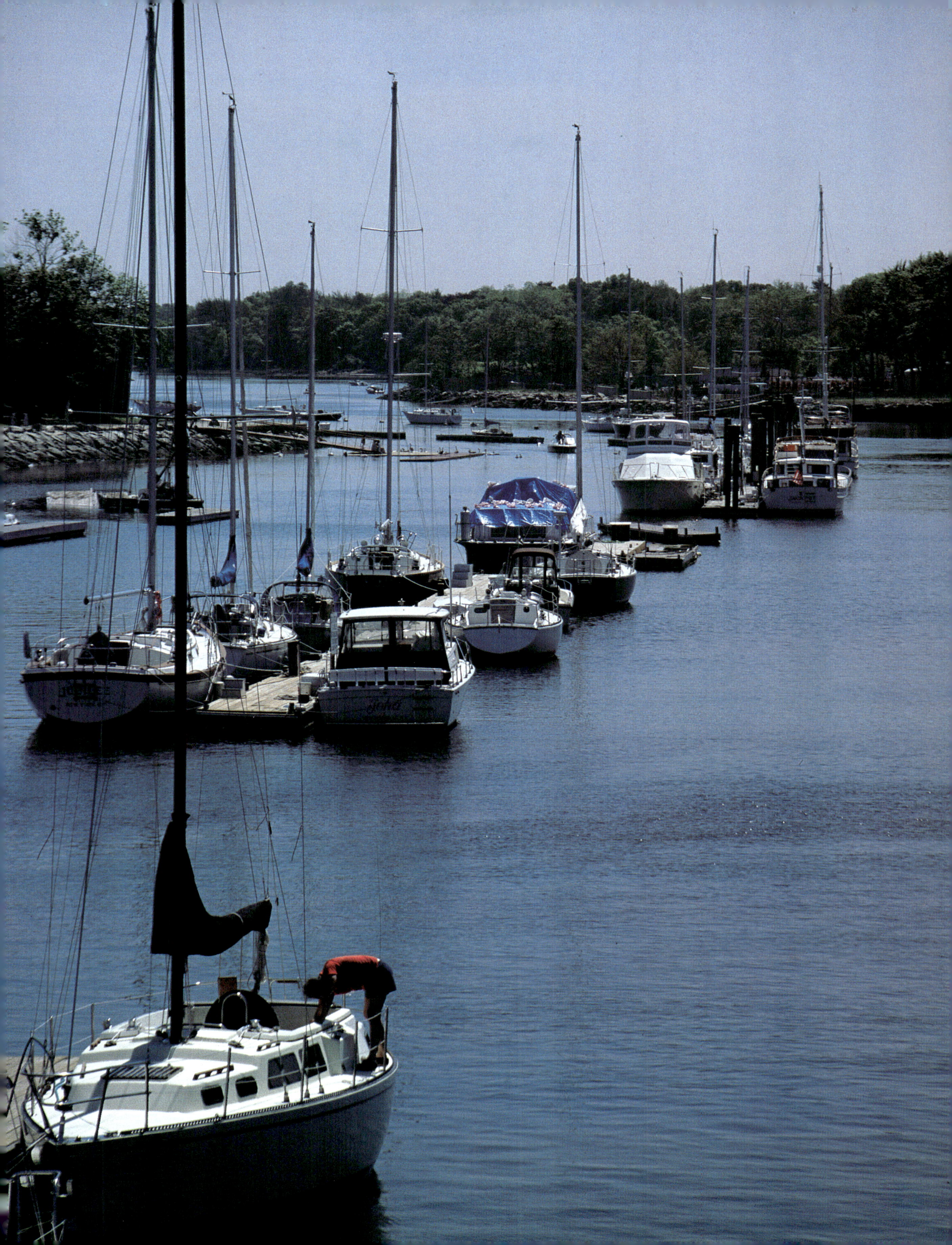

AN UNPARALLED QUALITY OF LIFE

PUBLIC SAFETY

Whether at home or at work, everyone wants to feel safe. Westchester affords its residents as low a crime rate as can be found anywhere for an area and population of its magnitude. This is made possible by the link between the police of the local cities, towns, and villages with the Westchester County Department of Public Safety. Officers of the latter diligently patrol the county's parkways, while the former maintain the safety of their respective communities' streets and homes. The emergency "911" calling system, adopted countywide several years ago, manned by paid and volunteer policemen, firemen, and ambulance services, provides the necessary quick response and has significantly reduced the number of fatalities and serious injuries.

VOLUNTEERISM

Westchester County has an abundance of public-spirited and civic-minded individuals. People here find the time to get involved in actions that improve their communities, whether it be in the schools, business organizations, or fraternal and religious groups. All of this adds to the quality of life the county has to offer.

Groups such as Rotary, Lions, Knights of Columbus,

Playland Amusement Park in Rye is the nation's first amusement park. *Photo by Joe Vericker.*

122 / Westchester County: New York's Golden Apple

Above, Bargain hunters browse the Farmer's Market in White Plains. *Photo by Joe Vericker.*

Right, Shoppers on Fourth Avenue in Mt. Vernon. *Photo by Joe Vericker.*

Junior League, parent-teacher associations, and garden clubs can be found in every community. People from all walks of life work collectively within these and other institutions to balance the demands of a robust economy, a clean environment, and a social order not only for themselves but for their neighbors as well.

Expositions, galas, dinners, and fairs are held regularly year round, planned and conducted by concerned citizens who donate their time and talents for the public good. These events, sponsored and operated by Westchester volunteers, do much to help the aging, the homeless, families in crisis, and others with special needs.

There can be no doubt that if you are looking for a lifestyle that combines a stable economy with family values and outstanding opportunities in the workplace, Westchester County is the place to be.

NEW YORK'S GOLDEN APPLE BECKONS!

Girl Scouts join Liz Edwards, PepsiCo employee and Westchester/Putnam Girl Scout board member, for recreation in Taconic State Park in Yorktown Heights. *Photo by Joe Vericker.*

Right, *Photo by Joe Vericker*

124 / WESTCHESTER COUNTY: New York's Golden Apple

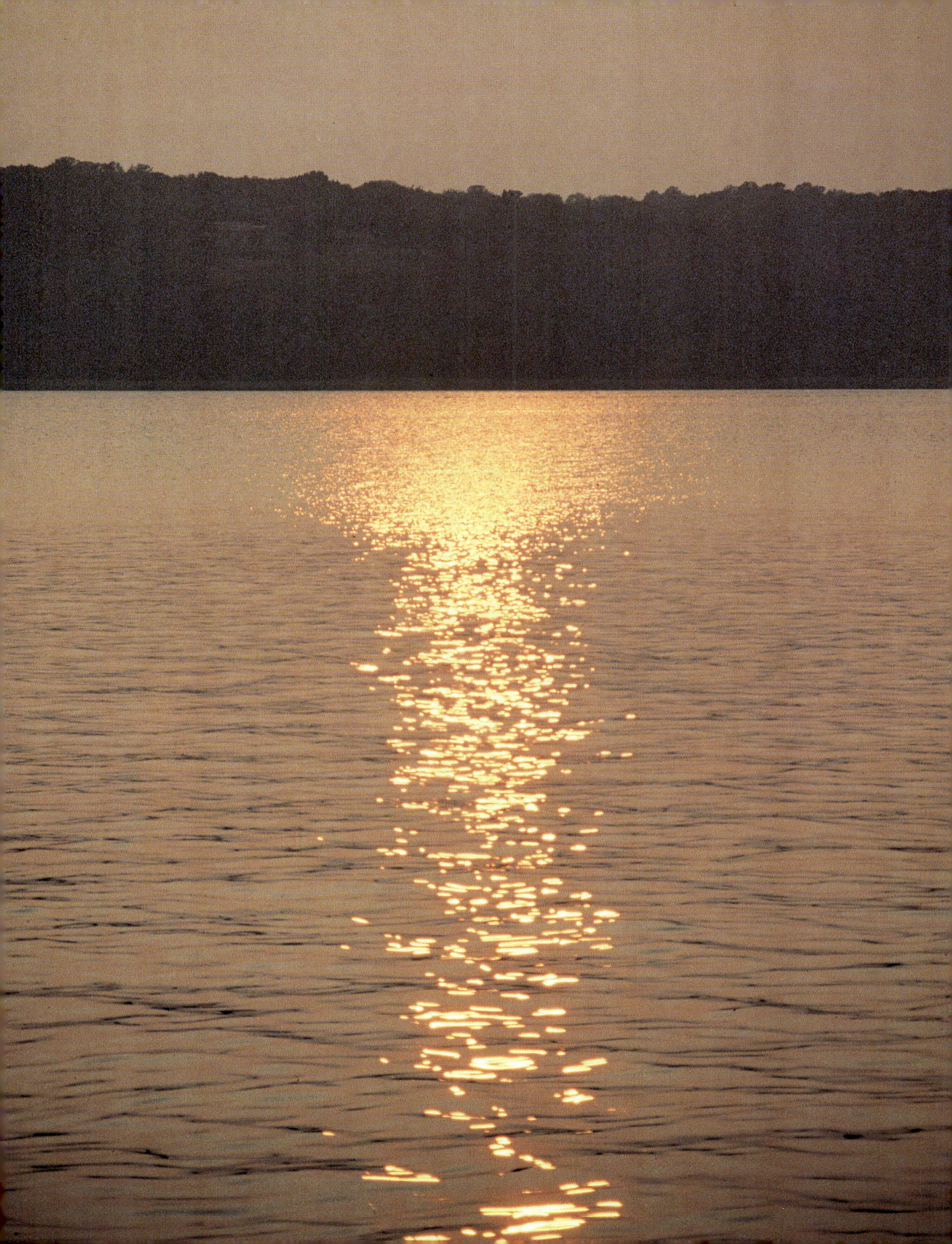

YONKERS
MOUNT VERNON
NORTH SALEM
EASTCHESTER
MAMARONECK
NEW CASTLE
GREENBURG
CORTLANDT
LEWISBORO
HARRISON
BEDFORD

Westchester County
New York's Golden Apple

PART TWO

Photo by Joe Vericker

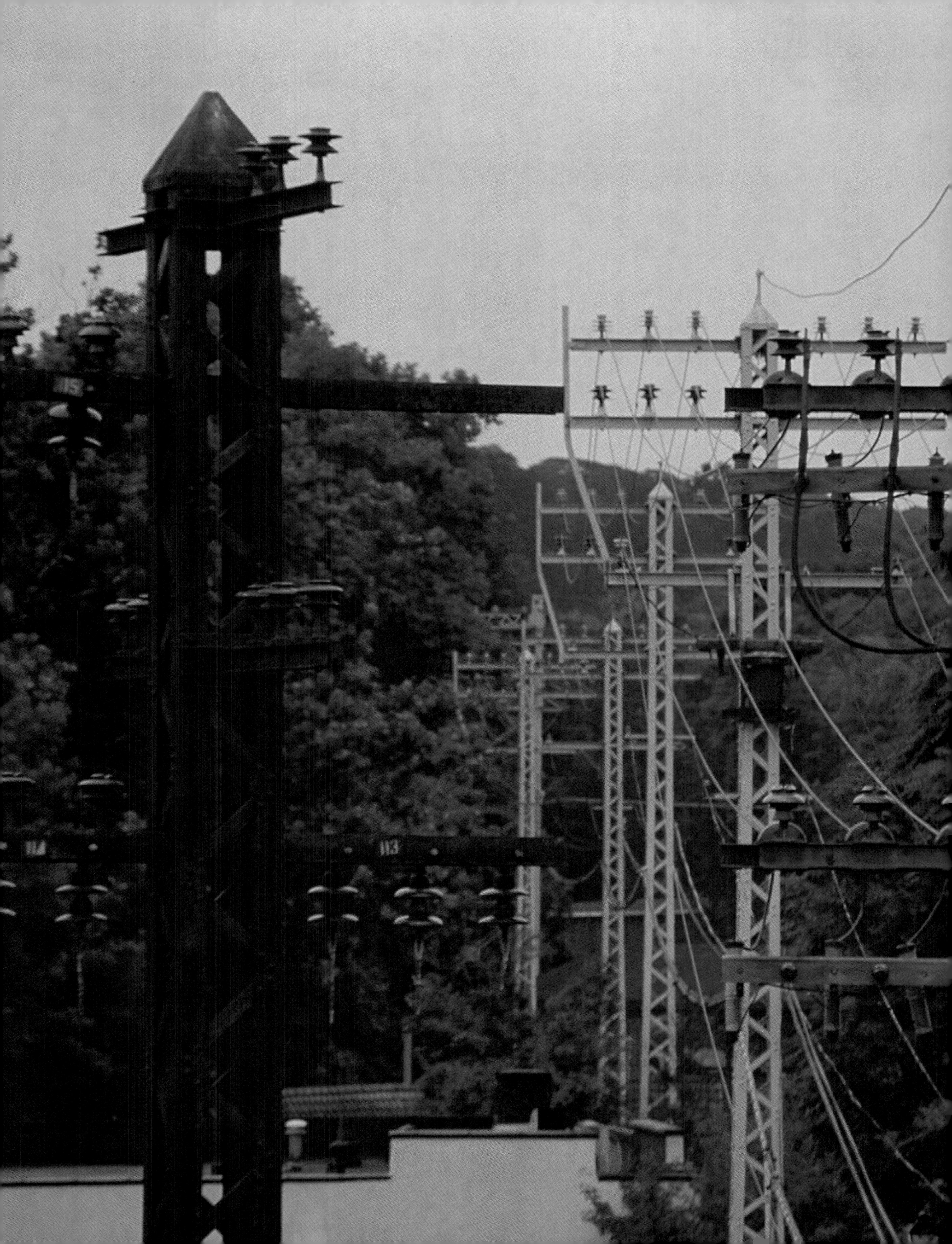
113

CHAPTER • NINE

Networks

The area's energy, communications, relocation, and transportation firms keep people, information, and power circulating inside and outside the area.

TRANSAMERICA LEASING
Page 130

THE READER'S DIGEST
ASSOCIATION, INC.
Page 132

MTA METRO-NORTH RAILROAD
Page 134

WESTCHESTER COUNTY
BUSINESS JOURNAL
Page 136

GANNETT SUBURBAN
NEWSPAPERS
Page 138

NEW YORK POWER AUTHORITY
Page 139

NYNEX CORPORATION
Page 140

WFAS AM & FM
Page 141

COLLINS BROTHERS
MOVING CORP.
Page 142

Photo by Joe Vericker

Westchester County: New York's Golden Apple / 129

NETWORKS

TRANSAMERICA LEASING

In 1994 Transamerica Leasing's container fleet became the second largest in the industry through its acquisition of the container assets of competitor Tiphook plc, a London-based equipment lessor. According to Charles E. Tingley, president and chief executive officer, this acquisition positioned Transamerica Leasing to meet the challenges of the industry in the coming decade, to deliver a level of service exemplifying the very best that the leasing industry has to offer, and to achieve efficiencies that will benefit its customers worldwide.

A pioneer of containerization and the use of rust-resistant corten steel in its containers, Transamerica Leasing was first organized in 1963 as Integrated Container Service. The company experienced modest gains in the years before its acquisition by the San Francisco-based Transamerica Corporation in July 1979. Since that time, the resources of a strong parent company have fostered a level of growth that has enabled Transamerica Leasing to amass one of the world's largest fleets of intermodal transportation equipment (intermodal equipment can be carried on ships or rail cars or hauled by truck) and to become the second largest lessor of standard containers. The company today is recognized as one of just a few mega lessors in the business.

Transamerica Leasing operates a worldwide container and chassis fleet of approximately 1.5 million investment TEUs. (An investment TEU values a variety of equipment types by equating them to the replacement cost of one 20-foot standard container.) Its extensive and diversified inventory includes standard and specialized dry cargo containers; refrigerated containers; tank containers; rail containers; and trailer chassis; and, in Europe, highway and intermodal semi-trailers. "Fifteen years ago, Transamerica Leasing could satisfy customer needs with just one type of container—the standard dry cargo steel container. Today, in response to customer demand, we operate 12 major product lines," said Tingley.

Transamerica owns the largest tank container fleet in the United States, Europe, and the Pacific with the widest range of tank types to ensure safe, secure, and cost-effective transportation for liquid and chemical products as well as hazardous cargo. The company's international operations offer one of the most diversified inventories of standard dry cargo containers, refrigerated containers, specialized containers, and chassis and tank containers in the industry. Transamerica Leasing is also one of the world's major lessors of refrigerated containers, offering equipment using environmentally safe materials. The company's refrigeration experts are recognized as the most experienced and technically proficient in the industry.

More than one-third of all the trailers and rail containers in the United States are owned or managed by Transamerica. In Europe, the company's Trailer Division, with its modern fleet of intermodal and highway trailers, is a leading provider of lease and rental trailers.

Transamerica not only leases its equipment to railroads, steamship lines, and motor carriers, but it also provides sophisticated, computerized management services that offer users around the world on-line access to key billing and operational information. With its primary mission defined as the provision of customer-driven service alternatives and customized solutions, the company takes pride in its ability to offer the in-depth marketing knowledge and technical expertise that help customers meet immediate as well as long-range requirements. The company's unparalleled flexibility in lease terms spans contracts that range from daily rentals and short-term operating leases to full payout finance leases that

World Headquarters: Transamerica Leasing has its world headquarters at 100 Manhattanville Road, in Purchase.

One of the newest of Transamerica Leasing's product lines is tank container leasing. These 20-foot containers, which can be transported safely and securely on road, rail, or ship, are designed for the bulk transportation of liquid cargoes such as foods, wines, liquor, and chemical products. Transamerica Corporation's famed Pyramid building in San Francisco is in the background.

enable customers to purchase equipment over time.

Based in Westchester County since 1985, Transamerica Leasing has grown into a worldwide network of more than 300 offices, depots, and other facilities in 50 countries on 6 continents. There are over 900 employees worldwide, with 300 based at the company's Purchase, New York, headquarters.

Transamerica Leasing views the move from New York City to Westchester as one of its most auspicious decisions in more than three decades of existence. The county's lower rents, income taxes, and occupancy taxes have enhanced the company's ability to compete as a low-cost operator. The Westchester years have also heralded the implementation of formal training programs worldwide at every level of the company, the systematic diversification of product and lease offerings, the introduction of new computer systems and applications, and the establishment of a company-wide continuous improvement process—all designed to keep Transamerica Leasing at the leading edge of its industry.

Charles Tingley foresees more changes of the sort that have made Transamerica Leasing an industry standout. "We are implementing several process changes and technology innovation initiatives, and we will be working to introduce more new products and businesses that will complement our existing product line," he said.

To complement its international marketing activities, the company strives to sustain a philanthropic presence in the metropolitan New York area. Transamerica Leasing is a long-time supporter of the New York City Opera through its provision of storage trailers for scenery. This is an important contribution to the Opera because there are no in-house storage facilities at Lincoln Center. An annual Transamerica Day at the Opera honors the company's special support. In Westchester, Transamerica Leasing contributes directly to the Boy Scouts and Girl Scouts, as well as various cultural and civic entities.

Transamerica Leasing also contributes to many worthy organizations through its employee matching gifts program and through its encouragement of and financial support for employee-initiated activities. One such project began in 1986 when several Westchester-based employees bought school clothes for 10 children living in local welfare hotels and shelters. Each year, as more employees joined in, this program grew, providing clothing for more and more homeless children. Financial support from Transamerica Leasing and assistance from the firm's legal department permitted the group to organize Back-to-School Clothes for Kids as a nonprofit, tax-exempt corporation. This program now outfits a significant number of underprivileged youngsters each year, boosting their morale as well as their desire to learn in the process. According to Tingley, good corporate citizenship is important to the company because "our corporate success is directly related to the well-being of the communities where we do business."

NETWORKS

THE READER'S DIGEST ASSOCIATION, INC.

The Reader's Digest Association, Inc. global headquarters in Pleasantville, New York, is noted for its well-maintained grounds and abundance of beautiful flowers.

Rejected by publishers across America, DeWitt Wallace decided to start a unique little magazine on his own in 1922. *Reader's Digest* has since sold more than 10 billion copies in the U.S. alone, and The Reader's Digest Association, Inc. has become a preeminent global publisher and direct marketer of products that inform, enrich, entertain, and inspire people the world over.

Along with its flagship magazine, Reader's Digest sells quality books, music, home videos, audio books, special interest magazines, and a growing line of multimedia products that bring the joy of learning to a whole new generation.

Reader's Digest markets its products primarily by direct mail, but is rapidly expanding into other distribution channels—including direct-response television advertising, interactive on-line services, catalogs, and door-to-door sales. The Reader's Digest World Wide Web site is just one example of how the company is tapping into the booming home computer audience. A variety of strategic alliances underscore the immense future value of the company's editorial content, database management skills, and respected brand name as it enters the electronic media market.

Quality Products, Loyal Customers

The Reader's Digest Association has about 1,200 employees at its landmark global headquarters, opened in Pleasantville in 1939, and another 4,300 in more than 50 locations worldwide. It became a publicly traded company on the New York Stock Exchange in February 1990 and has already built a solid reputation for increasing shareholder value.

The company's global success is driven by *Reader's Digest*, the world's best-read and best-selling magazine. Founded by Wallace and his wife Lila under a Greenwich Village speakeasy and reaching just 1,500 subscribers, its worldwide circulation now tops 27 million. Its 48 editions in 19 languages present a timely mix of local and international content. The magazine also offers a truly global advertising medium—with one call, a growing list of multinational advertisers can reach 100 million potential customers worldwide, in their local languages.

Through this unique global reach, The Reader's Digest Association has built customer databases worldwide containing more than 100 million households, a wealth of customer information that helps the company create and market well-researched, high-quality products of superior value. Reader's Digest sells:

- More than 52 million books a year, in over a dozen languages. Topics include reference, how-to, gardening, science, history, religion, and cooking.
- More than 9 million recorded music collections—from Bach to Big Band, Pavarotti to Presley.
- More than 5 million home video packages—travel, history, religion, nature, and comedy.

132 / WESTCHESTER COUNTY: New York's Golden Apple

NETWORKS

- Special interest magazines with a combined circulation of more than 2 million: *American Health*, *The Family Handyman*, *New Choices: Living Even Better After 50*, and *Moneywise*.

Building For The Future

This range of appealing, high-quality editorial content positions The Reader's Digest Association for exciting growth. The company has taken significant steps to pursue new customers, new products, and new distribution channels. These initiatives include introduction of interactive, multimedia CD-ROM versions of some of its best-selling books; alliances with the Public Broadcasting Service to create and broadcast television programming; with Avon Products, Inc. to target new customers for Reader's Digest products; with Meredith Corporation, to direct-market books, music, and CD-ROMs under *Better Homes and Gardens* and *Ladies Home Journal* trademarks; and with Dove Audio, Inc. to distribute audio-book versions of more than 800 titles—classics, children's titles, and contemporary best sellers.

A Part of The Community

While looking ahead to the new, The Reader's Digest Association continues to honor the long-time legacy of philanthropy and outstanding corporate citizenship begun by the Wallaces.

Exemplifying this spirit is the Reader's Digest Foundation, a charitable, grant-making institution funded by contributions from the Reader's Digest Association. Located at headquarters in Pleasantville, the foundation's employee and education programs make a difference wherever Reader's Digest employees live and work. A $500,000 foundation grant established the Tall Tree Initiative for Library Services, a partnership with area schools and libraries to create the finest possible learning environment for Westchester children.

Tall Tree is just one of many investments the foundation is making to help people reach their full potential. Area students are showing dramatic improvement through innovative education, literacy, and library programs which have flourished thanks to its Local Grants Program. And the foundation awards more than a half-million dollars yearly in college scholarships to employees' children and journalism students nationally.

Another way Reader's Digest makes a difference in the classroom is through its QSP, Inc. subsidiary, which has helped schools and youth groups in the United States and Canada raise more than $1 billion since 1963 for educational enrichment programs through sales of magazines and other items.

The Reader's Digest Art Collection is one more beloved facet of the Wallace legacy. Started by Lila Wallace nearly 50 years ago, this brilliant collection now includes more than 8,000 paintings, drawings, prints, photographs, and sculptures. Its works represent masters ranging from Monet and Renoir to Chagall and Picasso, along with contemporary greats such as Warhol and Rauschenberg. The company welcomes visitors to view the collection at its Pleasantville headquarters and provides knowledgeable guides to make such tours a memorable experience.

Of course, no look at Reader's Digest would be complete without mention of its famous sweepstakes, conducted by Reader's Digest companies around the world in their local countries. Since 1962 the company and its subsidiaries have awarded prizes totaling more than $240 million.

The Reader's Digest Association's superior editorial skills, data management expertise, and long-respected brand name position it for success as consumer media spending grows exponentially in the coming years. Known in Westchester and worldwide for a 75-year heritage of quality and service, the company is committed to building on its preeminence as a global publisher and meeting the exciting opportunities that lie ahead. ◆

The Reader's Digest Association, Inc. has a global database with information on more than 100 million households, providing a wealth of customer information that helps the company create and market superior products that appeal to people around the world.

The Reader's Digest Association, Inc. is a preeminent global publisher and direct marketer of magazines, books, music, and home entertainment products for people of all ages.

Westchester County: New York's Golden Apple / 133

NETWORKS

MTA METRO-NORTH RAILROAD

Metro-North Railroad is on track to meet the demands of today's increasing commuter population. To accomplish this feat, the railroad has initiated "Vision 2003," a series of goals designed to ensure a continued upward trend in customer satisfaction. Metro-North is determined to achieve a 98 percent on-time performance, an injury-free workplace, and an additional 10 million annual rides by the year 2003—its 20th anniversary.

"Our goal is to reach a point where, when people want superior transportation, they'll think of us. We intend to keep improving and deliver that level of superior service," said Donald N. Nelson, president of Metro-North.

"Also, as the federal government continues to place greater restrictions on counties, cities, and states to improve the air quality and reduce traffic, we'll certainly be playing a much larger role. As Westchester County's only railroad, we plan to be prepared to meet that challenge."

Metro-North was founded in 1983, when it assumed control of the Conrail commuter operations within New York State and Connecticut. At the time, the rail operation was deteriorating and approaching collapse.

However, through dedicated employee effort and the effective management of some $3 billion in capital outlay for new or rehabilitated stations, upgraded track and signal infrastructure, new repair and maintenance facilities, and new rolling stock, the railroad has been transformed into a recognized national leader in the commuter rail industry.

Metro-North's roots can be traced back to the New York and Harlem Railroad, which began service in 1832 as a horse-car line serving lower Manhattan. Metro-North now serves 120 stations in seven counties in New York State-Westchester, Putnam, Dutchess, Orange, Rockland, the Bronx, and Manhattan—and New Haven and Fairfield Counties in Connecticut. The railroad has a fleet of more than 800 rail cars and locomotives which operate over 339 route miles and 738 miles of track, and it employs some 5,500 workers.

Metro-North, an operating agency of the Metropolitan Transportation Authority (MTA), is the second largest commuter rail operation in the United States. The railroad provides more than 210,000 customer rides each weekday and, in 1994, broke the 60-million-rider mark last seen by the railroad during World War II. The railroad boasted an on-time service performance of 95.7 percent in 1995.

Ridership is expected to keep growing. While additional customers help Metro-North reduce its reliance on taxpayer subsidies, they also present many challenges—such as meeting the parking demand. The railroad has increased parking at several Westchester stations and opened a new station in Cortlandt in June. The railroad also encourages riders to leave their cars at home by providing expanded feeder bus service. The Westchester Avenue Shuttle, linking White Plains Station with major employment parks along the I-287 corridor, has shown continued growth since its inception in 1993. Also, at Tarrytown Station a weekend bus connection for historic Hudson Valley sites has proved successful over two seasons.

Improving safety and personal

Grand Central Terminal from Park Avenue South

Metro-North's new Genesis locomotive on the Hudson Line near Storm King

134 / Westchester County: New York's Golden Apple

NETWORKS

security—always a concern to railroad commuters—has been of paramount importance to Metro-North. The railroad has fully modernized its signal and rail traffic control systems. It has installed event recorders aboard locomotives that provide diagnostic and train-operation data. A state-of-the-art Operations Center at Grand Central Terminal opened this year.

Metro-North delivers safety messages to students in community schools through its "Metro-Man," a talking robot that helps students learn about safe travel in and around trains, stations, and tracks. "This program is fun and educational," Nelson said. "It introduces children to the railroad and lets them know that while riding the railroad can be fun, the tracks that run through their communities are not a playground."

Metro-North has completed a three-year expansion of its police force to include more than 200 officers, and increased their presence on trains, platforms, and stations. A multiagency police-security alliance now operates from a storefront office outside Grand Central Terminal, and provides customers passing through the area with an added level of security.

The railroad is working on a $47-million project to provide easier access to Grand Central Terminal. The North End Access project is expected to save customers who work north of the terminal nearly 10 minutes per day on their commute. Also construction is underway on a five-year, federally funded $120-million rehabilitation of the Park Avenue Viaduct and 125th Street Station. The two-mile viaduct carries more than 500 trains per day into and out of Grand Central Terminal. The 125th Street Station, which dates back to 1897, serves more than 4,000 customers every day.

Nelson said that the most visible of all Metro-North's capital program undertakings began in February 1996 with the kick-off of the "long-awaited" Revitalization of Grand Central Terminal. "The Main Waiting Room, the Vanderbilt Avenue taxi entrance, and the Incoming Train Room have already been restored to their original grandeur. This multi-year undertaking, with secured funding for a thorough restoration, will ensure returning the 'grand' to all of Grand Central," he said.

In Westchester, Metro-North's services have had a significant impact on the business community—more so than transporting executives around the region. As the railroad improves, so does the county's total economic and business development climate. Nelson said: "Now companies can relocate to Westchester and have an excellent transportation network that broadens their employment pool. The railroad also has helped improve property values, because it makes this area a more palatable place to work and live."

For the community in general, Metro-North participates in a number of events to support local organizations. The railroad takes part in the "Clearwater Festival," a celebration of the Hudson River held at Westchester Community College each year, and works with the county to offer discount travel packages to individuals enroute to Playland in Rye and Sleepy Hollow and Kykuit in Tarrytown. ◆

Metro-North customers boarding at Chappaqua Station

Open House at Metro-North Railroad's Harmon Shop

Westchester County: New York's Golden Apple / 135

NETWORKS

WESTCHESTER COUNTY BUSINESS JOURNAL

"Nobody knows Westchester business better than a Westchester business," according to informed sources at the *Westchester County Business Journal* in White Plains. In keeping with its motto, the *Business Journal* provides comprehensive coverage of local business news in Westchester.

"We are a local business with deep roots and commitment to the community," said Dee Del-Bello, publisher. "We share experiences with our business colleagues. That's why we can relate pertinent news and information with a passion."

The *Westchester County Business Journal* is a weekly newspaper for, and about, the business community in Westchester. Printed in tabloid format, the *Business Journal* contains a balance of hard news and features along with detailed records of transactions important to conducting business in the county.

More than 13,000 copies are distributed to subscribers and selected leaders in the county's business community. In addition, the *Business Journal* is available at newsstands throughout the county. With 3.2 readers per copy, the *Business Journal* provides advertisers with an audience of approximately 41,000 decision-makers in one of the most affluent markets in the United States. The *Business Journal's* targeted distribution and editorial coverage give advertisers ideal—and productive—marketing opportunities.

For three decades, the *Business Journal* has been covering news that gets down to business. As the economy and business environments have changed, the *Business Journal* has kept the county's private sector abreast of trends and developments that affect their industries. And, the *Business Journal* has gained a solid reputation for its local business "scoops" and for its fair, impartial, and accurate news coverage.

"We're highly focused, with an enthusiastic news team that knows the dynamics driving the business community," DelBello said.

The *Westchester County Business Journal* was founded by David Moore in the late 1960s. In 1971 Moore launched the *Fairfield County Business Journal*. Both publications were acquired in 1986 by American City Business Journals of Kansas City, Missouri. Two years later, American City sold the Journals to County Business Journal Publications, Inc., a publishing group in Pine Island, New York.

Westfair Communications, Inc. of White Plains purchased the *Westchester* and *Fairfield County Business Journals* in 1990 and, under the leadership of DelBello, has since expanded the papers' coverage, doubled the staff, boosted circulation, and implemented a long-term strategy for continued expansion.

"Because of our dedicated staff, we survived the economic slump of the late '80s and early '90s," DelBello said. "Our region was hit particularly hard. We're a better newspaper because of the staff's efforts and endurance during that period."

Today, the *Business Journals* are committed to covering their respective business markets as no other media does—both in the traditional sense and electronically via the Internet—while at the same time adding new features and special sections. In addition to news coverage, the *Business Journals* contain weekly editorial features, including:

- On the Record—quick-reading information on new businesses, incorporations, tax and mechanic's liens, deeds, patents, bankruptcies, foreclosures, new products, certifi-

Searching the pages of the *Journal* for information and business leads. *Photo by Jim Hunter.*

The Westchester bureau chief intently pursues a business scoop. *Photo by Jim Hunter.*

136 / WESTCHESTER COUNTY: New York's Golden Apple

cates of incorporation, corporate announcements, mergers and acquisitions, import-export news, and stock tips. The Record section also contains such special features as: Newsmakers, spotlights on executive appointments and promotions; Credits, Clients & Awards, highlights of companies' new clients, products, marketing strategies, and industry awards; Real Estate Update, information about recent commercial and residential transactions, including leases, sales, and executive promotions; and On the Agenda, listings of upcoming business meetings, seminars, workshops, and educational programs.

- Focus Sections—a comprehensive look at a specific industry group, its new products and services, and position in the business market.
- Business Lists—top-ranking businesses or organizations with pertinent facts about each company. And, at the end of the year, the lists are bound into a special *Book of Business Lists* publication.
- Faces and Places—a picture page of local business people in professional and social activities.
- HOTLINX—a biweekly two-page spread containing information on new technology, trends, and issues on the Internet and World Wide Web, new Web sites, and upcoming Net events.

On a monthly basis, the Business Journals publish special supplements and feature pages as well. These include:

- *How's Business?*—an in-depth look into a specific small business. The Journals profile a business and, working with the Entrepreneurial Center, Inc. of Purchase, examine problems facing that business and offer suggestions.
- Supplements—a comprehensive and up-to-date editorial examination of industry categories affecting local business. Industries include banking and finance, health care, real estate, entrepreneurs, how to start a business, and hospitality.
- Guides—the Business Journals periodically publish guides such as *Market Facts*, which examine their respective counties and provide charts and statistics about numerous markets and industries; *Arts and Leisure*, which provides information about local leisure activities; and *Health Care*, which offers lists and information about HMOs, PPOs, and other key sectors of the health care industry.

The Business Journals also publish periodical supplements highlighting towns and cities throughout Westchester and Fairfield Counties. The sections contain information about employment, real estate values and office markets, business and industry trends, and lists of municipal government officials.

"The vitality of the market shows through in our expanded coverage of small business," said DelBello. "Entrepreneurship is at an all-time high, and we try to convey the excitement and energy of this critical component of our economy."

The Business Journals also frequently host "Round-Table" discussions in which industry experts discuss and debate key issues affecting local business. The Business Journals then publish highlights of the discussions.

As an active member of the respective communities in which they serve, the Business Journals sponsor a number of events, business seminars and workshops, and awards celebrations. For example, the Journals joined with Lucent Technologies in sponsoring an annual High-Tech Super Start-up Star competition. The Journals also are actively involved with the Westchester County Association, Inc., The County Chamber of Commerce, Inc., Ernst & Young's Entrepreneur of the Year awards program, and the United Way Corporate Volunteer Council. ◆

A Journal *executive juggles the paper and a client at the same time.*
Photo by Jim Hunter

The Journal's *colorful front page sets the tone for up-to-the-minute local business news.*
Photo by Jim Hunter.

NETWORKS

GANNETT SUBURBAN NEWSPAPERS

For more than three decades, Gannett Suburban Newspapers has been providing complete coverage of news, issues, and events that affect the Westchester County communities they serve. "Gannett Suburban Newspapers continues to publish strongly independent local newspapers throughout the region," said Gary F. Sherlock, president and publisher. "Our priority must always be to report on the communities we serve with fairness and sensitivity."

Gannett offers its readers comprehensive local news and provides coverage of New York City, New York State, the nation, and the world. The company has local offices in Yonkers, New Rochelle, Harrison, Yorktown, Carmel, and West Nyack, and reaches 465,400 readers daily and 504,800 on Sunday.

Gannett Suburban Newspapers is owned by Gannett Company, Inc., which has 92 dailies, including USA Today, radio and TV stations, the largest outdoor advertising company in North America, and other communications interests. The company operates in 44 states, the District of Columbia, Canada, Guam, and the U.S. Virgin Islands.

Gannett was founded by Frank E. Gannett in 1906, incorporated in 1923, and brought public in 1967. Following the April 1, 1964, acquisition of the Westchester Rockland newspapers from the Macy family, the Gannett Company grew from a 15-newspaper operation to 24 dailies—overnight. The dailies and the communities they serve are the following:

- *The Reporter Dispatch*—Two editions that cover central and northern Westchester
- *The Putnam Reporter Dispatch*—Serving Putnam County
- *The Citizen Register*—Serving Ossining and Briarcliff
- *The Tarrytown Daily News*—Serving Tarrytown, North Tarrytown, Irvington, and Ardsley
- *The Daily Item*—Serving Port Chester, Harrison, Rye, and Rye Brook
- *The Daily Times*—Serving Mamaroneck and Larchmont
- *The Standard-Star*—Serving New Rochelle and the Pelhams
- *The Herald Statesman*—Serving Yonkers, Hastings on Hudson, Dobbs Ferry
- *Mount Vernon Argus*—Serving Mount Vernon
- *Rockland Journal-News*—Serving Rockland County
- *Review Press-Reporter*—Weekly serving Bronxville

Gannett's commitment to powerful, accurate reporting is evidenced by the consistent recognition it has received. Gannett has garnered such awards as the 1996 Society of the Silurians' "Excellence in Journalism Award" and the New York State Associated Press Association Awards for spot news reporting, depth reporting, and features. Gannett's photography has received awards from the New York Press Club, National Press Photographers, Women in Journalism, and Pictures of the Year.

Gannett was a leader in multimedia innovation with the 1993 launch of New York NewsLink, the online forum launched on CompuServe. Its World Wide Web site, *Westchester Today*, was launched in 1995 and features 45 "hometown" pages, a comprehensive guide to communities; a county home page about local government, services, issues, and events; as well as sports, entertainment, real estate, and restaurants.

Gannett supports many projects which benefit its community. The Gannett Foundation has provided hundreds of thousands of dollars in grants to the communities served by Gannett newspapers and continues to sponsor Lend-A-Hand, a program that helps people in need throughout the area. Gannett's current community efforts focus on crime prevention, education/literacy, and human needs programs. ◆

A variety of sections for a variety of interests: Gannett Suburban Newspapers' colorful daily and weekly sections offer everything from hometown coverage and perspectives to national and local sports, to business entertainment happenings throughout the area.

The paper of record for Westchester County: Hundreds of thousands turn to Gannett Suburban Newspapers each day for news about their hometown, local issues and events— and everything that affects their world.

138 / Westchester County: New York's Golden Apple

NETWORKS

NEW YORK POWER AUTHORITY

The New York Power Authority (NYPA) prides itself on its customer relations. "We've been successful because we approach customers on a partnership basis. What can we do to help them save money with their energy costs?" said Robert A. Schoenberger, chief NYPA's president and chief operating officer from his White Plains office.

"We supply power for almost all municipal purposes in Westchester County—we've saved them millions of dollars. We just signed a 10-year power supply contract with them. In today's market, with all the choices available, we were able to convince them to sign up with us. That's a measure of how well we service customers."

NYPA's goal is to provide customers with lower-priced electricity in an environmental-friendly way. In 1990 it launched the High Efficiency Lighting Program—HELP—that won several national awards. HELP was designed for NYPA's downstate government customers, but has been extended to state agencies, public schools, and county and local governments statewide.

The nation's largest non-federal public power supplier, NYPA provides 25 percent of the state's electricity. It is a nonprofit, public benefit corporation that finances, builds, and operates electric generation and transmission facilities. Based in White Plains, it employs about 3,000 people. More than 550 work in the White Plains headquarters and 800 work at the Indian Point Nuclear Power Plant in Buchanan.

The combined capacity of NYPA's 12 generating plants exceeds 7 million kilowatts (kw). Customers include the 51 municipal electric systems and rural cooperatives in New York state, 100 government agencies in New York City and Westchester, the state's seven major private electric utilities, designated industries, and the Niagara Frontier Transportation Authority. Projects are financed through sale of bonds, without tax monies or state credit, Schoenberger said.

In 1931 then-Governor Franklin D. Roosevelt and the state legislature established NYPA to develop the hydroelectric potential of the St. Lawrence River. The 800,000-kw St. Lawrence-Franklin D. Roosevelt Power Project began operation in 1958.

Subsequent projects include Niagara Power Project, Niagara Falls; Blenheim-Gilboa Pumped Storage Power Project, Schoharie County; James A. FitzPatrick Nuclear Power Plant, Oswego; Indian Point 3 Nuclear Power Plant, Buchanan; Charles Poletti Power Project, Queens; and Richard M. Flynn Power Plant, Suffolk County. NYPA also has five small hydroelectric plants: Ashokan Project, Ulster County; Kensico Project, Westchester County; Gregory Jarvis Power Plant, Utica; and two plants on the Mowhawk River.

NYPA also operates more than 1,400 circuit miles of transmission lines, including twin 199-mile, 345-kilovolt lines from Niagara Falls to Marcy, near Utica—the backbone of the state's transmission network.

NYPA plays a large role in Westchester's efforts to attract and retain businesses, Schoenberger said. In fact, he cited Ciba-Geigy Corp. as an example. Ciba, a research and manufacturing firm specializing in chemical, pharmaceutical, and health care products, considered relocating from Westchester to Connecticut. In response, New York State offered $13.25 in economic incentives, including low-cost electricity from NYPA. Ciba stayed within the town of Greenburgh. "One of the complaints about New York State is the high cost of doing business in terms of taxes, energy, and workers' compensation. We can help solve one of those problems by continuing to provide low-cost energy," said Schoenberger.

Also, as the utility industry undergoes major changes brought on by deregulation, Schoenberger said NYPA will be a key player. "The end goal has to be lower energy rates, or our region won't be competitive in the future. NYPA is a jewel—and we'll continue to be very bright as long as we do our jobs and run the authority as businesses even though we're a public entity." ◆

New York Power Authority's White Plains Headquarters

Indian Point #3 Nuclear Power Plant in Buchanan

NETWORKS

NYNEX CORPORATION

In order to stay profitable in an increasingly competitive global market, businesses must keep pace with the technological revolution. And NYNEX Corp. provides the means to help companies gain momentum on the information superhighway.

Terry Hewitt, a NYNEX cable splicing technician in New York, works along the Route 287 "Platinum Corridor" in Westchester County, New York.

In fact, NYNEX is working to ensure that all its customers—businesses, public service organizations, and residential consumers—remain at the forefront of these technological changes. The company provides customers with advanced tools such as voice, video, and high-speed data services; wired and wireless telecommunications; electronic and printed directory services; and access to information and entertainment.

And research is ongoing at such facilities as the NYNEX Science and Technology Center in White Plains, which employs 300 people. "We're spending approximately $100 million each year at the center developing new products and ways to make our phone network more reliable," said Meredith Pera, vice president and general manager for NYNEX in Westchester and surrounding counties.

Overall, NYNEX continues investing aggressively in its facilities—to the tune of some $2.4 billion a year—and delivering services to 17 million customers in the northeastern United States and selected markets worldwide.

Closer to home, NYNEX has installed nearly 100,000 miles of fiber optics in the region. And, in Westchester, more than 65 corporate parks, 75 businesses, and 4,700 residential buildings have become part of the high-speed fiber network. NYNEX invests about $175 million a year in network modernization in Westchester, and has formed alliances with a number of equipment and technology providers here. "We have a lot invested in Westchester County," said Pera.

Through its Integrated Services Digital Network (ISDN), NYNEX is making high-speed digital communications accessible and affordable throughout Westchester. ISDN lets users talk, receive and send data, and transmit images and video simultaneously, on the same line. The dial-up service utilizes standard telephone lines and computer systems, making it affordable for even home-based businesses.

As the telecommuting trend grows in Westchester—enabling employees to work at home or in satellite offices and still remain active team members—NYNEX is offering integrated programs of network services and support to help companies explore this option.

Through a jointly-owned subsidiary with Bell Atlantic, NYNEX also has been growing its mobile and wireless phone market. And the company is enhancing its ability to provide wireless cable television services through another joint venture with Bell Atlantic.

NYNEX technology plays a significant role in stimulating the region's economy, as well.

At the Special Services garage on Knollwood Road in Westchester, New York, technicians Bruce Sypher (left) and William White shovel snow in preparation for getting repair vehicles on the road during the Blizzard of '96.

The company pays $30 million a year in property taxes alone, and employs 2,700 people here. In addition, some 6,400 NYNEX employees—and 2,500 retirees—live here, Pera said. The company owns 60 buildings in Westchester and leases 30 more.

NYNEX is a major supporter of cultural, health care, community service, and educational nonprofit groups throughout the region. NYNEX has helped the Southern Westchester County BOCES put its elementary and high schools online, enabling students to access resources via the Internet and correspond with pen pals worldwide.

"Because we have so much invested here, there's a lot at stake for us," Pera said. "We want to be a good corporate citizen. As we say, 'We live and work in your hometown.'"

In April, NYNEX announced an agreement to merge with Bell Atlantic, another diversified telecommunications company at the forefront of the new communications, entertainment, and information industry. The merger, which may not be completed until 1997, will not change NYNEX's presence in Westchester County—although the merger is expected to speed the delivery of cable TV and other services to the county, and the two companies will eventually take the Bell Atlantic brand name. ◆

NETWORKS

WFAS AM & FM

WFAS is tuned in to the needs of Westchester. Whether it's breaking local news, in-depth traffic and weather reports, or the latest sports updates—if it's happening in the county, you'll hear about it on WFAS.

WFAS-AM 1230 began in Yonkers as WCOH during the 1920s. Following the Communications Act of 1932, it moved to White Plains and became WFAS. The station began serving a small market —mostly White Plains and Yonkers—providing local information to the rural population, summer residents, and early suburban migration.

WFAS soon gained a reputation as Westchester's "Storm Center" for winter school and business closings, and, as the population grew, so did the importance of the station's local coverage.

Today, the station, which is owned by Commodore Media, Inc., employs 25 full- and 10 part-time workers in Hartsdale. WFAS-AM 1230 is a full-service, middle-of-the-road format, providing extensive local news, weather from the WFAS Weather Center, and the most comprehensive local traffic updates. The station also features music from the 1940s, '50s and '60s, designed to appeal to the county's older listeners.

For sports fans, WFAS-AM offers play-by-play coverage of Manhattan College and New Jersey Nets basketball, Pace University and White Plains High School football, and a weekly "College Football Game of the Week" from the CBS Radio Network.

WFAS-AM's "Dean of Local Broadcasters," Bob E. Lloyd broadcasts live from this state-of-the-art studio.

WFAS's local and international news, traffic, weather, and commentaries are hosted by Westchester personalities. The station's local talk shows include lifestyle and community service, financial advice, cooking and gardening, health, and automotive problems.

Listeners also receive live local and national business updates from the offices of Gary Goldberg and Co., and Bob E. Lloyd, Westchester's "Dean of Local Broadcasters" for the past 25 years, kicks off each morning with contests and interviews.

In addition, WFAS's Traffic Network Center—combined with a network of 100 other public and private sources—provides complete traffic and train reports. The 24-hour network features Tom Baroni, who originated traffic network reporting in Westchester and Rockland Counties.

Westchester Radio 103.9 WFAS-FM is the leading adult contemporary music station in the county, playing hits from the 1970s, '80s, and '90s. WFAS-FM was the first all-compact disc station in the New York metropolitan area, and continues to provide listeners with music and commercial production produced with state-of-the-art equipment.

In addition, WFAS-FM benefits from the WFAS news department, the Traffic Network Center, Accuweather, and a 24-hour lineup of professional disc jockeys.

WFAS also works closely with its advertisers, helping them sell goods and services via unique marketing strategies and professional commercial production.

WFAS is equally concerned about the nonprofit segment of the market, and devotes numerous hours each week to promote hundreds of local causes. It participates in the American Heart Association's Annual Heart Radiothon, 5-K runs around Cross County Shopping Center, and the United Way's Annual Human Race.

One of the aspects that sets WFAS apart from its competitors is its heritage, according to station manager Peter Mutino. "WFAS-AM is the third oldest continuous operating AM station in the state." And WFAS-FM was one of the nation's first commercial FMs.

WFAS-AM and Westchester Radio 103.9 WFAS now reach more than 150,000 adult listeners in Westchester every week—more than most New York City stations. The station plans to continue to be a vital information and entertainment center for Westchester. ◆

WFAS-FM's Jay Michaels is the top-rated morning show host in Westchester County.

Westchester County: New York's Golden Apple / 141

Networks

COLLINS BROTHERS MOVING CORP.

Collins Brothers Moving Corp. is on a roll, and the firm's president, Frank E. Webers, has ambitious plans for growth.

The company was founded in 1910 by William Collins, who, via horse and wagon, moved furniture and other freight in Westchester and New York City. Collins' sons, William and Hugh, took over the business in 1958 and began moving household goods. At that time, there were three employees and two vans. Now, located at 620 Fifth Avenue, Collins Brothers has grown dramatically since Webers purchased the business in 1972. The company now has more than 100 vehicles and 325 employees.

Collins Brothers, a leader in the moving and storage industry, has a domestic household goods operation, an international division, a storage operation, and a commercial moving and storage division. Collins Brothers has two facilities in Brewster—a 50,000-square-foot warehouse and a recently opened 37,000-square-foot one—a 15,000-square-foot site for offices and warehousing in Larchmont, and a 30,000-square-foot office and terminal in New York City.

Collins Brothers' full-service, temperature-controlled storage facilities contain state-of-the-art security and sprinkler systems. All household goods are stored in specially designed storage vaults. The company also offers storage for office records, and receives and distributes new office furniture, fixtures, and electronic equipment.

As a top Atlas Van Line agent, Collins Brothers is able to handle household goods relocations to and from any place in the United States. Collins Brothers also is one of the largest international agents in the Atlas Van Lines' system, handling hundreds of shipments worldwide. The company consistently receives awards from Atlas for safety, superior packing, and customer satisfaction. In addition, Collins Brothers has won a number of other awards from Atlas Van Lines and corporate customers.

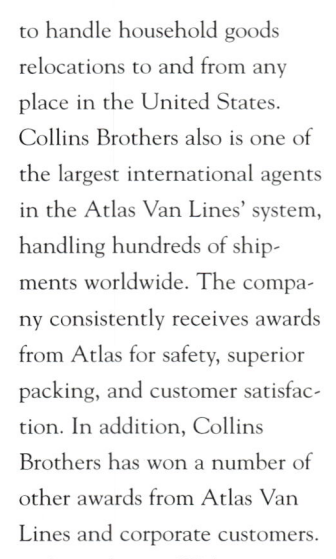

According to Webers, Collins Brothers is one of the largest commercial office movers in New York City and the largest in Westchester County. "We can handle any size commercial relocation. Our team of professionals designs and implements a marking and tagging system to ensure all items are placed in proper location at destination, which means there is no down time when employees return to work after the move."

Webers intends to keep growing the business, both locally and nationally. His goal is to open another full-service facility in the Northeast in order to service the ever growing customer base.

Webers credits much of the company's success to its employees. "We have a longevity of service here—more than one-half of our employees have been here at least 10 years. In this business, that's unusual. There are certain skills required in the moving business, and we train our people to be professionals at what they do. We provide our customers with experience and quality that no other can match." ◆

142 / Westchester County: New York's Golden Apple

Photo by Joe Vericker

CHAPTER · TEN

Manufacturing, Distribution & Technology

Producing and moving goods for individuals and industry, manufacturing, distribution and technology firms provide employment for many Westchester County residents.

J. F. Jelenko & Company
Page 146

Hitachi Metals America
Page 148

International Paper
Page 150

Philips Research Briarcliff
Page 152

Bally, Inc.
Page 154

IBM Corporation
Page 156

Bayer's Business Group Diagnostics
Page 157

Elmsford Sheet Metal Works, Inc.
Page 158

Tetko Inc
Page 159

Photo by Joe Vericker

144 / Westchester County: New York's Golden Apple

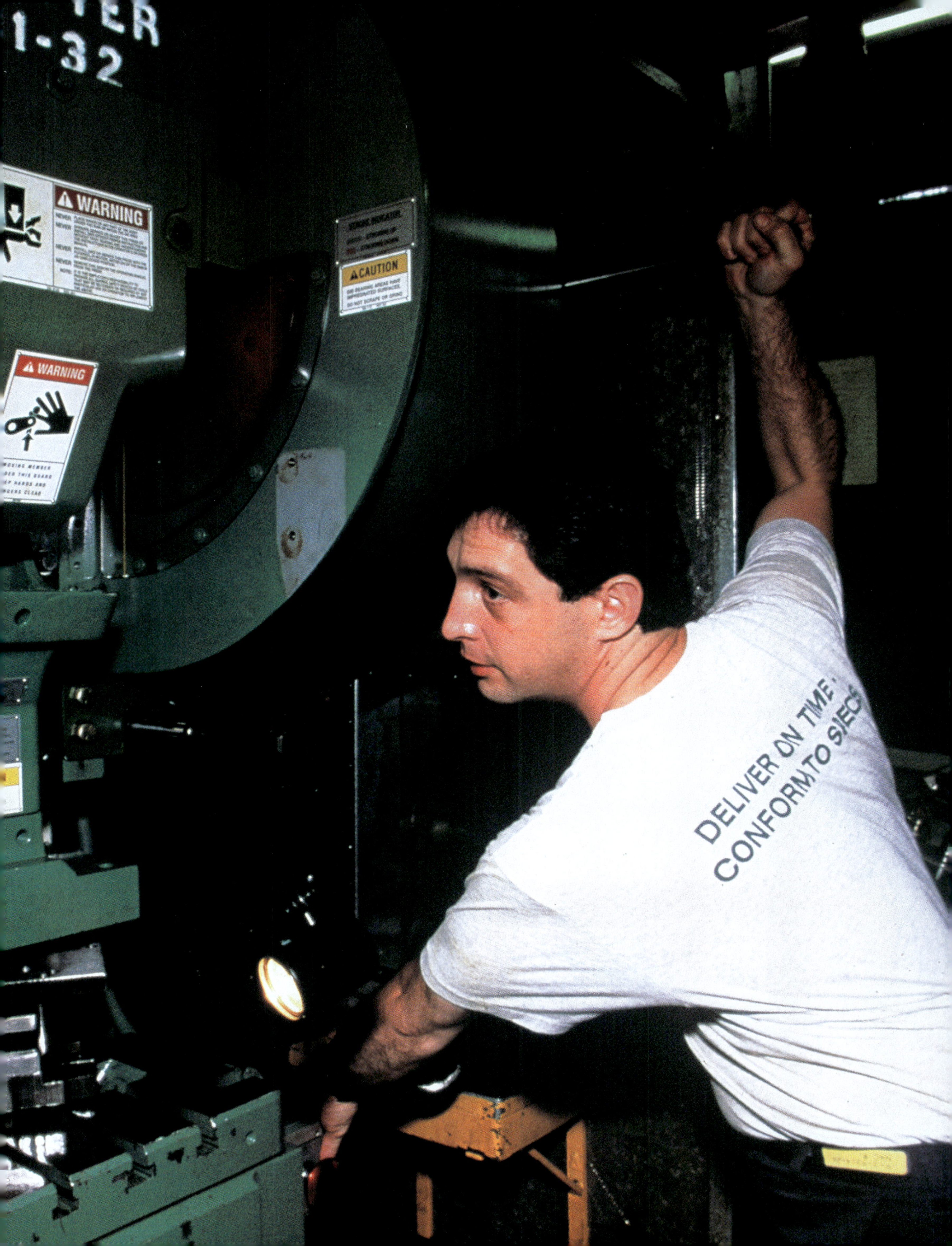

WARNING
CAUTION
WARNING
DELIVER ON TIME
CONFORM TO SPECS

MANUFACTURING, DISTRIBUTION & TECHNOLOGY

J.F. Jelenko & Company

A campus-like setting is home for Jelenko's educational programs for dental health.

Founded in 1912 by Jess Jelenko Sr., J.F. Jelenko & Co. has supplied the finest products and customer service to the dental laboratory industry for over 80 years. His commitment to excellence guided the company's growth as a manufacturer of dental gold alloys from its modest beginning in Lower Manhattan to national prominence and a growing international presence. A man of vision, Jess Jelenko established a research and development function and planned for expansion into foreign markets, creating a foundation for industry leadership that remains viable and dynamic. Today, in addition to its broad line of precious metal dental alloys, J.F. Jelenko & Co. provides dental laboratory equipment and a wide range of consumable dental supplies. It is a major supplier to the dental laboratory industry, both in the United States and throughout the world.

Jelenko moved its operations to a 25,000-square-foot building in New Rochelle in 1964 to expand its manufacturing and administrative functions, and established a training facility to better support its commitment to dental education. Four years later, the company was sold to the Pennwalt Corporation. This corporate change provided new avenues of national distribution and strengthened international sales.

In 1980 Jelenko relocated to a 75,000-square-foot building on 7.5 acres in a conveniently-located, campus-like setting in Armonk, New York. Its new headquarters were designed so as to consolidate manufacturing, research and development, and administrative operations in a facility that would enhance the company's ability to provide technical training and seminars for staff, customers, dental students, and area dentists. Most Jelenko employees work at this facility and are residents of Westchester County.

Company executives actively support dental education by serving on industry and academic boards and advisory committees. Jelenko also supports many community groups including the County Chamber of Commerce, the Armonk Fire Department, the Westchester County March of Dimes and United Way. Employee involvement in community and charitable activities is encouraged.

Acquired in 1986 by management and investors commit-

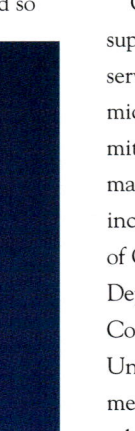

This three-unit bridge, fabricated from Jelenko alloy, exemplifies the beauty of technology and artistry working together, as all Jelenko products do.

146 / Westchester County: New York's Golden Apple

MANUFACTURING, DISTRIBUTION & TECHNOLOGY

ted to the standards of excellence established by the Jelenko family, J.F. Jelenko & Co. continues to advance its tradition of industry leadership by developing innovative, cost-effective, and environmentally-sensitive products and services that successfully meet changing dental health needs and regulations. Its sophisticated precious metal dental alloys, technologically advanced laboratory equipment, and broad range of quality dental products include attachments, porcelain, consumable items, and accessories that are recognized worldwide. Its internal quality standards are in full compliance with the United States Food and Drug Administration's Good Manufacturing Procedures, and have earned the company ISO 9001 certification for its Quality System from the demanding International Organization for Standardization.

While "gold has been the premier dental restorative material for patients for over 2,000 years and it will continue to be based on its superior biocompatibility and long term durability" according to Robert Owen of the World Gold Council, J.F. Jelenko & Co. has also played a vital role in developing high-quality, lower-cost alternatives. Today, the company manufactures more than 60 different alloys which offer the excellent physical properties that are the hallmark of its precious metal alloys.

Jelenko's emphasis is on quality products and precise product performance. Of special significance, Jelenko's precious metal alloy OLYMPIA was chosen by the Dental Implant Clinical Research Group as the control alloy for its landmark clinical study to evaluate the influence of design, application and location of dental implants on clinical performance and crestal bone response. The company is also recognized as a leader in the development of the porcelain-to-metal bonding technique, and as the first company to offer microfine grain structure and white-gold alloy with non-greening properties.

Responding to a query about the future of dental education, Dean R. Bruce Donoff of the Harvard School of Dental Medicine said, "Demographic changes in this country, namely the increasing age of the population, combined with improvements in oral hygiene, will result in dentists treating patients with more chronic diseases. As a result, students we are training today to be dentists in the twenty-first century will need to be more medically oriented than yesterday's dentist." Jelenko's ongoing commitment to dental education will ensure that useful and effective products are widely available for meeting the oral health care needs of this changing patient population.

A technician programs one of Jelenko's state-of-the-art continuous casting machines.

Jelenko is in the forefront of designing, manufacturing, and servicing a diverse line of laboratory equipment which includes handpieces, ultrasonic cleaners, turbine vacuum systems, furnaces, and casting machines. Jelenko's technological know-how and market experience significantly aid laboratories in producing their best work on time and with cost-effectiveness.

For over 30 years, Jelenko has offered refining services. Customers can return precious metal in any form for redemption in check, credit, or coins. State-of-the-art assay equipment and techniques are utilized to ensure the customer accurate valuation and fast turnaround.

Customer service is the key to the company's longevity and success. Jelenko's reputation as an industry leader is enhanced by the teamwork of its highly valued employees. All departments and functions participate in the exchange of ideas and new techniques, and share the latest developments in alloys, consumables, and equipment.

Sustaining a leadership role in a constantly evolving industry is a challenge. To do so, J.F. Jelenko & Co. will continue to seek alliances throughout the world to more effectively provide its products and services, pioneer the development of new alloys and products for use by dental professionals, keep actively involved with dental education, and employ the best people to provide the highest quality service. ◆

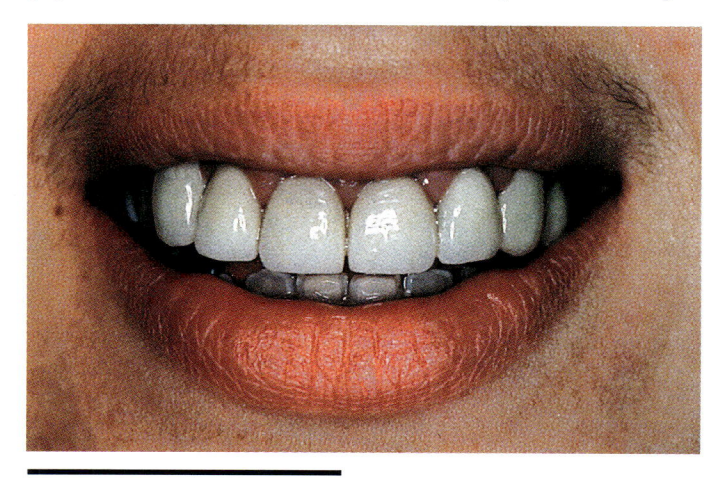

A great smile achieved using Jelenko products. When you look great you feel great.

MANUFACTURING, DISTRIBUTION & TECHNOLOGY

HITACHI METALS AMERICA

Hitachi Metals, Ltd. arrived in North America in the early 1960s with less than $50,000 in capitalization and a single product (steel strip for razor blades); its four employees operated out of a small office in New York City. Today, Hitachi Metals America, Ltd. is a major American manufacturer with corporate headquarters in Purchase, New York, annual revenues exceeding $500 million, and more than 2,500 employees throughout the United States.

Now in its fourth decade of operations in the United States, Hitachi Metals America, Ltd. (HMA) is a wholly-owned subsidiary of Tokyo-based Hitachi Metals, Ltd., one of the major members of the Hitachi Group Companies. HMA's main business lines are castings, steel-related products, magnetic products, and electronic materials. These products are manufactured primarily in the United States and sold mainly to the automotive, steel, telecommunications, computer, and consumer products industries. The company's position as a highly respected manufacturer and supplier results from its distinctive approach to customer service and its commitment to providing superb technical support. Because HMA takes a solutions-oriented approach to customer needs, its technical support services are often called upon by customers for assistance in resolving complex and demanding production, fabrication, and distribution problems.

During its early years of operation, HMA's only business was importing specialty steel from Japan. By the early 1970s, the company's imports had expanded to include castings and pipe fittings. Then HMA began to purchase U.S.-based companies, which led to its expansion into magnets. During the 1980s and early 1990s, Hitachi Metals America, Ltd. continued to diversify into electronic materials. The addition of new production facilities and product lines, introduction of new technologies, and increased production capacity have enabled the company to play an important role in the expansion of markets for small, fuel- efficient automobiles, personal computers, cellular telephones, and telecommunications products.

In 1991 Hitachi Metals America, Ltd. was reorganized into four product-based operating divisions: casting products, magnetic materials, electronic materials, and material trading. This step was taken to integrate the production and marketing of products manufactured in the United States by the various company units that comprise the Hitachi Metals Group. As a result of this restructuring, HMA can fill customer orders significantly faster and at the lowest cost.

Hitachi Metals America's largest market -and one of its oldest -is the automotive industry. HMA products are located throughout the automobile, and all four of its product lines support automobile sales, directly or indirectly. The company's automotive products, which include magnetic devices, high-grade ductile iron and aluminum castings, and aluminum wheels, are sold to manufacturers, assemblers, and fabricators of automotive parts and components, and directly to the three largest U.S. automotive manufacturers and U.S. facilities of foreign manufacturers.

HMA products for the business, industrial, and consumer electronics market include magnetic, electronic, and metallic parts for computer hard drives; computer peripherals, such as printers; telecommunications products; and switching mode power supplies. The company has achieved outstanding success in this industry because it is committed to the rapid development and application of advanced technology. This commitment enables HMA to create highly customized products on a consistent basis, giving it one of the industry's fastest time-to-market cycles.

Corporate headquarters in Purchase, New York

Cast aluminum wheels manufactured in Ohio at AAP St. Mary's, a subsidiary of Hitachi Metals America, Ltd.

MANUFACTURING, DISTRIBUTION & TECHNOLOGY

The computer industry is one of today's fastest growing markets, and the demand for personal computers, workstations, and compact laptops is expected to continue well into the foreseeable future. HMA manufactures a critically important component for the computer hard disk drive assembly: the magnetic recording head slider assembly, which performs the read/write function. The ongoing development of faster operating systems, memory-hungry software, and multimedia applications are creating insatiable demand for more storage capacity at higher density levels. HMA is enhancing its advanced DMIG (Double Metal In Gap) magnetic head technology and seeking to pioneer new technologies. Through these efforts, the company expects to play a significant role in this dynamic industry.

Another fast-growing HMA market is telecommunications, particularly cellular and cordless telephones, satellite communications systems, and beepers, which utilize microwave components developed by HMA. The company is one of the leading suppliers of ferrites (magnetic substances composed of iron oxide combined with one or more metals) and custom-designed telecommunications magnets and components to some of the largest telecommunications and electrical product manufacturers. HMA's superior engineering and product performance have set industry benchmarks and laid the foundation for meeting the increasing demand for higher levels of capability and speed in

Magnetic materials for the communications and automotive industry manufactured at plants in Edmore, Michigan, and China Grove, North Carolina

Cast automotive parts manufactured in Erie, Pennsylvania, and Blossberg, Pennsylvania, as well as in Japan for the worldwide market

information storage and transmission technologies. The electronics industry represents one of the brightest opportunities for HMA products in the coming years.

HMA also supplies diversified specialty products and components for the personal care and household products markets and the general construction and home-building industries. HMA materials are used in the production of razor blades, saw blades, cutlery, drills and taps, metal cutting tools, paper cutters, and shadow masks for television screens. In addition, HMA is a major producer of speaker magnets for sound and entertainment systems, high quality mill rolls for the steel industry, and malleable and cast iron piping components for water and gas supply products.

HMA's abiding commitment to technological leadership and outstanding customer service has been its wellspring for past and present accomplishments. And it will be the engine that drives the company toward the key goals it has defined for becoming stronger and more competitive in the twenty-first century: improving profitability to fund growth and offset economic downturns; expanding production capacity; identifying new supply sources exportable to Japan to offset the impact of foreign currency fluctuations; and developing new technology-driven parts and components that add value in the marketplace and differentiate HMA from its competitors.

While Hitachi is a global organization, its spirit of philanthropy nurtures the development of strong roots in the communities where its employees live and work. HMA encourages employees to volunteer within the community, and many do—collecting food for the hungry, providing clothing for children from impoverished families, and donating time and money to charitable organizations involved in health, human services, and education. Local activities are coordinated by three Community Action Councils (CAC), one of which is based in Purchase, New York, and supported by the Hitachi Foundation, which provides direct grants as well as matching funds in communities across the United States.

From a fledgling operation to a marketplace leader, Hitachi Metals America, Ltd. has achieved remarkable success in three decades. Its commitment to advancing technology, superior customer service, and the creation of custom-designed products that meet the needs and specifications of consumers will serve as the cornerstone for continued progress in the years ahead. ◆

MANUFACTURING, DISTRIBUTION & TECHNOLOGY

INTERNATIONAL PAPER

International Paper is on the cutting-edge of the forest products manufacturing industry.

The company, which specializes in paper, packaging, forest, and specialty products, is headquartered in Purchase, New York, and has more than 400 facilities throughout the Americas, Europe, and Asia. International Paper's products are used by customers in 130 nations.

In 1995 International Paper enjoyed net earnings of $1.2 billion on sales of $19.8 billion—making it a solid player in its field. And as the company begins gearing up to celebrate its centennial as a New York State corporation in 1998, its management has no plans to slow down its rapid expansions or scale back its impressive growth.

"International Paper's success has been built upon three principles that will serve us well in the twenty-first century," said John T. Dillon, chairman and chief executive officer of International Paper. "We will continue to provide a broad range of products and services that consistently meet and exceed customer expectations; we will constantly improve the quality and efficiency of our operations; and we will insist upon a business environment that develops and uses the full potential of all of our employees."

And Dillon said that Westchester County will continue to be an integral part of and benefit from International Paper's success. "Westchester County is a vital part of this management model. It offers the educational, economic, civic, and lifestyle resources that attract and nourish the extraordinary people who make possible world-class organizations."

The company's roots date back to 1898, when 20 paper mills in the states of Maine, New Hampshire, Vermont, and northern New York were merged to form International Paper. During that time, International Paper was producing about 60 percent of the newsprint being used by consumers in the United States.

Today, International Paper produces paper, packaging, and forest products for customers throughout the world. These lines are complemented by related specialty products and an extensive distribution division.

International Paper is one of the largest producers of high-quality printing and writing papers in the world. Through its Hammermill, Springhill, Strathmore, and Beckett franchises, the company serves markets for uncoated paper, fine papers, and more than 100 grades of recycled papers. The company is a leading manufacturer of coated papers used in magazines and catalogs, and heavyweight papers designed for folders, tags, and tickets.

International Paper's Aussedat Rey, Zanders, and Kwidzyn operations produce paper and pulp in Europe, with brands that include Aussedat Rey's Reymat, Zanders' Ikono and Chromolux lines, and Kwidzyn's Pollux. The company also is one of the leading producers of paper, fluff pulp, and dissolving pulp for international markets.

Printing papers

Packaging

MANUFACTURING, DISTRIBUTION & TECHNOLOGY

Specialty products

In the packaging industry, International Paper is one of the largest producers of containerboard and corrugated boxes, and the company is among the top providers of agricultural packaging in Europe. Its Everest bleached board is used for folding cartons, liquid packaging, and food service products throughout the world. The company's aseptic packaging system keeps liquids fresh without refrigeration, while its kraft division offers one of the largest arrays of kraft paper and packaging in the industry.

International Paper also distributes paper, industrial products, graphic arts supplies, and other goods worldwide. In North America, ResourceNet International comprises more than 280 distribution facilities; overseas, Aussedat Rey and Scaldia cover the growing European markets. The company said that it plans to continue expanding its product line and geographic areas to enhance the value of its products.

The company also has a specialty products division, which complements its core paper, packaging, and forestry operations. This division develops imaging products, such as plates, film, and papers, for the photography and graphic arts markets. Specialty panels produce CraftMaster door facings, siding, decorative products including Fountainhead solid surfacing, and Nevamar high-pressure laminates, foam products, and furniture components.

International Paper's specialty industrial papers are used for various applications, such as pressure sensitive labels. The company's nonwovens producer—Veratec—is one of the leading manufacturers of spunbound fabrics for consumer disposable products; Arizona Chemical reprocesses papermaking byproducts for specialty applications; and a petroleum operation develops oil and gasoline reserves.

In the United States, International Paper owns or manages more than six million acres of timberlands—making it one of the largest landowners in the country. The sawlogs and pulpwood that are harvested from the company's forests represent about 33 percent of its U.S. fiber needs. The company is a leading U.S. producer of southern pine lumber, and a range of panel and other wood products, such as oriented strand board.

International Paper prides itself on being an industry leader in innovative and cutting-edge technologies—whether that means satisfying a single customer's need for stronger, lighter packaging, or an entire community's need for recreation land and recycling, or a future generation's need for clean air and water.

The company's philosophy is to remain "firmly dedicated to environmental leadership, from conserving the world around us to protecting the health of our employees and the communities in which we operate." And, throughout the world, more than 88,000 International Paper employees work to support the company's goal every day.

In an effort to demonstrate its commitment, the International Paper Company Foundation was incorporated in 1953, and has since sought and funded programs to address the social and civic needs of numerous communities.

International Paper is an active supporter of all the communities in which it operates- and Westchester County is no exception. The foundation has provided grants to a number of local organizations in Westchester County, including Westchester County Parks, Recreation, and Conservation; Council for the Arts in Westchester; Food-People Allied to Combat Hunger, Inc.; Friends of Karen; Mental Health Association of Westchester County; New Orchestra of Westchester; College Careers; Hospital Chaplaincy, Inc.; and the White Plains Hospital Center.

International Paper also has had a significant impact on the economy in Westchester County. In 1987 the company's operations center was relocated to Memphis, Tennessee and the company relocated its corporate headquarters from New York City to Two Manhattanville Road in Purchase; it employs about 120 people in the county. ◆

Forest products

Westchester County: New York's Golden Apple / **151**

MANUFACTURING, DISTRIBUTION & TECHNOLOGY

PHILIPS RESEARCH BRIARCLIFF

For more than half a century, Philips Research Briarcliff has been quietly formulating technological breakthroughs right in Westchester's backyard. And its work has impacted numerous industries—from the health care field, where Philips' highly sophisticated technology improves medical imaging processes, to the electronics market, where a simple chip expels unwanted "ghosts" from television sets in people's homes.

Although based on a 100-acre campus in Briarcliff Manor, "The direct applications of the work we do goes far beyond Westchester County," said Dr. Peter Bingham, president of Philips Research Briarcliff.

Philips Research Briarcliff is the U.S. research facility for Philips Electronics N.V., a global electronics leader with more than 250,000 employees worldwide and annual sales of $40 billion. The labs play a major role in the development and improvement of a range of Philips products sold under the brands of Philips, Magnavox, Norelco, and PolyGram.

Philips is a recognized leader regionally and internationally,

Peter Bingham, president, Philips Research Briarcliff

Members of the Philips High Definition Television (HDTV) project team work on the digital broadcast systems that will deliver the next generation of home entertainment.

Bingham said, noting that many of its scientists play a significant role among the world's top government and university-led scientific bodies and standards organizations.

The labs recently celebrated its 50th anniversary in Westchester, and Bingham reflected upon the company's interesting history—and impressive founder, the late Dr. Anton Philips.

During World War II, when the Nazis invaded the Netherlands, Anton Philips fled to the United States. As the Germans were occupying his family's Philips Electronics N.V. labs in Eindhoven, Philips began developing X-ray technology and equipment in the United States. When the Netherlands was freed, he traveled back to Eindhoven to supervise the company. In 1945 he founded Philips Research Briarcliff in the United States and, in 1946, the labs opened in a stone mansion on a 13-acre estate in Irvington. In 1963 the company built its current site in Briarcliff Manor.

During the first 25 years, Philips Research Briarcliff specialized in material physics, cryogenics, and sophisticated X-ray analysis. Some of its research was undertaken to support the needs of the U.S. military during World War II; the labs received a post-war U.S. Army-Navy production award for those efforts.

Although Philips branched out into other directions after the war, it continued to conduct research in support of the U.S. government's objectives. In 1969 Philips built the necessary apparatus and assisted in performing analysis of rock samples gathered from the first moon landing. And Philips built the first cryogenic system used in the infrared "night vision" surveillance system of the RF4C military plane.

Today, Philips Research Briarcliff focuses on advanced electronics, broadcasting systems, and emerging information technologies. Over the past decade, Philips has been granted more than 280 patents. In addition to its U.S. operations, Philips has research facilities in France, the United Kingdom, and Germany. The labs are a division of Philips Electronics North America Corp. in Manhattan, and the parent company remains based in the Netherlands.

In Briarcliff Manor, Philips employs 300 people. The team focuses on five technologies: digital television and multimedia, lasers, medical imaging, lighting, and software. The facility has attracted some of the top researchers worldwide, and Briarcliff scientists also are charter members of the Grand Alliance—the Federal Communications Commission-sponsored organization charged with making high-definition television a reality.

Much of Philips' research is concentrated on television, audio, and related technology. The labs' scientists have contributed to a number of innovations, including the universal remote control device, picture-in-picture television, video coding, video compression, and projection television.

Philips developed the Emmy award-winning Ghost Cancellation Reference signal which eliminates transmission echoes or "ghosts" caused by the video signal bouncing against buildings and terrain. The interference produces staggered reception and multiple, slightly overlapping images and Ghost Cancellation clears them up.

152 / Westchester County: New York's Golden Apple

MANUFACTURING, DISTRIBUTION & TECHNOLOGY

Philips is active in medical information science as well. The labs' software programs help radiologists locate and detect microcalcifications in patients that appear long before clinical symptoms of breast cancer arise.

Philips also researches specific ways to help businesses operate more efficiently. The labs developed the prototype for the first industry-wide multimedia network for supermarkets and food wholesalers—SuperMarket Trade Network—an on-line retail communications system that links the entire food chain together.

In laser technology, the labs are working on semiconductor blue lasers to replace conventional infrared lasers and improve the storage capacity of optical recording systems.

Despite the numerous areas in which Philips is involved, it continues its original work in lighting. The company began as a lightbulb manufacturer and today is the leading producer of lighting products. For example, the labs developed the Micro-Lamp—an ultra-miniature, long-lasting, and low-cost lighting device that incorporates semiconductor technology. "By implementing electronics-based lighting, we are helping protect the environment and save people money," Bingham said.

Research shares about one percent of the company's $40 billion annual revenues. "That's pretty generous," Bingham said. "By plowing money back in research, Philips is demonstrating its commitment to maintain a leadership position.

Philips Research Briarcliff, Briarcliff Manor, New York

We're well-positioned for the future as a global leader in information technology and the application of information technology. But that doesn't mean we won't be active in other areas."

Philips prides itself on the ability of its researchers to work in an "open, collegial environment" in which ideas and discoveries are exchanged freely, Bingham said. "We're developing a challenging work environment in our research labs. We recruit the cream of the crop, who then work with our experienced staff. This creates a group of colleagues who are exciting to work with and have a mutual spirit of trust."

In an effort to bring new products and technologies to the market quickly, Philips collaborates with research partners and works with government agencies. The labs work with International Business Machines Corp., 3M Corp., and the M.I.T. Media Lab. In addition, Philips Research Briarcliff has awarded grants to scientists at Stanford, Rensselaer Polytechnic Institute, and Georgia Tech. "These cooperations are mutually rewarding," Bingham said. "It helps us gain insight into their talents and lets us bring the best global talent to our partners."

Philips also collaborates with its community. The labs sponsor educational programs like the Philips Science Education Initiative, a project that each summer unites elementary school teachers with Philips' researchers to develop different ways to teach science to students. "This program gives teachers hands-on, practical knowledge," Bingham said. In January 1996 Philips Research Briarcliff honored New York area high school students for "thought-provoking glimpses of technology in the next 50 years." At an awards presentation, 26 students received prizes in a regional scholarship competition—Your Technology Future: Imaging The Next 50 Years. "The contest gives students a boost towards science and technology education." ◆

David Koo and Philips researchers discuss the Ghost Cancellation (GCR) system that eliminates "ghosts"—unwanted television images—that plague millions of TV sets each year.

Westchester County: New York's Golden Apple / 153

MANUFACTURING, DISTRIBUTION & TECHNOLOGY

BALLY, INC.

Bally, Inc., a leading Swiss international manufacturer, has been designing and producing superior quality men's and women's footwear and leather accessories for more than a century.

The business was started in 1847 by a silk-ribbon manufacturer, Carl Franz Bally. He later took the reins of his family's business and began manufacturing elastic tapes which tailors and shoemakers were just beginning to use. Carl Franz's idea proved successful—his Swiss quality wares attracted the interest of even the French boot- and shoemakers.

Shortly thereafter, during a trip to visit some customers in France, Carl Franz noticed a pair of ladies' shoes in the window of a Paris bootmaker. He wanted to purchase the shoes for his wife but realized he did not know her size. Bally's solution? He purchased the bootmaker's entire range. That experience lead Carl Franz to begin manufacturing elegant shoes himself. In 1851, Bally's first series-produced shoes were produced in his own factory in Schönenwerd. The fledgling company flourished and soon enjoyed enormous success throughout the world.

The entrance on Madison Avenue opens to an elegant store with dramatic high ceilings and open spaces. The store opened in August 1995.

Today, Bally is comprised of retail and wholesale operations worldwide. The U.S. company is a wholly owned subsidiary of Contraves USA; its parent company is Oerlikon Buhrle AG in Switzerland. Bally companies are located in Switzerland, France, Belgium, Luxembourg, Great Britain, Netherlands, Germany, Austria, Italy, the United States, Canada, Hong Kong, Singapore, Australia, Japan, and South Africa.

The company has 550 retail stores throughout the world, including 64 in Switzerland and 46 in the United States. In the United States, 75 percent of Bally's business is generated through third-party customers, including such upscale department stores as Nordstrom and Saks Fifth Avenue, as well as smaller, independent shoe retailers.

Bally's premium products are manufactured in its own factories, the balance being produced in third-party factories in Italy. Bally has six factories specializing in the highest quality footwear—three in Switzerland, two in France, and one in the United Kingdom.

In Westchester County, Bally maintains corporate offices and a distribution center in New Rochelle. Bally moved to New Rochelle in 1981, expanded its presence there in 1986, and today employs 120 people at One Bally Place. The company also has corporate offices, a wholesale operation, and showroom on Fifth Avenue in Manhattan; a recently opened store on Madison Avenue and 59th Street; a men's shoe store on Madison Avenue; and several stores in New Jersey.

"We are the only globally recognized footwear company in the world," said Richard Wycherley, president of Bally, Inc. in New Rochelle. "Our specialty is comfort and fit. We specialize in shoe-making skills that have been lost in the mass manufacturing process. Also, we are always looking for the finest, softest leather. We are not just looking for beauty, but how to design the longest-wearing shoes as well."

While the company is inter-

The Copley Plaza store in Boston was remodeled in January 1995 to fully reflect Bally's total international image.

154 / Westchester County: New York's Golden Apple

MANUFACTURING, DISTRIBUTION & TECHNOLOGY

nationally renowned for its men's and women's shoes, Bally also produces a line of men's and women's leather accessories, including handbags and wallets, which account for 25 percent of Bally's total U.S. sales. The company also manufactures a line of leather clothing.

Bally has been aggressively expanding its presence throughout the United States. In addition to its Madison Avenue expansion, the company has opened new stores in Waikiki, Hawaii; King of Prussia, Pennsylvania; Boca Raton, Florida; Vancouver, British Columbia; Roosevelt Field in New Jersey; and at airports in Atlanta and Los Angeles.

"We are concentrating on obtaining more penetration in the domestic American market," said Wycherley. "Our customer base is now 40 percent tourist, and, while we plan to retain that share, we want to grow our domestic business."

In addition to expansions, Bally has been refitting its existing stores throughout the world. The stores are being remodeled in cooperation with a renowned Parisian interior designer. The new look constitutes a key element of Bally's international corporate identity—the design is characterized by the subtle use of natural materials in delicate shades of brown, beige, and off-white, carefully balanced architectural forms, and atmospheric lighting.

"We have developed a vision for Bally," Wycherley said. "We are updating our retail image and conducting major renovations, from London to Tokyo. We are improving all of our stores, developing a strong, consistent marketing plan, and getting a strategy and vision for our footwear—what we stand for and what our products are."

Customer service is a top priority at Bally, and the company has developed a program that is tailored for the international training requirements of a global company. Through its "Bally Art," the company has invested in the professional development of its retail sales force. The program consists of one training module for sales personnel and three training modules for store managers in which small groups are brought together for two-day seminars.

"We have in place a special training course that we have been conducting worldwide for three years," Wycherley said. "In this course, we discuss how to meet and greet our customers and how to conduct sales in our shops. We are trying to make shopping at Bally an even more enjoyable experience."

One of the reasons Bally is able to concentrate on its image is because it needn't worry about market share, Wycherley said. "We have relatively few competitors here. We're global, so our main competition is in other parts of the world. Nobody has the strength and distribution that we do worldwide, so we are less worried about competing and are able to spend more time on marketing efforts."

"We are aiming for a totally consistent image worldwide," he added. "This is very important for our products and customers. We are in the process of creating one corporate image, one consumer approach, and have made significant steps towards that goal. We plan to have a consistency worldwide, so a consumer can buy the same product and receive the same service in Tokyo or New York." ◆

The ladies' section of Copley Plaza shows off the rich warm colors and materials of the global design.

Bally's newest store opened in Waikiki April 1996. Like many of its store openings, the event is marked with a party that raises funds for the less fortunate—"Bally Cares."

MANUFACTURING, DISTRIBUTION & TECHNOLOGY

IBM CORPORATION

IBM Corporation in Armonk has been at the forefront of technology for more than 75 years. As advances in network technology present new global market opportunities, IBM is prepared to guide its customers into the twenty-first century.

One of IBM's advantages over competitors is its "global reach," said Robert N. Sellar, area community relations manager. "'International' is our first name—we are ubiquitous. A lot of companies don't have that reach, and many now want to expand into the global marketplace. We've been in 158 countries for quite some time, and we have folks there with a deep and broad knowledge of those markets."

IBM is the world's largest computer manufacturer and information technology services company, with some 80,000 people providing consulting, systems integration, and solution development services worldwide. IBM also is the world's largest software company with major offerings in mainframe operating and application software and through the acquisitions of Lotus Development Corp. and Tivoli Systems, Inc.

IBM's history dates back to the late 1800s, when Thomas John Watson was recruited as a salesman for National Cash Register (NCR), a manufacturer of automated punch-card tabulating machines. In 1911 NCR was acquired by Computing Tabulating Recording Co. (CTR). Watson was hired to run CTR, and he renamed the company IBM Corporation in 1924.

IBM moved its corporate headquarters from New York City to Armonk in the mid-1950s. IBM North America is based in White Plains, and IBM has locations in Somers, Yorktown Heights, Mount Pleasant, Hawthorne, and Tarrytown. Countywide, the company employs in excess of 7,000 people.

IBM has a significant impact on the county's economy. Annually, it generates more than $3 million in sales tax to Westchester. In addition, IBM recently invested approximately $70 million to construct a 283,500-square-foot headquarters in Armonk to replace its former facility.

IBM, the world's leading computer manufacturer and information technology services company, is headquartered in Armonk, New York, with additional locations across Westchester County including facilities in Somers (pictured), Yorktown Heights, Mt. Pleasant, Hawthorne, and Tarrytown.

IBM has a tradition of supporting its communities. In Westchester, IBM provides over a quarter million dollars to local organizations, and its employees are involved in local schools through mentoring programs, Junior Achievement, the United Way of Tri-State, and the Westchester Arts Council, among others.

Like many corporations countywide—and nationwide—IBM has focused on cost-cutting strategies to remain competitive. Chairman and CEO Louis V. Gerstner implemented a massive restructuring in 1993 which helped IBM rebuild a strong financial foundation.

IBM is investing in technologies to enhance "network computing," which expands global networks that support the Internet to bring people together to collaborate, share ideas, and solve problems.

In 1995 IBM reported record revenues of $70 billion and earnings of $6.3 billion, and was number one in U.S. patents issued for the third consecutive year. In addition, the company has been investing in technology, in high-growth areas such as semiconductor manufacturing, and in its workforce—IBM hired 15,000 people last year.

"Year after year, we have been able to increase our value and capabilities and make dramatic enhancements to our products," Sellar said.

As part of IBM's strategy, the company is investing in "network computing," which expands global networks that support the Internet to bring people together to collaborate, share ideas, and solve problems. IBM plans to continue creating technology to enhance powerful networks' role in worldwide communications. "That's the next wave and that territory is very familiar to us. That's where our expertise is critical," Sellar said. And IBM will keep working with its customers to help them exploit these networks. "We're very customer-driven, and we'll stay focused on customer satisfaction." ◆

MANUFACTURING, DISTRIBUTION & TECHNOLOGY

BAYER'S BUSINESS GROUP DIAGNOSTICS

Bayer's Business Group Diagnostics focuses on developing accurate, cost-effective, and efficient diagnostic systems that enable clinical labs, health care providers, and self-testers to diagnose and manage disease. With a customer offering that includes in-home blood glucose monitoring systems, physician office systems, and high volume, automated clinical laboratory systems, the company's goal is to advance the quality of health care around the world.

Headquartered in Tarrytown, New York, the Diagnostics Group is one of the four largest diagnostics companies in the world, serving customers in five categories of in vitro diagnostics: clinical chemistry, diabetes, hematology, immunodiagnostics, and urine chemistry. Bayer's Diagnostics research is conducted primarily in Tarrytown, New York, and Elkhart, Indiana. The company provides customers in 100 countries with well-known and highly respected products under the brand names Ames and Technicon. Worldwide, the Group employs 5,000 people at 40 locations, including 700 in Tarrytown.

In the United States, Diagnostics is a division of Bayer Corporation, an $8-billion research-based company with diversified businesses in health care, chemicals, and imaging technologies. Eight U.S. Bayer Corporation divisions develop, manufacture, and market the 8,000 products in Bayer's portfolio, which include Bayer® Aspirin, *Alka-Seltzer*®, and Agfa film. The parent company, Bayer, is based in Leverkusen, Germany.

With an annual investment of $10 million in research and development, the Diagnostics Group explores a range of scientific disciplines—from classical chemistry to molecular biology—and conducts research into engineering and software.

To enhance its customer offering, the Diagnostics Group has formed many strategic alliances. Examples include an agreement to develop new cervical cancer detection systems, and another to jointly commercialize biochemical bone-markers.

A company history of pioneering spirit is reflected in the important technological "firsts" Bayer has brought to its customers. The company is a long-time leader in dry reagent technology and was first to bring automation to clinical chemistry. In 1941 the company, under the name Miles Inc., revolutionized in vitro diagnostics when it launched CLINITEST® effervescent urine sugar testing tablets—the first convenient and accurate test to detect the presence of sugar in urine. In 1964 Miles developed DEXTROSTIX®, the first dry reagent blood glucose test, which enabled millions of people with diabetes to monitor blood-sugar levels quickly and conveniently in their homes.

In 1989, in an effort to expand its customer offering of diagnostic systems, the company acquired Technicon Instruments Corp. of Tarrytown. The acquisition enabled Bayer to combine its ability to simplify processes of complex testing with Technicon's capability to automate test analyses.

Miles has been a member of the Bayer family since 1978 but due to legal restrictions was unable to use the Bayer name in North America. However, following Miles' 1994 acquisition of Sterling Winthrop's North American over-the-counter drug business, Miles officially changed its name to Bayer and regained the rights to the Bayer Cross trademark in the United States. Now unified under the name Bayer, the company is better positioned to meet customer needs by delivering products and services that reflect the global Bayer commitment. ◆

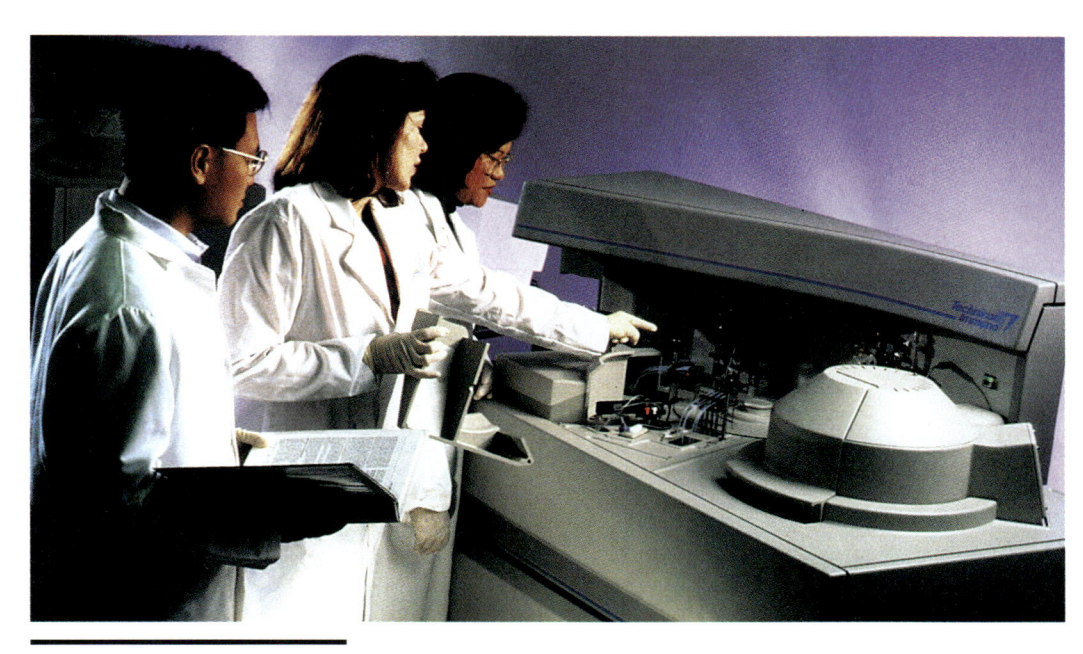

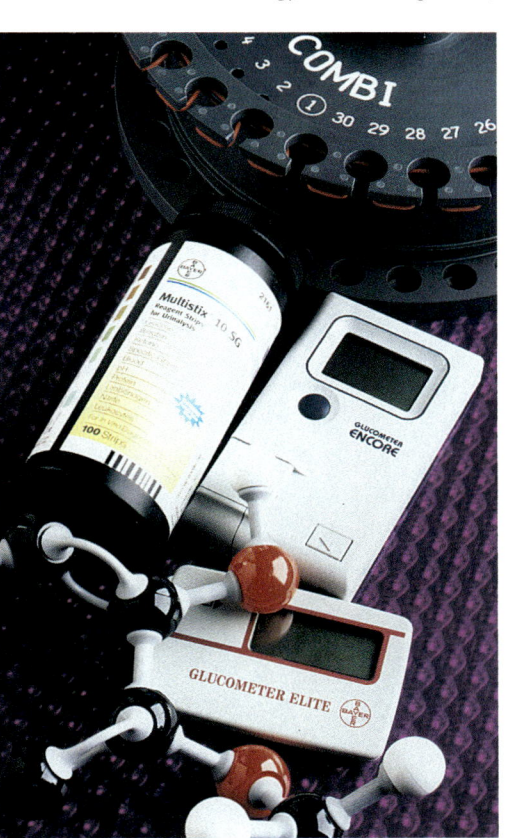

The TECHNICON® IMMUNO 1® system is meeting customer needs in clinical laboratories around the world. The fully automated system offers one of the broadest immunodiagnostics test menus available in the industry.

Bayer's Business Group Diagnostics offers a wide range of diagnostics products and services to meet diverse customer needs.

MANUFACTURING, DISTRIBUTION & TECHNOLOGY

Elmsford Sheet Metal Works, Inc.

At Elmsford Sheet Metal Works, Inc., President and CEO Joseph Massaro's modus operandi is "Work hard; play hard; take care of business." On summer nights it's not unusual to find Massaro's team gathered on the cedar deck abutting his Peekskill office—firing up a barbecue and laying down plans for future projects.

"These people aren't my workers—they're my friends," said Massaro. "Many of us grew up together; I've been having coffee with some of these guys since we were teenagers."

Massaro credits much of Elmsford Sheet Metal's success to this "friendly" environment. "I have an open-door policy. You don't have to go through a chain of command—we handle problems right away. Everyone here cares—that's what makes this company work."

Elmsford Sheet Metal was founded by Massaro's uncle, Vincent Gervasi, in 1946. Gervasi operated from his Elmsford home but, following rapid growth in 1950, moved into a building up the road. The company later relocated to larger space and in 1972 settled into its present quarters—a 25,000-square-foot facility on five acres in downtown Peekskill. In the meantime, Massaro had joined the company and, together with Gervasi, purchased the building at 4000 Arlo Lane. Although Massaro eventually bought the business, the two remain partners in ownership of the building.

Today, Elmsford Sheet Metal is a leader in its field. Working with flat coils of metal, the company designs, manufactures, and installs air-conditioning and heating ducts in commercial buildings. It employs 100 people, and covers seven counties in New York, as well as Fairfield and Litchfield Counties in Connecticut. The company has a full-time maintenance crew to take care of equipment and owns five trailers for shipping products.

"We're one of the top 25 privately owned sheet metal companies in the U.S.," said Massaro, who is president of SMACNA, Southeastern New York (Sheet Metal and Air Conditioning Contractors National Association, Inc.). "And we are the top in this area. We're involved in many of the major jobs in Westchester."

Left to right: Elmsford Sheet Metal's President and CEO Joe Massaro, Frank Suda, and Don Trier

Those "major jobs" include work at Westchester County Airport, the former General Motors plant in North Tarrytown, White Plains Hospital, and Hudson Valley Westchester Hospital Center in Peekskill. The company has a satellite office in Fishkill, where it is doing work for International Business Machines Corp. Projects also have been handled in Kuwait, Moscow, Cuba, and off the coast of Africa.

The sheet metal business is extremely competitive, Massaro said, but Elmsford Sheet Metal has established "a reputation for bringing the job in on time, and on or under budget. And we've finished every job we ever started. That's what has kept us alive. Also, we're the largest one here, so we can do jobs that no one else—locally—can do."

Quality and efficiency have always been a priority of Massaro. In 1974, when construction was minimal and sheet metal shops were failing, he took action. In an effort to increase productivity, he capitalized on experience with computers in the office and decided to integrate all automatic sheet metal manufacturing processes under computer control. The team created and installed a fully computerized sheet metal design, layout, and manufacturing system for its own shop, and Massaro formed East Coast Sheet Metal Fabrication Corp. to market the system and train other companies to use it. Today, the software is sold worldwide. ◆

MANUFACTURING, DISTRIBUTION & TECHNOLOGY

TETKO INC

Tetko Inc, headquartered in Briarcliff Manor, supplies top-quality screening fabrics and related products to industries worldwide. The company is part of a Swiss organization that is internationally recognized as the leading manufacturer of precision woven fabrics used in filtration, sifting, shielding, and screen printing applications.

Building on centuries of silk-weaving experience, Tetko's affiliated mills have developed the technology to weave synthetic fabrics that have become the standard against which others are judged. This achievement made them first in the industry to earn ISO 9001 certification—an internationally recognized standard of quality.

Tetko also provides a broad line of woven wire cloth, equipment, and supplies produced by leading international manufacturers. The company serves a number of industries, including medical diagnostic equipment and instrumentation, mining and mineral processing, automotive, textile, graphic arts, glass and ceramic, food processing, aerospace, and chemical or pharmaceutical processing.

Tetko's history dates back to the 1830s, when its Swiss mills began exporting silk bolting cloth for flour sifting throughout the world. "In the early twentieth century, Tetko evolved as an importer of woven materials primarily made of silk for military applications and screen printing," said Peter E. Lohaus, president. "Then silk was replaced and substituted by polyester, so we began to weave fabrics for filtration. We grew and added product lines to expand our market share."

Tetko established its presence in the United States in 1923 and relocated from New York City to Elmsford in the mid-1950s. Today, Tetko employs 125 people in New York State: 61 in Westchester, and 64 at its Buffalo plant.

In a fully staffed 4,600-square-foot screen printing laboratory in Briarcliff Manor, the company conducts ongoing tests on all products needed to print on various substrates. At its Filtration Division lab, in Depew, New York, Tetko evaluates filtration, sifting, and electronic shielding requirements, and continually inspects fabrics and wire cloths. At this facility and in Kansas City, Missouri, Tetko uses state-of-the-art fabrication processes to manufacture custom components and finished products from the same high-quality fabrics and wire cloth.

Tetko has distribution centers in New York and Los Angeles and has sales and marketing offices nationwide.

While the industry is competitive, Lohaus said Tetko has an edge over its rivals. "We are unique. We manufacture a broad product range and produce the finest materials and fabrics. We are known as specialists who provide fine fabrics made of yarn as thin as a hair." Lohaus also stressed the company's focus on customer service and satisfaction as key to remaining competitive in the industry.

Tetko's fabrication facilities can produce both finished and semifinished parts in virtually any shape for a variety of end-use applications.

Tetko has made "numerous breakthroughs" in its industry, Lohaus noted. "In the development of commercial jet engines, we have come up with a new range of products that we are selling to the aircraft industry."

Tetko's location in Westchester has added to the company's success, Lohaus said. "The internationality of the greater New York area has benefited us. Our business requires highly educated individuals, and in Westchester we have access to a stable, well-educated workforce. Also, we purchase products from local sources and we have an excellent relationship with the banking community and other support groups.

For the future, Tetko has ambitious plans for growth, Lohaus said. "We really feel the U.S. market is extremely viable for us. We plan to hold on to that market and expand through both internal growth and acquisitions. And, we have big plans for adding new product lines." ◆

The Briarcliff Manor location of Tetko Inc in Westchester County

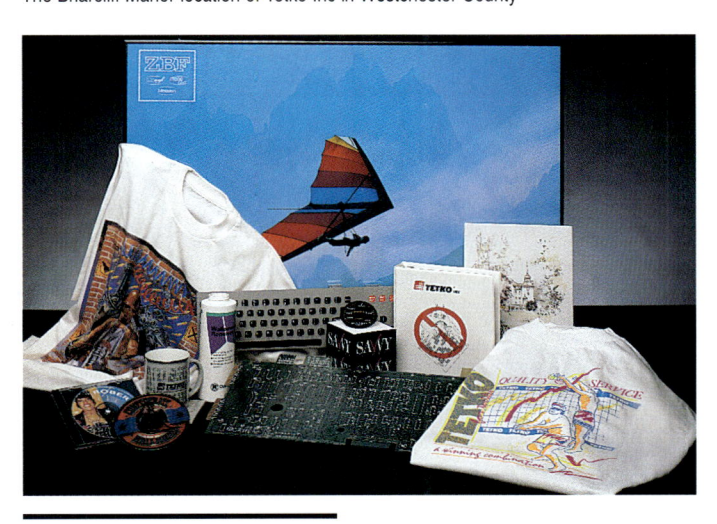

Tetko's product line features the best product innovation available for each step of the screen making process. The result is optimum print quality, time after time.

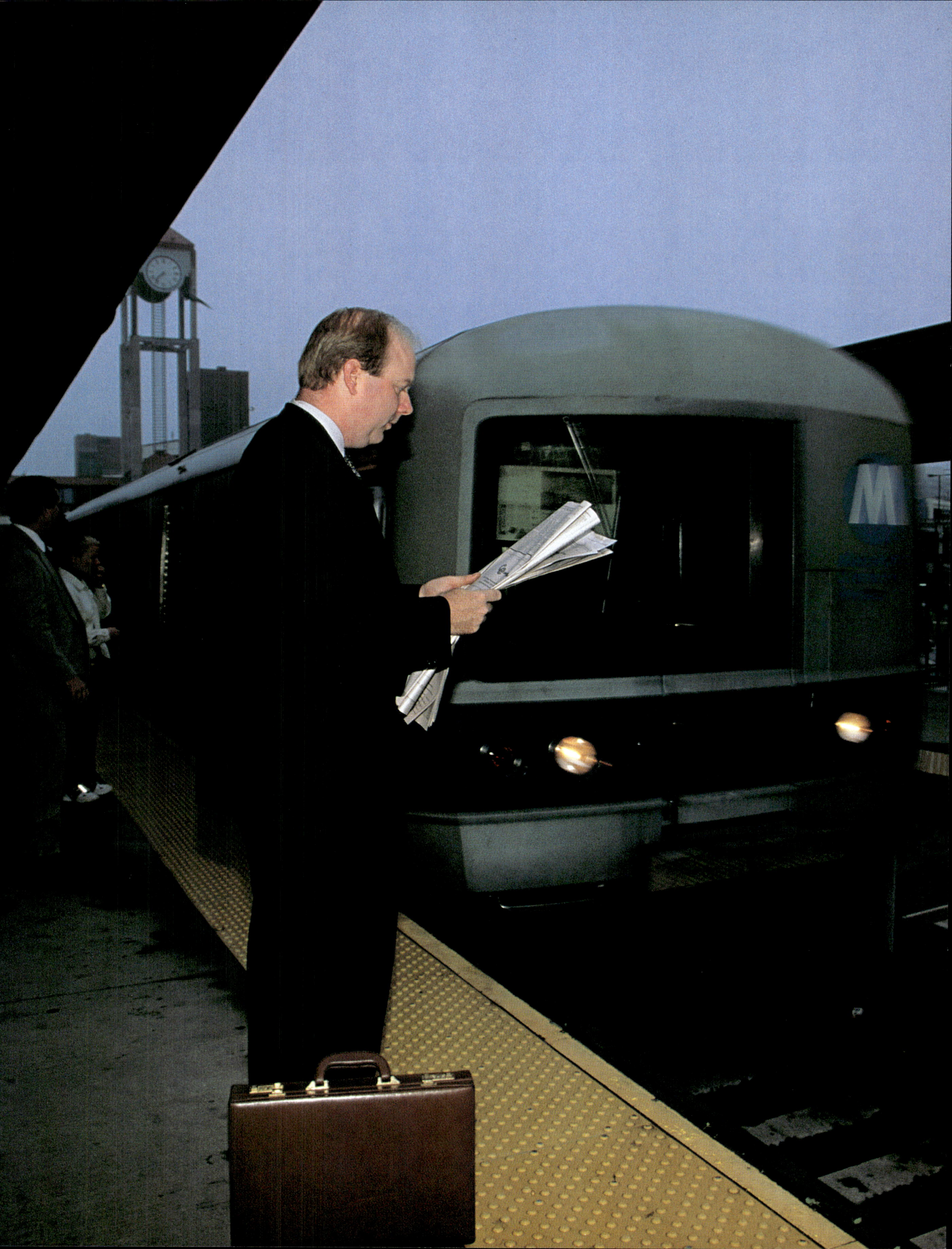

CHAPTER • ELEVEN

Business, Professions & Finance

Westchester County's mix of business talents and resources strengthens the professional community.

THE COUNTY CHAMBER OF COMMERCE, INC.
Page 162

BLEAKLEY PLATT & SCHMIDT
Page 164

TARRYTOWN HOUSE EXECUTIVE CONFERENCE CENTER
Page 166

THACHER PROFFITT & WOOD
Page 168

MASTERCARD INTERNATIONAL INCORPORATED
Page 169

SHAMBERG MARWELL HOCHERMAN DAVIS & HOLLIS, P.C.
Page 170

Photo by Joe Vericker

Westchester County: New York's Golden Apple / 161

BUSINESS, PROFESSIONS & FINANCE

THE COUNTY CHAMBER OF COMMERCE, INC.

The County Chamber means business. So does Harold E. Vogt. He has to. As president and chief executive officer of The County Chamber of Commerce, Inc., Vogt has in mind the interests of thousands of business people.

"Our goal has always been to be on target in specifically addressing the common and special interests of only one constituency—our members. The business climate, the impact of its components on the ability of business to operate and grow, and Westchester's general economic vitality and well-being are the target upon which we set our sights," said Vogt.

The County Chamber of Commerce, Inc. (a.k.a. Westchester County Chamber of Commerce) in White Plains—"Westchester's largest, broad-based business organization"—is a private, not-for-profit corporation funded by annual membership dues.

Founded in 1904 as the White Plains Board of Trade, the County Chamber today boasts 3,000 member companies and individual professionals, 97 percent of which are small businesses. And unlike other local organizations, it's always "business first" at The County Chamber, Vogt said.

According to its mission statement, the Chamber "does not profess to be a social club, philanthropic entity, or 'old boys network' . . . is not a multifarious assortment of nebulous partnerships which frequently suffer paralysis from analysis, are often driven by capitulation and acquiescence and frequently expend valuable resources and time in mustering consensus rather than simply pursuing the obvious."

Simply put, the Chamber is dedicated to identifying and addressing the business community's concerns.

"We are here to serve the needs of the business community," Vogt said. "All other esoteric things going on in the county are secondary. We're a 'business first' organization. That distances us from other area associations. We don't get involved unless there is a direct relationship with business."

The Chamber's commitment to business is evidenced by its accomplishments. It has initiated and advocated a number of pro-business programs, including the following:

- Westchester Regional Small Business Loan Program. Through its affiliate—the Westchester Regional Business Community Development Corp. (WRBDC)—the Chamber established a three-year, $4.2-million loan program for small businesses. The loan capital is provided by seven participating banks. The loans, which are guaranteed by the United States Small Business Administration and administered by WRBDC, range from $5,000 to $50,000 or more, depending on qualifications.
- Alliance for Watershed and Water Quality Protection. Founded by the Chamber and other business, labor, professional, and civic organizations in the Westchester-Putnam-New York City watershed area, the alliance has worked to ensure a "reasonable and rational approach" in New York City's initiatives to protect its watershed in Westchester and Putnam Counties.
- Legislative and regulatory action. The Chamber has pursued a number of legislative issues on behalf of the county's business community, including workers' compensation reform, English as the official language, telecommunications reform, Superfund reform, tax reduction, and the Westchester County budget.

The Chamber's transportation initiatives include taking a leadership role in lobbying for Congress to remove the Employee Commute Option/Employee Trip Reduction mandate from the Clean Air Act; and founding the Coalition for Better Transportation in the Tappan Zee Corridor to support improvements proposed by the State Department of Transportation for Interstate 287.

The Chamber also strives to be a source of information for its members and the business community at large, Vogt said. He pointed out that through its bimonthly *Westchester Commerce* magazine, the Chamber provides county business news and information to 10,000 business, professional, and community leaders. And the Chamber circulates 5,000 copies annually

The County Chamber's prime goal is to specifically address the interests and concerns of the business community.

BUSINESS, PROFESSIONS & FINANCE

of its *The Golden Apple Guide to Business and Livability in Westchester County, New York*—a business directory and livability information publication.

The Chamber produced the Economic Development Video, an 11-minute, five-language video touting the county as a good location for business and investment. The video is used in foreign and domestic economic development outreach initiatives.

In addition, the Chamber participates in cooperative publication ventures, such as *The Westchester County Economic Development Book*, a four-color publication containing economic development information about the county; and *Westchester County: New York's Golden Apple*, a hard-cover coffee table book about the county and its business community.

As an added benefit to members and the business community in general, the Chamber provides access to business growth, expansion, and networking opportunities as well as informational seminars, Vogt said. These include "A.M. Breakfast Club" networking sessions; Spotlight on Your Business, an after-business-hours product and service mini-expo and networking reception; Golden Apple Business Exposition; and various issue- and topic-specific meetings, seminars, and workshops.

The Chamber also sponsors "The Westchester 50," which honors 50 of the largest nominated privately-owned local businesses each year; the annual "Secretarial Success Awards Program"; and the "Annual Golden Apple Business Community Golf Outing."

The Chamber has a host of affiliate corporations, such as the Westchester Convention and Visitors Bureau, Ltd. The bureau is Westchester's official tourism agency and promotes the county's hospitality industry and solicits meetings and tourism business for the county.

Other affiliates include the following:

- Westchester/Rockland/Putnam Health Plan Purchasing Alliance, Ltd. The alliance's goal is to design health care protection products to be underwritten by health care packagers and/or carriers; market and enroll subscribers to plans in the tri-county area; and address health care cost containment and provider issues.
- Westchester Regional Business Community Development Corp. The not-for-profit corporation was established to enhance employment opportunities, attract and assist new business investors, promote and encourage retention and expansion of existing businesses, and assist businesses in complying with governmental regulations and utilizing opportunities available through government agencies.

The Chamber strives to be a source of information for its members and the business community at large. Its bimonthly *Westchester Commerce* magazine provides county business news and information to 10,000 business, professional, and community leaders.

Harold Vogt means business. Vogt is president and chief executive officer of The County Chamber of Commerce, Inc., and is pictured here with the Chamber's first Golden Apple Award.

As a major player in Westchester's business community, Vogt has witnessed a number of dramatic changes that have reshaped the county during the past decade: The county has shifted from manufacturing toward a more service-driven business community; the commercial real estate market toppled during the recession; several large companies relocated from the county; and downsizing became the buzzword within the corporate community.

As a result, many large corporations have been forced to tighten their belts, thus limiting their involvement in local initiatives, Vogt said. But smaller businesses have been emerging as the driving force behind the county's economy—a trend Vogt expects will continue well into the next decade.

"The midsized and smaller firms seem to hold the best hope for regenerating and reinvigorating our economy. And we will continue our strong involvement in economic development initiatives and provide the best services possible to all businesses in our community."

Westchester County: New York's Golden Apple / 163

BUSINESS, PROFESSIONS & FINANCE

BLEAKLEY PLATT & SCHMIDT

Bleakley Platt & Schmidt has evolved over the 60 years since its founding in 1937 into the largest law firm between New York City and Albany.

Located at One North Lexington Avenue in the heart of downtown White Plains, the office is near both the county courthouse and the new federal courthouse.

The firm has over 45 lawyers divided into departments serving the Greater New York and Connecticut area. The departments are civil litigation, including real estate assessment litigation and eminent domain, negligence (including product liability and personal injury), real estate, land use and municipal law, banking, health law, corporate and commercial, trusts and estates, insurance, employment, immigration, tax, environment and education law.

Left to right: Frederick J. Martin, senior partner; Mary Ann Zeolla, office manager; and William F. Harrington, managing partner.

Litigation Law: *(front row, left to right)* Partners William H. Mulligan Jr., William P. Harrington, *(back row, left to right)* Richard N. Pitassy, Hugh D. Fyfe, and Timothy P. Coon

Bleakley Platt & Schmidt is three times the size it was just 15 years ago. The senior partners have recognized that as law becomes more complex and new areas of practice develop, it is essential to develop special expertise.

Along the way, the firm has boasted some of the top legal minds that have practiced in Westchester County. Foremost was its founder, William F. Bleakley, Supreme Court Justice, gubernatorial candidate and Westchester's first County Executive. Other legal giants have included Charles L. Brieant Jr., Chief Judge of the southern district, and Thomas L. Platt, Chief Judge of the eastern district respectively, of the United States District Court. Three

164 / Westchester County: New York's Golden Apple

BUSINESS, PROFESSIONS & FINANCE

other former members of the firm served on the Appellate Division, second department of the State Supreme Court—Justice James D. Hopkins, who had succeeded Judge Bleakley as Westchester County Executive before attaining great distinction on the Appellate Division, and Appellate Justices Arthur B. Brennan and Frederick G. Schmidt. Additional alumni have sat as judges of the Supreme, County, and Surrogate courts.

Collectively and individually, Bleakley Platt & Schmidt's current partners and associates have vast experience in their respective fields. They have previously worked for governments and large corporations, as well as public and private not-for-profit agencies. They are skilled in their specialties and committed to their clients. In turn, they are served by state-of-the-art technology, including computer-aided research, litigation support, and document preparation. The result is an efficient and effective response by the firm to its clients' diverse legal problems.

Bleakley Platt & Schmidt's client roster, a virtual "who's who" of Westchester County, encompasses *Fortune* 500 companies, major title companies, municipalities, banking institutions, health care providers, foundations, not-for-profit corporations, closely held corporations, condominiums, insurance companies, and individuals from all walks of life. Bleakley Platt & Schmidt is committed to treating even a "routine" legal matter with the same respect and attention.

The law firm's partners and associates have demonstrated their commitment to serving their local communities, whether it be as elected officials, by providing pro bono legal services to individuals in need and to not-for-profit agencies or by serving as volunteers on a wide-ranging number of civic, religious, and social organizations.

Under the leadership of the current partners, the old Bleakley Platt traditions have been nurtured and expanded by careful selection of the best young talent available in the Westchester-Fairfield area. By doing so, the firm is poised to provide continuing professional leadership into the next century.

Some things, however, will never change. Integrity, competence, and hard work will always be paramount at Bleakley Platt & Schmidt. ◆

Trusts & Estates and Tax Law: *(left to right)* Partners Mary Ellen Manley, Janice H. Eiseman, Raymond M. Planell, Lester Berkelhamer, and Brian E. Lorenz

Real Estate Law: *(left to right)* Partners Joseph P. Harrington and Joseph B. Glatthaar

Westchester County: New York's Golden Apple / 165

BUSINESS, PROFESSIONS & FINANCE

TARRYTOWN HOUSE EXECUTIVE CONFERENCE CENTER

Tarrytown House Executive Conference Center offers guests the modern conveniences of a technologically sophisticated meeting facility combined with the charm and grandeur of the estate's historical past.

Tarrytown House was founded as a conference center in 1964 by entrepreneur Bob Schwartz. "He [Schwartz] was the mastermind of conference centers," said Jeffrey H. Weggeman, director of sales and marketing at Tarrytown House. "So this facility was the nation's first conference center."

The property's history dates back to the 1800s, when the areas overlooking the Hudson River became the locality for dazzling estates. Two of these estates—the stone house of the Biddle family and the Greek Revival mansion of the King family— make up the central part of Tarrytown House.

The restored, elegant mansions are situated amid 26 lush private acres of landscaped gardens and manicured lawns, and views of the Hudson River add to the site's splendor. In addition to the Biddle Mansion and King House are the Carriage House, Westchester House, Rockland House, Fairfield House, the Atrium, and the Cottage House. Also, the 5,500-square-foot Mary Duke Room was opened recently as an addition to the Biddle Mansion. The wing is named for the estate's owner, Mary Duke Biddle, who was renowned for hosting exclusive New York society events during the 1920s and 1930s.

Today, Tarrytown House is a premier executive conference center that handles approximately 8,000 meetings per year, ranging from 2 to 350 people. The facility is managed by Dolce International, a conference center management company.

Tarrytown House has undergone several changes over the years—including millions of dollars in renovations to keep the property updated—but has maintained its historic spirit, Weggeman said. "One of the unique aspects of the Tarrytown House is that it is an 'estate' conference center. We are dedicated to accommodating corporate meetings, but the historical mansions and spectacular views of the Hudson add an unmatched charm to this facility. It has a campus feel to it. Also, the location is key for us. We're close to the railroad, 25 miles north of Manhattan, and close to southern Connecticut and New Jersey."

For its executive clientele, Tarrytown House handles a variety of events, including board meetings, holiday parties, sales meetings, training seminars, promotions, weddings, and retirements. Some frequent clients include Ciba-Geigy Corp., the Dutch airline KLM, and PepsiCo, Inc. "We are the meeting place for corporate decision makers," Weggeman said. "We offer an important service to the business community by providing a venue for groups to meet and plan competitive strategies."

The facility offers a CMP—complete meeting package—for overnight conference guests, which includes all meals and gratuities, continuous refreshment breaks, meeting and breakout rooms, audiovisual equipment, deluxe guest rooms, and use of all recreational facilities. The day conference package includes continental breakfast, buffet lunch, gratuities, and continuous all-day refreshment breaks; a main meeting room with standard audio/visual requirements; and complete use

The Greek Revival mansion of the King family at Tarrytown House offers accommodations for private meetings for groups of 10 to 18, and banquets for up to 100.

Inside the King House, the Grand Salon (shown) provides an atmosphere of elegance for meetings or private dining.

BUSINESS, PROFESSIONS & FINANCE

of on-site recreational facilities. In addition, both packages include individual conference planners to assist with preplanning and on-site servicing, and professional audio/bvisual communications technicians to assist with A/V needs. Guests also may utilize the Conference Services Desks for faxing, copying, and secretarial services.

Tarrytown House has 30 different meeting rooms, comprising 30,000 square feet of meeting space. The King House offers accommodations for private meetings for groups of 10 to 18, and banquets for up to 100, with 10 guest rooms, meeting rooms, and private dining in the Grand Salon. The Tarrytown Room offers front screen projection for between 110 and 220 attendees, while the Mary Duke Room provides meeting space for up to 400 and dining for up to 350 people.

The facility's 148 guest rooms—80 of which were recently renovated—are designed to reflect the estate's heritage. The rooms contain either king-size beds or two double beds; work/study areas; direct-dial telephone with voice mail, data port, and message alert; and television with videotape players.

Tarrytown House offers several dining options. Formal dining is available in the main dining room, the Winter Palace, a glass-enclosed restaurant with views of the Hudson. For casual dining, the recently renovated Sleepy Hollow Pub offers American-style fare in a relaxed atmosphere. Private dining is also available in the glass-enclosed Sun Porch, Garden Room, or Music Room. In addition, richly paneled libraries and card rooms, the Mary Duke Room, terraces, and outdoor gardens are available for receptions.

The facility also offers a Recreation and Fitness Center with weight training equipment, an exercise area, a sauna and whirlpool, racquetball, and table tennis. The exercise room includes Stairmasters,™ rowing machines, free weights, and computerized treadmills. The center's staff includes a certified physical fitness instructor, and individual or group aerobic classes and "stretch breaks" are available.

The facility has indoor and outdoor pools, lighted tennis courts, volleyball, bowling, billiards, and cards. Also, the estate grounds contain walking and jogging trails. And for team-building exercises, Tarrytown House offers the Cradlerock™ Corporate Adventures Course. Guests may also utilize the Metropolitan Golfers Club, which offers members a private, toll-free personal service for reserving dates and times on more than 40 public and semi-private clubs and 25 private clubs in the area.

Although executive meetings comprise 70 percent of Tarrytown House's business, the facility also caters weddings,

The Tarrytown House Executive Conference Center has 30 different meeting rooms, comprising 30,000 square feet of meeting space.

The restored stone house of the Biddle family is situated amid the 26 lush private acres of landscaped gardens and manicured lawns that make up the site of the Tarrytown House Executive Conference Center.

bar/bat mitzvahs, and accommodates weekend and transient guests. "Tarrytown House is a gorgeous venue for many wonderful events, such as balls, galas, weddings, bar/bat mitzvahs, and fundraisers for the people of our community," said Weggeman.

For leisure travelers, Tarrytown House offers a Great Estates Bed and Breakfast weekend package. For a special price, guests stay at Tarrytown House and receive discounts on admission to historic sites such as Sunnyside or Philipsburg Manor. A trolley service is available to transport guests from Tarrytown House to the historic sites.

The Tarrytown House also holds a Judith Crist Film Festival Weekend twice a year. The festival, named for the famous film critic, presents five to seven new-release movies for viewers to watch and critique. Over the past 25 years, the festival has attracted such notables as Gregory Peck, Woody Allen, and Paul Newman. ◆

Westchester County: New York's Golden Apple / 167

BUSINESS, PROFESSIONS & FINANCE

THACHER PROFFITT & WOOD

Thacher Proffitt & Wood embodies the size, knowledge, and experience of an international law firm, yet has built a solid reputation by maintaining the simple philosophy of focusing on client service. The firm takes pride in its ability to anticipate and respond to client needs.

Founded in 1848, the firm has offices in White Plains, New York City, and Washington, D.C. and 160 lawyers with a strong reputation worldwide in commercial and financial transactions and litigation. Thacher Proffitt is organized into six practice groups, corporate, real estate, litigation, tax, private client, and international.

"The firm's White Plains office has experienced significant growth in recent years," said Thomas M. Leslie, the attorney who manages the White Plains office. For example, when he joined that office five years ago, there were two lawyers on staff. Today, the office has 11 full-time attorneys.

"The growth I've seen in Westchester County has been twofold." Leslie said. "Banks and other corporations have been moving their executive offices from New York City to Westchester County or lower Fairfield County (Connecticut), or they are now making decisions here that were traditionally made in New York City. Westchester and White Plains have a unique opportunity to capitalize on those changes."

"While many of the companies that have moved to Westchester County are large corporations, there is also a significant market for small to mid-size companies that may also have a need for a law firm with our banking, corporate, and corporate finance experience."

"Westchester is a great place for our type of business," he said, adding that technological advances enable the firm to provide Main Street clients with "Wall Street sophistication."

In addition, a 161,300-square-foot U.S. Courthouse opened in the city last year. "I expect the new courthouse will have a dramatic effect on the legal community here, and in particular, our firm." Leslie said. "We are an established leader in the community for handling matters involving foreclosures and other real estate litigation, lender liability claims, and bankruptcy and creditor disputes. Our attorneys in White Plains and New York have the sophistication and experience to address all types of commercial litigation impacting our Westchester client base."

One of the unique aspects of the firm is its billing system. "We recognized a long time ago that legal services had to be correctly priced in order to expand in our market," said Leslie. "We have taken a value-added approach to billing. Value-added billing means pricing the delivery of legal services commensurate with the benefit being derived by the client. This billing system has been one of the major reasons for our success."

Thacher Proffitt & Wood is "very active" in community affairs. Leslie said. "This firm has an aggressive program in which management requires every lawyer to devote some time to *pro bono* work. We believe this is a valuable contribution to the Westchester community and we hope to build on these efforts each year." ◆

Photo by Peter North

Photo by Peter North

168 / Westchester County: New York's Golden Apple

BUSINESS, PROFESSIONS & FINANCE

MasterCard International Incorporated

MasterCard's new global headquarters at 2000 Purchase Street in Purchase, New York, provides an exceptional work environment for the 900 employees currently on-site.

MasterCard International Incorporated—one of Westchester's newest corporate residents—is a global payments company comprising more than 22,000 member financial institutions, as well as 2,000 employees and 34 offices in 6 regions worldwide. Currently marking its 30th year of operations, MasterCard is an industry leader with a universally recognized and respected family of brands.

That family of brands—MasterCard®, Maestro®, and Cirrus®—represents a full range of payment products and services, including credit, online and offline debit, ATM cash access, remote banking and bill payment, stored value, and travelers cheques. The brands all share the promise of quality, and the interlocking circles—the visual symbol of that promise—have been incorporated into the distinct logos of each brand to communicate the complementary relationships among them.

More importantly, MasterCard's superior brands and global transaction-processing network deliver what today's consumers want most: safe, secure access to their money anytime, anywhere. The network provides near-perfect around-the-clock availability, facilitating authorization of transactions from almost anywhere in the world in about two seconds. Transaction volume over the network has expanded 69.1 percent since 1992, reflecting the explosive growth of the payments business.

In fact, there has never been a more exciting time to be in the payments business. By almost every measure, 1995 was MasterCard International's most successful year ever. Overall, MasterCard's business worldwide grew by more than 18 percent in 1995. MasterCard volume rose 17.8 percent to $467.7 billion; cards in circulation increased 13.2 percent to 272.3 million; and by year-end, MasterCard cards were accepted at more than 12 million locations in 220 countries and territories worldwide—a 9.9 percent increase over 1994 levels. From this position of strength, MasterCard has the opportunity to help its member financial institutions shape the future of money in the years ahead by redefining the way people around the world pay for goods and services.

And as MasterCard enjoys success, it also is enjoying its new status as a Westchester corporate citizen. MasterCard relocated its headquarters in October 1995 from Manhattan into a majestic, 472,600-square-foot facility at 2000 Purchase Street in Purchase, New York. The building, designed by noted architect I.M. Pei, formerly served as IBM's North American headquarters. Concurrent with the relocation, MasterCard installed a state-of-the-art technical infrastructure that now links its offices worldwide. That infrastructure, combined with an open office environment, enables employees to work together more effectively.

"MasterCard means 'smart money,' and we made a 'smart decision' when we moved to Westchester," says William I Jacobs, MasterCard's executive vice president of Global Resources, adding; "Westchester offers the kind of environment we wanted for our employees. Our new headquarters affords us the opportunity to build a successful team approach to business." ◆

BUSINESS, PROFESSIONS & FINANCE

SHAMBERG MARWELL HOCHERMAN DAVIS & HOLLIS, P. C.

Shamberg Marwell Hocherman Davis & Hollis, P.C. is a full-service law firm that is renowned nationally for its representation of clients with real estate interests, especially with regard to zoning, land use, and environmental issues. The firm's clients range from major multinational corporations and financial institutions to regional developers, municipal entities, title insurance companies, and non-profit organizations to closely-held businesses, individuals, and families.

Founded by Stuart R. Shamberg in 1970, the firm's adherence to its founder's principles of integrity of professional conduct, the maintenance of the proper relationship with adversaries, excellence of work, and the delivery of efficient, resolution- driven, cost-effective services has enabled it to attract legal talent of the highest caliber. Shamberg Marwell attorneys represent a wide spectrum of academic and professional training; they continually advance and expand their knowledge by attending continuing legal education programs, and they share their expertise by publishing regularly and speaking to professional and lay groups.

The firm's guiding principles are also reflected in its commitment to Westchester's communities. Shamberg Marwell lawyers serve in leadership positions on business, professional, and charitable governing boards and as members of school boards and special task forces.

In addition to its concentration in all aspects of real estate law, Shamberg Marwell attorneys practice with equal effectiveness in the areas of banking and finance; municipal law; corporate law and general business counseling; syndications; and matrimonial, elder, and education law. They also have a particularly strong trusts, estate planning, taxation, and administration practice. The breadth of their legal expertise and community knowledge enables them to devise creative solutions and provide responsive, productive representation for clients.

At Shamberg Marwell, the formation of "client service teams" creates a collegial environment in which attorneys' experience and judgment are shared across the boundaries of individual areas of expertise. By working in this uniquely cooperative way, the firm develops a thorough understanding of each client's needs and goals and successfully builds strong, close attorney-client-community relationships, many of which now span the life of the firm itself.

In a typical development project, the firm first becomes involved in real estate acquisition, structuring the transaction to embody the client's goals. Then they "quarterback" the administrative approval process, working with expert environmental and planning consultants to obtain the necessary approvals and permits at federal, state, and local levels. Finally, the firm provides business and contract counseling throughout the process, culminating in project completion.

While Shamberg Marwell prefers to resolve matters without resort to litigation, it has an extensive litigation practice in the trial and appellate courts. At both the state and federal level, the firm focuses on land use, environmental, commercial, title defense, real estate, personal injury, foreclosure, and family law. The firm regularly handles matters involving unconstitutional "takings" of property rights, challenges to illegal impact fees and zoning regulations, civil rights claims, and the illegal exercise of governmental authority. Many are landmark cases which have created an extensive body of law placing limits on the exercise of governmental authority and established important legal precedents.

After more than a quarter century of diversified regional legal practice, the ethical and professional standards of the Shamberg Marwell Hocherman Davis & Hollis attorneys are reflected in their team approach to problem assessment and resolution. The firm maintains enthusiastic confidence in Westchester County's virtually unlimited growth potential and looks forward to assisting its clients in meeting legal opportunities and challenges in the years ahead. ♦

The Board of Directors of Shamberg Marwell Hocherman Davis & Hollis, P.C., *(left to right)* Henry M. Hocherman, John S. Marwell, Stuart R. Shamberg, and P. Daniel Hollis III

The attorneys of Shamberg Marwell Hocherman Davis & Hollis, P.C. in front of the firm's office building at 55 Smith Avenue, Mt. Kisco, New York

Photo by Joe Vericker

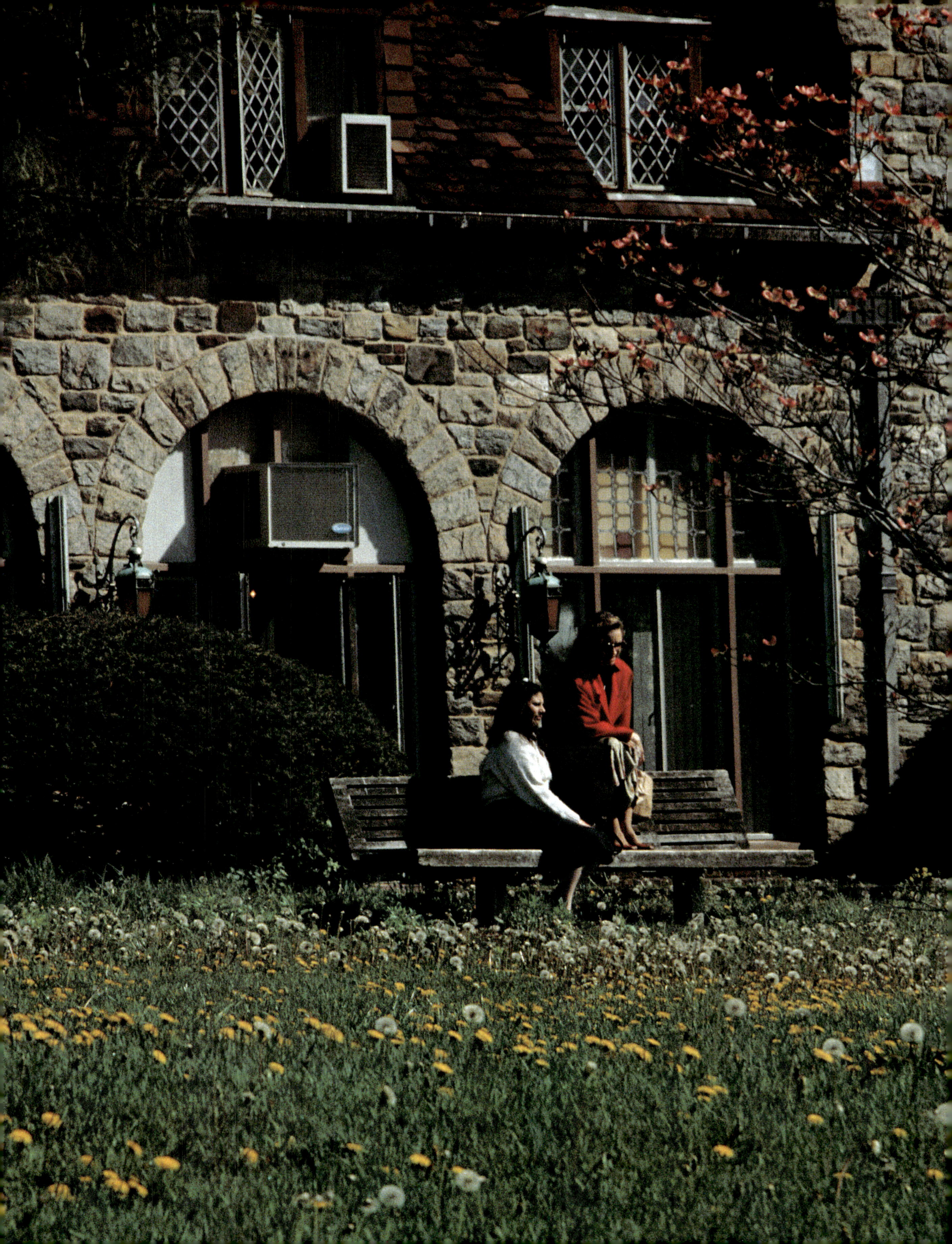

CHAPTER · TWELVE

Education & Quality of Life

Educational institutions and recreation and leisure-oriented communities all contribute to the high quality of life found in Westchester County.

Iona College
Page 174

Mercy College
Page 176

Heritage Hills of Westchester
Page 178

Keio Academy of New York
Page 180

The Ursuline School
Page 182

Iona Preparatory School
Page 183

The Westchester Business Institute
Page 184

The Masters School
Page 185

Monroe College
Page 186

Photo by Joe Vericker

EDUCATION & QUALITY OF LIFE

IONA COLLEGE

Iona College in New Rochelle assures its graduates are well-positioned to meet the challenges of a technologically advanced world. This is evidenced by its multi-million-dollar investments in technology.

The College's Helen Arrigoni Library/Technology Center puts students and faculty on the cutting edge of the information age. The multimedia, state-of-the-art facility allows opportunities for extensive on-line research via a worldwide network of libraries and databases. The center is also equipped to allow students to experiment with new technology, work on interactive group projects, and search Iona's 240,000-volume library.

Iona offers academic majors which prepare students for the information and technology age, including management information systems, computer and information sciences, as well as programs in mass communication. The Journalism Lab gives students hands-on experience in electronic publishing, and state-of-the-art multimedia classrooms combine text, audio, illustrations, music, voice, and full-motion video on the same screen. Students also have access to more than 500 networked computers, while skills workshops, study groups, and tutoring are available at the Samuel Rudin Academic Resource Center.

Iona is a private, coeducational institution whose mission is to develop students as complete people, independent thinkers, and moral adults. The College was founded by the Congregation of Christian Brothers in 1940. Today, Iona is one of the largest independent colleges in New York State. The College boasts an enrollment of 5,500 students and more than 60 areas of graduate and undergraduate education.

Iona's full-time undergraduate school is comprised of some 3,000 students from 22 states and 46 countries. About one-third of the students live in campus residence halls, while the rest commute from home or off-campus locations. Annual tuition and fees are $12,200, representing perhaps the best value of any college in the metropolitan region.

The College's location is ideal. Being in Westchester provides people with a suburban setting, yet enables Iona to be close to downtown Manhattan—it's a 25-minute train ride.

Iona offers bachelor of arts, bachelor of science, and bachelor of business administration degrees in nearly 50 concentrations. Most classes contain fewer than 20 students. Iona offers small classes to enable interaction, and its programs are designed so students receive a broad-based education.

Money Guide, a publication of *Money* magazine listed Iona College as one of the nation's 10 best private commuter schools in 1995.

Also, all courses are taught by faculty members, not graduate students. Iona's professors include published authors, award-winning researchers, executive officers of national academic associations, and consultants to major corporations.

"We prepare our graduates to be leaders in business, and our track record stands out," says Nicholas J. Beautell, dean of Iona's Hagan School of Business. As examples, he notes that Iona graduates are top executive leaders at corporations such as American Express, AT&T, Texaco, and Ciba-Geigy.

In 1995 the College inaugurated as its seventh president James A. Liguori, CFC, who had been executive vice president of Iona since 1993. Previously, Brother Liguori was superintendent of schools for the archdiocese of Newark, New Jersey; associate superintendent of schools for the archdiocese of New York; and headmaster of Iona Preparatory School. Liguori succeeded John G. Driscoll, CFC, who was the College's president for 24 years, continuing Iona's commitment to the tradition of the Christian Brothers and American Catholic higher education, and that of welcoming students of all faiths and backgrounds.

In addition to a classic liberal arts program, Iona provides a diverse range of study, including telecommunications, criminal justice, educational computing, and business ethics. Students may choose from day, weekend, or evening programs at the New Rochelle, Manhat-

The mission of the faculty at Iona College is to develop students as complete people, independent thinkers, and moral adults.

174 / Westchester County: New York's Golden Apple

EDUCATION & QUALITY OF LIFE

Iona's full-time undergraduate school is comprised of approximately 3,000 students from 22 states and 46 countries. About one-third of the students live in campus residence halls.

tan, or Rockland County campuses. Iona students have the opportunity to study abroad in Europe, the Middle East, South America, and the Orient.

Iona's graduate program in Pastoral and Family Counseling educates and trains family counselors in Ireland. The three-year program enables students to travel to the United States to study at Iona for one summer.

Iona provides religious programs ranging from worship, spiritual direction and personal support, to interfaith retreats and open campus discussions about current ethical and moral issues.

Iona's Career Services Office helps students develop skills in resume writing and interviewing techniques, offers a corporate internship program, and provides on-campus recruitment for seniors.

The Honors Program is designed to develop individual intellectual leadership within a close community of students. The program includes one-on-one work with a faculty mentor, special honors seminars and interdisciplinary courses, an extensive study-abroad option, and a seminar research project.

The "One-on-One" Science Program, funded by Ciba-Geigy, teams talented students and science faculty members to conduct original research into contemporary environmental problems.

Iona also offers degrees and training in pre-dentistry, pre-law, pre-medicine, pre-chiropractic, and physical therapy. The Columba School offers associate, baccalaureate, and graduate degree programs for adult learners. The Hagan School of Business offers the master of business administration in seven concentrations, and the Graduate School of Arts and Sciences offers master of arts and master of science degrees.

In addition to academic life, sports and social activities abound at Iona. Students may choose among 21 Division I teams, intramural and club sports, and more than 90 student clubs and activities. The 1996 men's basketball team won the regular-season championship of the Metro-Atlantic Athletic Conference (MAAC).

Iona is actively involved in the community, as well. In fact, with the help of a two-year Department of Housing and Urban Development grant, the College has opened an Information Access Center in Ryan Library. The center, designed for minority and women-owned businesses, but open to the public, contains 30 computers, and offers training, research, and on-line banking services.

The College also encourages students to participate in community projects. Iona students' volunteer work includes Big Brother and Big Sister programs; local soup kitchens; Midnight Run, which brings food and clothing to homeless people in Manhattan; and project S.W.A.P., an inner-city building reclamation project.

The College's ongoing pursuit of academic excellence has helped it gain national recognition. Iona was listed as one of the nation's 10 best private commuter schools in the 1995 edition of *Money Guide*, a publication from the editors of *Money* magazine. ◆

Iona College's suburban setting is ideal—by train, it's only 25 minutes from downtown Manhattan.

Westchester County: New York's Golden Apple / 175

EDUCATION & QUALITY OF LIFE

MERCY COLLEGE

Mercy College's mission is to reach out and provide all students with an opportunity to achieve a quality education. To fulfill this mission, the college offers a number of degrees, activities and services, innovative programs, flexible scheduling, affordable tuition, and multiple locations.

Dean for Admissions Joy Colelli said: "We were one of the first colleges in our area to offer night classes and weekend programs. And by offering a low tuition, we've made private education very affordable as well."

Mercy College offers 70 graduate and undergraduate degrees through a curriculum of liberal arts and sciences. Pre-professional and professional programs are available, as well as graduate programs in business, education, and allied health science.

Mercy's 156 full-time and more than 500 part-time faculty instructs some 7,000 students in day, evening, weekend, and "Distance Learning with Modem" sessions; the student/faculty ratio is 17 to 1. Sixty percent of the full-time faculty and 64 percent of the graduate faculty have earned doctorates.

Mercy attracts students from Westchester County and the New York, New Jersey, and Connecticut metropolitan areas, as well as a large contingent of international students from the Pacific Rim, Central Europe, and Ireland.

The College was founded by the Sisters of Mercy in 1950 as a junior college for women. The College received full accreditation from the Middle States Association in 1968, and the Sisters of Mercy gave the college as a gift to the board of trustees. The College became independent, nonsectarian, and coed, offering undergraduate and graduate degrees. A bilingual program was created, and an expansion was completed which doubled the size of the physical plant.

Mercy offers graduate programs leading to master of science degrees in Nursing, Human Resource Management, Learning Technology, Organizational Leadership, Occupational Therapy, Physical Therapy, Acupuncture and Oriental Medicine, and a Tri-certificate in Education.

Today, Mercy has branches in the Bronx, White Plains, and Yorktown plus 10 Extension Centers in Brooklyn, Manhattan, Queens, Mt. Vernon, Yonkers, and Dover Plains. The main campus, situated on 100 acres along the Hudson River in Dobbs Ferry, comprises 7 buildings which house classrooms, science laboratories, a TV/radio

Verrazzano Hall houses administrative offices and classrooms.

Students can enjoy the peaceful ambiance of the Mercy Residence Hall Courtyard.

176 / Westchester County: New York's Golden Apple

EDUCATION & QUALITY OF LIFE

studio, the main library, and a 300-bed residence hall.

Students at all Mercy's Extension Centers access the main library, which provides a collection of more than 300,000 volumes, and extensive audiovisual materials. In addition, the major athletic facilities are located in Dobbs Ferry, including five outdoor tennis courts, a swimming pool, a soccer-baseball field, softball field, and a running track.

At the Yorktown Campus, students have access to 28 classrooms, library, labs, a writing center, learning center, lounges, a fitness room, and a community room. The Yorktown Campus offers programs leading to all Mercy baccalaureate degrees.

The White Plains Campus offers undergraduate programs, a master's degree in Human Resource Management, and a Paralegal Certification Program. The campus has 14 classrooms, a lounge, a computer classroom, a computer lab, and a 17,000-volume library.

The Bronx Campus is the largest of the branch campuses, with classrooms, science and computer labs, a 15,000-volume library, a cafeteria, a student lounge, and an exercise room. The campus offers 16 majors, specialization and certificate programs, continuing education courses, bilingual programs, and master's degrees in Education, Tri-certificate, and Learning Technology.

Mercy College accepts students from more than 100 countries, and those who need to learn English enter Mercy's Westchester Institute for the Study of English—WISE—prior to pursuing degrees.

Mercy's view to the west—a glorious sunset over the Hudson River

Mercy offers 70 undergraduate courses through "Distance Learning." Via a computer and modem, students can register for a class and "log on" at their convenience. Colelli said: "In a regular classroom, students sit and observe, but some don't participate. In Distance Learning, the only way to participate is to actually log on. Students read, ask questions, and communicate through a modem. And you can do this anytime you want."

Mercy's EDGE Schedule (Executive Development and Growth Experience) is an accelerated degree schedule designed for individuals with two years of college who are seeking career advancement. Each student earns a bachelor of science degree in Interdisciplinary Studies in Business Leadership.

"Classes are taught sequentially, so you're learning one thing at a time," said Colelli. "This makes the work manageable, especially if you have a family and are working full time. Also, you never get closed out of a class and you know your schedule for the next year."

Part of Mercy's mission is to make college affordable, so full-time students pay a flat fee of $3,600 per semester. Basically, students pay for only 12 credits, regardless of how many additional credits they take. In light of cutbacks in government funding for higher education, Mercy introduced a flat-fee tuition program in 1995.

Collelli said: "When the state reduced some of the education funding, we had to respond. Most colleges simply raised the tuition to close the gap. But we decided to be innovative and lower our tuition, and create a flat tuition fee. And we've been very excited by the success. We've had a 12-percent increase in new students, and the number of credits they took has increased by 18 percent."

Mercy also has a Small Business Development Center on the Dobbs Ferry campus. Started in 1991, the Center's five staffers provide free counseling to entrepreneurs and small-business owners who need assistance in marketing, financial matters, or business plans. The Center is funded by the state and federal government, and Mercy.

"The Center's mission is to increase the probability of success for people who want to start a business," said director Tom Milton, associate professor in the College's Department of Business Administration. "We try to help them avoid making mistakes. That's very important because, without us, they might have plunged into a venture and wasted time and money."

Milton said the Center serves a "wide spectrum" of individuals, with a high representation from the Latino and African-American communities, and a large number of women. "The Center also is available to students, and many take advantage of it," he said. ◆

Westchester County: New York's Golden Apple / 177

EDUCATION & QUALITY OF LIFE

HERITAGE HILLS OF WESTCHESTER

The golf courses are the centerpieces for quality living at Heritage Hills.

Heritage Hills of Westchester offers its residents more than a condominium community. In addition to the serenity and the natural beauty of bucolic Somers, Heritage Hills provides a unique "lifestyle situation" for its 3,500 residents.

"We don't just build homes—we provide a lifestyle," said Douglas C. Delano, vice president and general manager of Heritage Hills.

Heritage Hills is comprised of clustered homes situated in private courtyards. Given the nature of the community, residents can enjoy both the peaceful country setting, as well as an active lifestyle by participating in the large number of social, cultural, and recreational activities available.

The community has more than 140 clubs and organizations, and residents choose from a host of entertaining events, such as Broadway shows and outdoor concerts, Fourth of July picnics, and New Year's Eve celebrations.

The landscaping at Heritage Hills is maintained by a full-time, year-round staff that provides all exterior home and grounds maintenance, including painting homes' exteriors, mowing the lawns, and clearing the roads and sidewalks of snow. These professional services allow residents to spend their time working on other things—such as toning up in the fully equipped fitness center or practicing their swing on the championship golf courses. Heritage Hills also offers tennis courts and swimming pools, nature trails and jogging paths, and a private country club. "Our residents are able to enjoy all the recreational activities here, but don't have to worry about maintenance of their properties," said Delano.

Most of Heritage Hills' residents have come from within Westchester County, or from Long Island, Manhattan, New Jersey, or Connecticut, Delano said. He said that residents are from a diversified business and educational background including such fields as medicine, law, engineering, and education. Many are working professionals, while others choose Heritage Hills for a weekend retreat or a complete schedule of leisure activities. "Heritage Hills has added a significant number of experienced professionals to the area," Delano noted. Many of these new residents have become active in the town, he said, from volunteering for local nonprofit organizations to serving on town boards.

The lifestyle at Heritage Hills reflects the spirit of its residents, who participate in a number of activities, including ballroom dancing, art discussion, chess, Japanese flower arranging, and yoga. Residents also are active in various clubs, such as the Book Discussion Club, Bowling Club, Computer Club, Fine Arts Clubs, Gourmet Club, Garden Club, Women's Club, Travel Club, and Scrabble Club. Bil-

EDUCATION & QUALITY OF LIFE

liards, folk dancing, aerobics, poker, and woodworking are also popular at Heritage Hills. In addition, the community offers a Chamber Music Society, Jazz Discussion Group, Philatelic Society, Shakespeare Reading Group, and the Top Hatters tap dancing group. The Community Center contains art studios, a private library, and a complete theater which the Drama Club uses for regular performances.

The development of Heritage Hills commenced in the 1970s by Henry J. Paparazzo, founder and chairman of Heritage Development Group. The Southbury, Connecticut-based development company has built a number of residential communities in the region. In fact, in creating Heritage Hills, the developer used the experience garnered from its first large project—the 2,750-unit Heritage Village in Southbury—which received the Urban Land Institute's Award for Excellence in 1982.

The developer's design philosophy has proved successful. Heritage Hills of Westchester has enjoyed continued recognition since its inception. The community has received several prestigious awards, including the National Association of Home Builders' Decade 1970 Award for Project Design in 1975, the *American Institute of Architects/House and Home* magazine's Homes for Better Living Award in 1976, and the Western Wood Products Association's Design Award in 1976.

One of the unique aspects of Heritage Hills lies in the developer's design and use of the land. Heritage Development Group has accentuated the natural beauty of the land—more than one-third of the 1,100-acre property has been preserved as open space. Each home has been painstakingly designed to complement its environment—an environment that provides for pleasing views from each home's windows. The buildings have been constructed with natural materials—such as stained wood siding—to blend with the natural beauty of the surroundings, including numerous old stone walls.

The newest neighborhood of 99 homes—Westridge at Heritage Hills—has been developed with the Heritage tradition and philosophy of luxury village living. Westridge offers 12 attached and detached floor plans, with prices starting at $175,000 for the one-bedroom Guilford unit, to $450,000 for the three-bedroom Columbia unit.

New detached home designs add to the exciting offerings at this national award-winning community.

The new homes include kitchen appliances, air conditioning, fireplace, carpeting, patio or deck, and one or two garages. Association fees cover trash removal, exterior building and grounds maintenance, including snow removal, and fire and liability insurance. A Society Fee includes all recreational facilities except golf; Golf Club membership is available.

Heritage Hills has its own 24-hour security patrol, private water and sewage treatment systems, and private roadways. Heritage Hills also offers shuttle-bus service to and from local shopping areas and the local Metro-North commuter railroad station (Manhattan is a one-hour ride). Residents enjoy the convenience of having two small shopping centers at the main entrance to Heritage Hills on Route 202.

In addition to sustaining its own residents, Heritage Hills benefits the entire community by contributing to the economic vitality of Somers, Delano said. "Heritage Hills is the largest community of its kind in the region, and has a significant positive effect on its town—it represents 20 percent of the population and 23 percent of the tax base."

Heritage Hills' economic benefit to Somers will continue to increase. Development at Heritage Hills is ongoing, Delano said, noting that the company recently sold its 2,000th home. He said the developer expects Heritage Hills to comprise almost 3,000 homes within the next few years. "Our objective is to maintain the high standard of quality as we proceed with the completion of Heritage Hills." ◆

Westchester County: New York's Golden Apple / 179

EDUCATION & QUALITY OF LIFE

KEIO ACADEMY OF NEW YORK

Keio Academy of New York in Purchase is an internationalized private academic institution that focuses on educating today's students to become tomorrow's global leaders. In order to achieve its mission, Keio Academy incorporates a unique bilingual and bicultural educational curriculum, and follows the traditions of Keio's founder, Yukichi Fukuzawa.

Keio Academy of New York was established in 1990 by the Keio Gijuku (Keio Private School System) of Japan. Keio Gijuku also operates Keio University, one of the most prestigious private schools in Japan. Yukichi Fukuzawa founded Keio Gijuku in 1858; the English translation of *gijuku* is "public school." Fukuzawa's goal was to establish a school that would serve as a place for mutual help and teaching for faculty, students, and alumni.

Today, Keio Gijuku operates nine graduate schools, a university with eight faculties, a junior college of nursing, five senior high schools (which includes Keio Academy of New York), three junior high schools, an elementary school, and three university hospitals.

Keio Academy was inaugurated in the United States primarily to meet the needs of Japanese living overseas, according to President and Headmaster Dr. Noriyuki Sugiura. "In the mid-1980s, a lot of Japanese business people were traveling overseas and staying in the United States," he said. "One of their major concerns was the education of their children. They wanted to send their children to a high school similar to the ones in Japan."

Situated on 27 acres of land in Purchase, Keio Academy of New York is a four-year coeducational, independent secondary school accredited by the New York State Board of Regents. The school also is authorized as an "overseas educational institution," thereby satisfying regulations of senior high school education by the Ministry of Education in Japan. The curriculum is administered under the guidelines of both Japan and the United States.

One of the benefits of Keio Academy is that all students are automatically permitted to enter Keio University in Japan. "Admission to Keio University is very competitive, so this is very important to parents," said Sugiura. Students also are able to obtain qualifications of other colleges or universities in Japan, or can apply to any colleges or universities in the United States.

Some 450 students attend Keio Academy; 80 percent of the students live on campus, while 20 percent commute from within the tristate area. Although 99 percent of the students are Japanese, the school welcomes all nationalities. In fact, Keio Academy attracts candidates from across the United States and the world.

Since many students are living away from their parents for the first time, counseling is essential to promote students' emotional and social well-being. Thus, Keio provides counseling from a cross-cultural perspective. The school also encourages parents to contact counselors for updates on their children's progress.

The school has 90 people on staff, including both Japanese and American teachers. Classes, which average about 25 students, are conducted in Japanese, English, or in both languages, depending on the instructor.

Students are required to speak both Japanese and English. The library offers 28,000 volumes of Japanese books and 8,500 volumes of English books; the school is planning to expand to 45,000 volumes in total. In addition, magazines, videocassettes, and compact discs are available. In the near

Situated on 27 acres of land in Purchase, Keio Academy of New York is a four-year coeducational, independent secondary school accredited by the New York State Board of Regents.

Keio Academy offers an active sports life for students.

future, the school also plans to use the Internet to develop links between Keio Academy's computers and those of its sister schools in Japan.

Keio Academy's emphasis on bilingual instruction is designed to help students attain, both linguistically and culturally, a global viewpoint and outlook. The school also focuses on "active" education, thereby encouraging students to observe, think, and express themselves. "There are some other Japanese schools in the tristate area, which are supported by Japanese government and business," Sugiura said. "Teachers are sent from Japan and the curriculum is strictly Japanese. At Keio Academy, we have designed a different concept to produce a different type of student. Those schools are training students to become good Japanese business people in Japan. We are training students to become good international businesspeople."

In addition to academic achievement, Keio Academy also stresses development of students' character. "We focus on service to the community and teaching students to become independent persons," Sugiura said. "Through a long-term development approach, we train students to develop the ability to provide leadership for the twenty-first century. Most students will become international businesspeople."

Keio Academy also offers an active sports life for students. In addition to required physical and health education classes, students may participate in club or intramural sports, junior varsity, or varsity athletic teams.

Keio Academy focuses on educating today's students to become tomorrow's global leaders.

To expand students' cultural perspective, Keio Academy arranges optional field trips for students to Lincoln Center and the Metropolitan Museum of Art, as well as to shopping areas, Broadway shows, skiing areas, and amusement parks. For traditional Japanese culture, the school offers a "Japanese Culture Room," where students and parents occasionally hold tea ceremonies and flower arrangements.

Now that Keio Academy has firmly established itself within Westchester's educational community, the school plans to focus on fine-tuning its curriculum, Sugiura said. "For the past five years, we have been concentrating on the physical aspects, such as building the facility, recruiting teachers, and establishing the curriculum. Now, we are taking a step forward and improving the quality of our curriculum."

Keio Academy also is working to develop strong relationships within the community, Sugiura said. "New York has the largest Japanese population in the United States. And it is the center of economic activity, the arts, international politics and business, and has a strong educational tradition. So we try to learn from other schools in this area. We also want to interact with other schools, government, and businesses. Keio Academy has a very strong Japanese program, and we'd like to offer that to the business community."

In addition, Keio Academy is an institutional member of the Japan Society, a nonprofit organization supported by the Japanese government and Japanese businesses that provides information about Japanese society and culture. "We are working to expand their program here, and be the local liaison for them," Sugiura said. "We would like to offer a lecture series and symposiums here for local people interested in the Japanese economy, business, the arts, and culture." ◆

Eighty percent of Keio Academy's students live on campus, while 20 percent commute from within the tristate area.

EDUCATION & QUALITY OF LIFE

The Ursuline School

"Give me your daughters as little girls, and I'll give them back to you as young women." That is the principle of The Ursuline School's principal, Sr. Jean Baptiste Nicholson. And during her 22-year tenure, she has maintained that philosophy.

Ursuline in New Rochelle is a private, Catholic, college preparatory school for girls in grades 6 through 12. The school's goal is to provide a challenging, intellectually stimulating, student-centered environment which requires academic and personal achievements. In fact, the United States Department of Education has twice recognized Ursuline as a Blue Ribbon School and cited it for "excellence in private education."

"We have a very prestigious academic program," Sr. Jean Baptiste said. "This year, four students are National Merit finalists, and nine others have received Letters of Commendation. Furthermore, 100 percent of our students go on to college and most to graduate school. The academic program includes six languages, including Latin and Greek, and advanced placement courses in seven subjects. In addition, we have an impressive art program, with nine upper level courses. The academic program is supported by a computerized library and computer facilities throughout the school." Equally outstanding is Ursuline's athletic program; the school fields 23 teams in 10 sports and has won championships at the sectional, county, and state levels. The Sisters of the Order of St. Ursula founded the school in 1897 at Leland Castle in New Rochelle. In September 1929, the school was moved to its present location. Today, Ursuline is still administered by the Sisters of the Order of St. Ursula and is staffed by 80 sisters and lay teachers. It is accredited by the New York State Board of Regents and the Middle States Association of Secondary Schools and Colleges.

In addition to its location, other aspects have changed as well. Originally, Ursuline was an elementary and high school, but the grammar school closed in the 1960s. The school also has become ethnically and racially more diverse—minority students comprise 24 percent of the population.

One thing that hasn't changed, however, is the school's mission. "Our focus has always been to prepare young women for college," said Sr. Jean Baptiste. "Now, we prepare them as women leaders in the world. Today's students bring with them all the different needs of a complex society, so we've increased our support services to teach them what they need in order to become effective members of today's competitive global society."

The school offers programs in Personal Development, Peer Counseling, and Peer Ministry, in which students are trained to develop their own gifts and to help others develop theirs. Through these opportunities, students build self-esteem, learn decision making, and clarify their values and religious beliefs. Through its faculty advisement program, each student has her own advisor, which insures personal attention and care for each individual. The school has always been marked by close relationships among students, parents, and faculty.

More than 4,000 students have been graduated from Ursuline, and the school boasts a number of lawyers, doctors, authors, and other professionals. Jurate Kazickas, '60, a freelance writer, was the first female reporter and photographer to cover the Vietnam War, while Ellen Mooney Hancock, '61, was one of the top female executives at IBM.

Ursuline will celebrate its centennial in 1997. As it begins its second century, it hopes to continue to provide an atmosphere in which its students will become women of strength and women of wisdom. ◆

EDUCATION & QUALITY OF LIFE

IONA PREPARATORY SCHOOL

Iona Preparatory School in New Rochelle educates young men to be "life-long learners" by providing a structure that nurtures each student's talents, and offering a gospel-centered, value-oriented, Catholic environment.

"We teach students how to learn," said Brother William Stoldt, CFC President of Iona Prep. "We practice what we preach by how we live and by what we teach."

Iona Prep, founded by the Christian Brothers, is a private Catholic school for young men, grades 9 through 12. Iona is fully accredited by the New York State Board of Regents and the Middle States Association for Secondary Schools and Colleges.

Iona's goal to prepare students to be "the Christian leaders of the next millennium" begins before the first day of class, with an in-depth orientation period that involves the student, his parents or guardian, and input from his sending school.

Freshmen are placed in classes according to their talents, strengths, and needs. The Superior Talent Enrichment Program—S.T.E.P.—is limited to the top 30 incoming freshmen. S.T.E.P. is team-taught, interdisciplinary, and centers on a core curriculum of English, social studies, religion, and Latin.

During the next three years, students study English, Latin, science, mathematics, health, computer, music, foreign language, social studies, and fine arts. In senior year, in addition to required courses, students design their own elective courses in preparation for college, including an extensive advanced placement program. The school boasts a 100-percent college acceptance rate.

The lay teachers and Christian Brothers of Iona Prep work to instill Christian values, enhance critical thinking, develop leadership skills, and prepare students for future studies. The more than 8,000 Iona Prep alums provide social, athletic, and academic support.

Iona has an enrollment of 750, which "is an ideal number," according to Edward O'Neill, headmaster. "Our enrollment allows us to offer a wide range of programs and, at the same time, know each student as an individual." Student-teacher ratio is 15 to 1, and classes average 23 students. All students are encouraged to be active in after-school activities which include extensive interscholastic sports, intramurals, and many other activities.

Recently, Iona has invested in three major building additions. Opened in 1983, the D'Urso Technology Center houses a student computer lab, faculty computer room, boardroom, and president's office. The Verni Arts Center, which contains the music and arts program, opened in 1986, and the Matthew Heffernan Gymnasium opened in 1995.

And the future of Iona?

"It's very bright," Brother Stoldt said. "Our future lies in graduating young men who respect others, who want to keep learning, who have the technological skills for the workplace, who have the ability to communicate, but most of all, have high values. We will continue to provide young men with the best possible academic education, balanced with a strong athletic and co-curricular program." ◆

Westchester County: New York's Golden Apple / 183

EDUCATION & QUALITY OF LIFE

THE WESTCHESTER BUSINESS INSTITUTE

Keeping abreast of rapidly changing technology presents challenges for employers and employees alike. As companies continue to streamline operations to stay competitive, they seek individuals who can handle heavier workloads and do those jobs more efficiently. And, at many businesses, computer knowledge is no longer a "plus"; it's a prerequisite.

"Companies are increasingly demanding more technological skills," said Karen J. Smith, senior executive vice president of the Westchester Business Institute in White Plains. "We can't send out graduates without computer skills, regardless of their majors. Companies require employees have that hands-on knowledge."

And WBI is meeting those requirements head-on, providing students with a host of multilevel business career-oriented programs. WBI, a coeducational, collegiate business institute, offers programs leading to associate degrees and diplomas. The institute has 1,000 students from Westchester, Rockland, Putnam, and Fairfield Counties, and employs 100 full-, part-time, and adjunct faculty. It is fully accredited, and offers full- and part-time programs, with day, evening, and weekend classes.

WBI was founded in New Rochelle as the Westchester Business School in 1915. The school was expanded and acquired by current chairman Ernest H. Sutkowski, who in 1959 relocated it to White Plains. Although WBI started as a secretarial training school, the changing job market during the 1970s prompted the school to begin seeking degree-granting status as a two-year private business college. WBI then enhanced its secretarial and administrative secretarial programs, and added business administration, accounting, management, marketing, computer systems management, and computerized office programs.

One of the unique aspects of WBI is its "career-relevant" programs, Smith said. "We have a very focused curriculum. For example, if a student comes to WBI and takes accounting, that student will have 10 separate accounting courses [rather than a mix of liberal arts and accounting classes]. This way, students know that every penny they spend on tuition goes directly toward enhancing their abilities to become successful in the workplace."

WBI also offers shorter diploma programs, such as computer programming and word processing, which provide students with specialized job skills to jump-start or upgrade their careers. They are designed for students who have advanced skills or education and want to be employable or promotable in the shortest possible time.

Through its placement program, WBI works with about 3,000 companies, ranging from small businesses to major corporations. "In Westchester, we have witnessed a huge growth in small and mid-sized businesses, and that's where most of our students are being placed," Smith said, noting that the school has a 95-percent placement rate.

In order to keep current of the latest business trends, WBI consults with the College Advisory Council, a panel of local business professionals. "We meet with them four times a year and use their judgment and real-world experience to guide the changes in our curriculum," Smith said.

WBI's location benefits the institute as well, she said. The accessibility to White Plains has helped draw more students, and the city's substantial business base provides surroundings conducive to WBI's programs.

As for the future, Smith said WBI will continue expanding from a technological stance, but is not planning to boost enrollment. "We don't want a dramatic increase in student population. We plan to maintain a level of quality for our students." ◆

Students at WBI work with the latest in computer equipment to keep abreast of today's rapidly changing technology.

EDUCATION & QUALITY OF LIFE

THE MASTERS SCHOOL

The Masters School prepares students not only for college but also for the real work of life in communities and in the world. Situated on 96 acres in Dobbs Ferry, this boarding and day school is comprised of a coed high school, a girls middle school (grades 5-8) and a parallel boys middle school (grades 5-8). Boarding starts in grade eight.

The curriculum includes advanced placement courses in every discipline as well as honors and regular college-prep sections. Most graduates have taken four years of math, English, science, history, and language, and many students have completed the AP sequence in either studio art, music theory, or computer science. Graduates attend such colleges as Wellesley, Dartmouth, and Barnard, and such universities as Columbia, SUNY, Cornell, Yale, Princeton, and Harvard. All students are involved in an extensive co-curricular program; this includes dance, three major dramatic productions, orchestra, community service, and varsity and junior varsity sports.

One of the unique practices of The Masters School is that it uses the Harkness method of classroom teaching—round-table seating in small numbers. "This method of teaching ensures equal participation and involvement," said Pamela Clarke, head of the school.

Students at The Masters School come from 12 states and 12 countries, creating a diverse and vibrant community.

"Students are facing each other around an oval table, learning from each other as well as from the teacher."

The middle schools are parallel and separated by gender because recent studies show that these junior high years are very important to the personal development of young women and young men. Also consistent with current research is the schools' practice of teaching mathematics in gender-separate classes. Cooperation and collaboration are important, as is leadership; boys and girls share major leadership positions to ensure collaboration and to minimize competition between students.

Small classes feature seminar-style teaching and encourage collaborative learning.

While competition is not stressed in the classroom, it is expected and demonstrated on the fields and courts. The Masters School is a member of the 27-school Fairchester League and competes in soccer, field hockey, volleyball, cross-country running, basketball, fencing, lacrosse, tennis, baseball and softball. The school is preparing to build a skating arena and has nine tennis courts, three playing fields, a fencing room, dance studio, fully equipped gymnasium, weight room, cross-country running and ski trails, and a low ropes course.

Community service is also important; all students belong to MISH (Masters Interested in Sharing and Helping), and their efforts include visiting senior citizens, volunteering for the Midnight Run to aid the homeless, helping at local day-care centers, tutoring students at Children's Village, and organizing a Special Olympics.

In addition to exchange programs in England, Switzerland, Russia, Australia, and South Africa, the school offers a unique opportunity to juniors and seniors called CITYterm. Qualified students come from other high schools (as well as The Masters School) to participate in this multidisciplinary one-semester program of urban studies. This intense, group learning experience offers students a chance to combine history, literature, and science with politics, economics, and sociology in pursuit of understanding the issues that face our cities. Admission to the CITYterm and to The Masters School is competitive. ◆

Westchester County: New York's Golden Apple / 185

EDUCATION & QUALITY OF LIFE

MONROE COLLEGE

At Monroe College, the staff and faculty have one goal—to provide each student with an "education for life." The college achieves this mission by offering a quality curriculum, flexible class schedules, ongoing counseling, and lifetime career placement.

Monroe College was founded as a business school in the Bronx in 1933 by Mildred King and Harry Jerome. In 1972, through the efforts of Jerome's son—current President Stephen J. Jerome— Monroe was officially accredited as a two-year college by the state Board of Regents.

Today, Monroe is a private, coeducational college offering associate and bachelor's degrees in business-related fields. Some 3,000 students are enrolled at the Main Campus on Fordham Road in the Bronx, and 800 at the Branch Campus on Main Street in New Rochelle. The college is accredited by the Middle States Association of Colleges and Schools and authorized by the Board of Regents of the University of the State of New York to confer associate degrees in applied science and occupational studies and bachelor's degrees. Students may earn degrees in accounting, business administration, computer science, hospitality management, and office administration.

Monroe's classes are small—usually fewer than 25 students—to ensure personal attention from the 250 full-time and adjunct faculty members. Students also receive academic advisement, career guidance, counseling, and a range of academic support services. Financial aid is available to eligible applicants and is received by 90 percent of students.

"Monroe is a family-type environment," said Rhoda Kaufman, associate director of admissions. "The faculty really gets to know the students, and we encourage them to succeed. We change people's lives."

Monroe's students represent diverse backgrounds, ages, and experiences. The student body is comprised of recent high-school graduates, individuals who are currently working and seeking career advancement or new careers, as well as those interested in continuing their education.

"A large percentage of our students—about 40 percent—go on to four-year colleges, while others go directly into the workforce," said Marc Jerome, director. "We have a diverse student body. We have a growing number of international students, from the Caribbean, Africa, and Europe."

The latest technology is incorporated into the classroom experience.

To accommodate students' schedules, the college offers the Monroe Flex-Schedule, which allows students to earn associate degrees in less than two years, while attending day, evening, or weekend classes as few as two days or two nights per week.

Monroe's Learning Centers offer comprehensive services and facilities such as tutors, computer programs, and audiovisual materials. In addition to tutorial workshops, students volunteer to assist their peers.

Career Services Centers provide Monroe alumni lifetime career placement, as well as career and transfer counseling, workshops, career fairs, and seminars. Monroe graduates have been placed at such companies as Xerox Corp., International Business Machines Corp., the Bank of New York, and Ciba-Geigy Corp.

Monroe graduates also are eligible to transfer to four-year colleges. Monroe graduates have continued their education at such colleges as Brooklyn College, Columbia University, Lehman College, Pace University, and Polytechnic University.

In addition to class work, students take part in a number of clubs and activities, including talent shows, speakers' programs, volleyball, and the college's two newspapers—*Campus Talk* and *Monroe Media*—which contain news about the college and programs, upcoming events, poetry, and feature articles. Students also participate in a variety of special events, including food drives for the homeless, blood drives, the homecoming dance, and ethnic festivals. ◆

Classes are kept small, usually fewer than 25 students, so everyone receives personal attention.

186 / Westchester County: New York's Golden Apple

Antique automobile at Kykuit.
Photo: Mick Hales/courtesy Historic Hudson Valley.

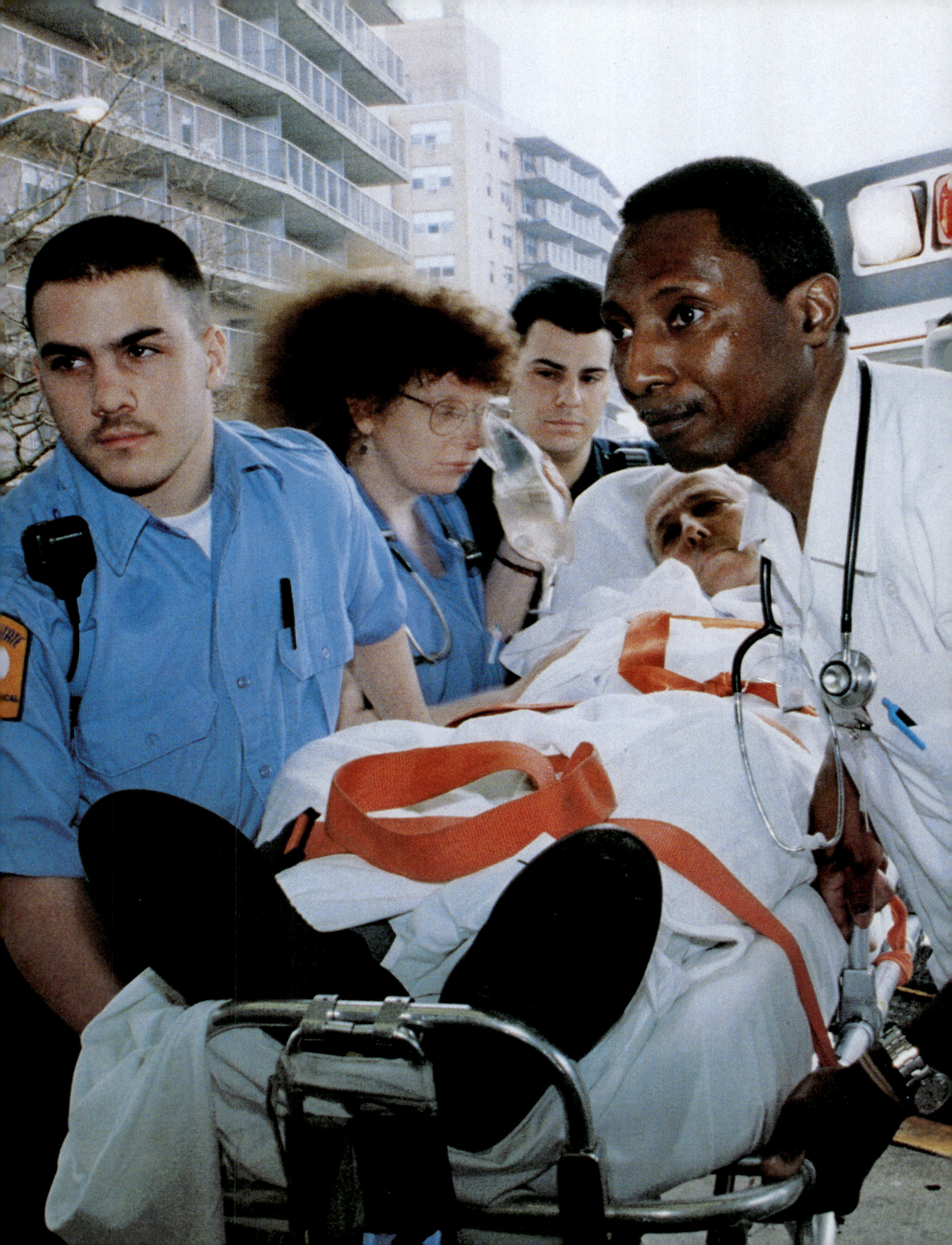

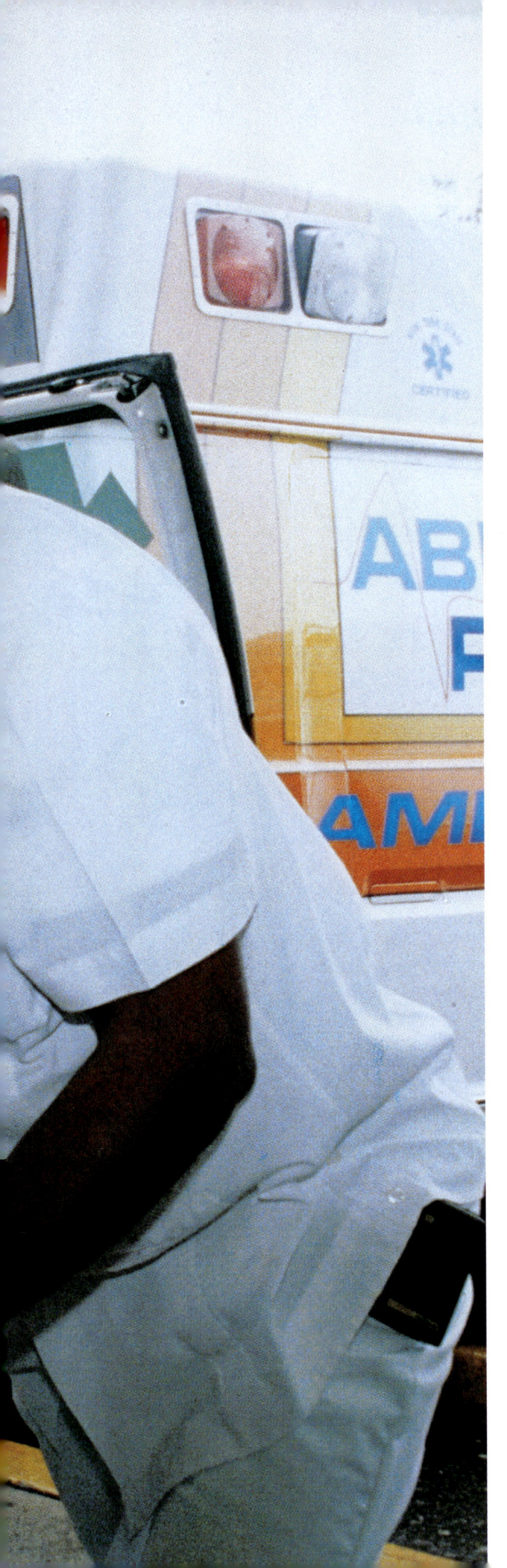

CHAPTER · THIRTEEN

Health Care

The Westchester County area's progressive medical community is shaped by compassionate caring, keen minds, and modern facilities.

Westchester County Medical Center
Page 190

White Plains Hospital Center
Page 194

United Hospital Medical Center
Page 196

Sound Shore Medical Center of Westchester
Page 198

St. John's Riverside Hospital
Page 200

Saint Joseph's Medical Center
Page 200

Yonkers General Hospital
Page 201

Northern Westchester Hospital Center
Page 202

The Bethel Homes
Page 204

Photo courtesy of Westchester County Medical Center

Westchester County: New York's Golden Apple / 189

HEALTH CARE

WESTCHESTER COUNTY MEDICAL CENTER

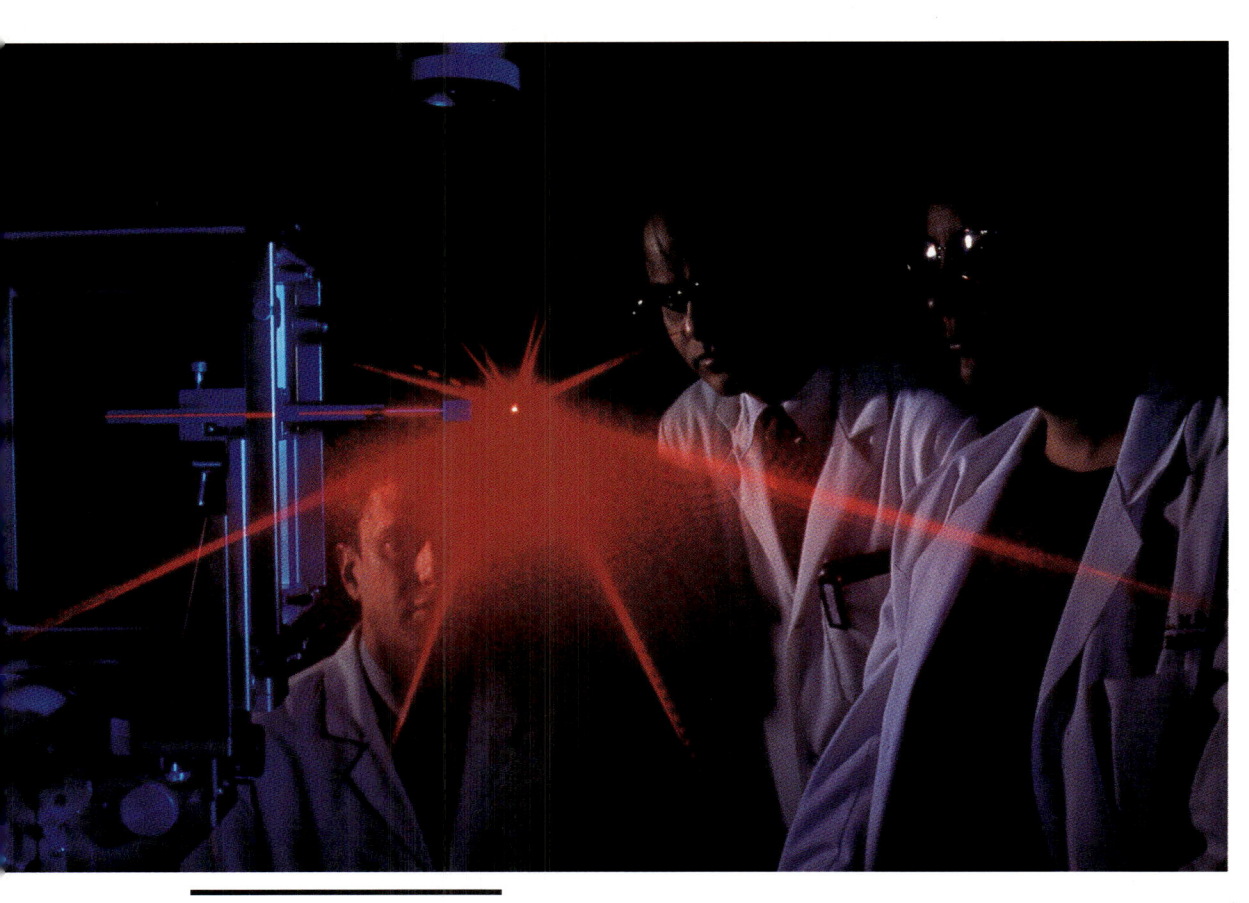

With cutting-edge technologies such as "knifeless" surgery for inoperable brain tumors, the medical center offers the latest procedures, treatments, and medications.

The Westchester County Medical Center has been serving the health care needs of Westchester County since 1977. And staying on the cutting edge of medical advancements has helped the medical center earn an impressive reputation in Westchester's health care community. "We are a world-class hospital doing national and international research," said Edward A. Stolzenberg, commissioner of hospitals at Westchester County Medical Center.

Situated on a 560-acre campus in Valhalla, the medical center is a tertiary and trauma care center that provides health-related services to more than 3.6 million people. It is a center of national and international clinical and biomedical research, and a training center and resource for the local medical community.

"As a tertiary care hospital, we are very fortunate to be in Westchester County," Stolzenberg said. "This location provides us with an opportunity for growth and development since we do not compete with the community hospitals."

Through its affiliation with the New York Medical College, Westchester County Medical Center (WCMC) is a major academic institution, Stolzenberg said. Staff and student training is an ongoing process, and the medical college's Office of Continuing Education sponsors a number of programs each year for faculty and community physicians. "As the only medical school in the seven-county Hudson Valley region, we help the medical industry through new initiatives in physician training and managed care," he said.

Dr. George E. Reed, medical director at Westchester County Medical Center, agrees with Stolzenberg. "To have a teaching hospital in the area is extremely important to the community," he said. He pointed out that national and international studies of new operative procedures, drugs, and innovative technological advances often are based at the medical center.

"The benefits of the research being done here, including the use of new drugs and protocols that our patients can take advantage of, are immeasurable," Dr. Reed said.

In addition to his position as medical director, Dr. Reed is the chief of cardiothoracic surgery. He is known worldwide for his initiatives and expertise in heart valve replacement.

The medical center also boasts many other world-renowned doctors, such as Dr. Khalid Butt, who performed the first intestinal transplant in the world. Dr. Butt is chief of transplantation and vascular surgery for Westchester Medical Center. Dr. Michael Gewitz, director of pediatrics and chief of pediatric cardiology, has just been named one of the best doctors in America by *American Health* magazine. Oncology Chief Dr. Tauseef Ahmed has an international reputation for his pioneering work in bone marrow transplants.

"These top doctors help the medical center continue as a strong player in the competitive and turbulent health care industry," Stolzenberg said.

"We have one of the most highly regarded cardiology and cardiac surgery programs on the East Coast. We have world-class physicians here, so patients do not have to travel into New York City to receive quality care. The medical center provides the highest quality of service, and we are well-known for the kind of care we provide. At Westchester County Medical Center, you're not just a case number."

"Also, we have a better physical plant than in New York City —we have a campus setting," he added. "And our accessibility makes it easier for patients' families to come and visit them. That is extremely important, especially with children. We make sure the parents are accommodated—we want to take care of the entire family."

190 / Westchester County: New York's Golden Apple

HEALTH CARE

Nurses also play a vital role in the services and care provided at the medical center. Members of the medical center's nursing staff are recruited based on their commitment to patient care, Dr. Reed said. Nurses frequently lecture nationally, and conduct advanced skill training for other nurses in the region. In addition, the medical center's team includes social workers, pharmacists, therapists, technicians, dietitians, nutritionists, and volunteers who offer their services to a variety of departments and programs.

Another aspect that sets the medical center apart from its New York City competitors is its "cutting-edge care." As part of its comprehensive specialized care, the medical center has established six "Centers of Excellence." They are the Heart Center; Trauma Care, including a Burn Center; the Children's Hospital; the Transplant Program; the Cancer ; and the Neurosciences.

The Centers of Excellence were designed in an effort to "create a seamless continuum of care for patients at every level, from their primary community physician to specialty and sub-specialty physicians at Westchester County Medical Center," Stolzenberg said.

"While every specialty service at Westchester Medical Center offers top quality medicine, we have chosen to further concentrate our efforts on quality in specific areas," he added. "We're putting more of our energy into these resources so that we can provide better services in a less costly fashion. For example, we are not trying to treat 'every' cancer patient—we want to concentrate on those that need bone-marrow transplants. And we're at the cutting edge of technology because our work is done with an umbrella of research behind it."

The Heart Center offers medical and surgical expertise and advanced technology in cardiology and cardiac surgery. A team of physicians performs thousands of procedures each year, such as cardiovascular surgery and angioplasty. The center's technology includes the latest instrumentation in a new biplane digital cardiac catheterization suite and an electrophysiological laboratory suite to evaluate the electrical pathways of the heart. In addition to the Coronary Care Unit, a consolidated cardiology unit is served by the most sophisticated hardware and telemetry monitoring capabilities.

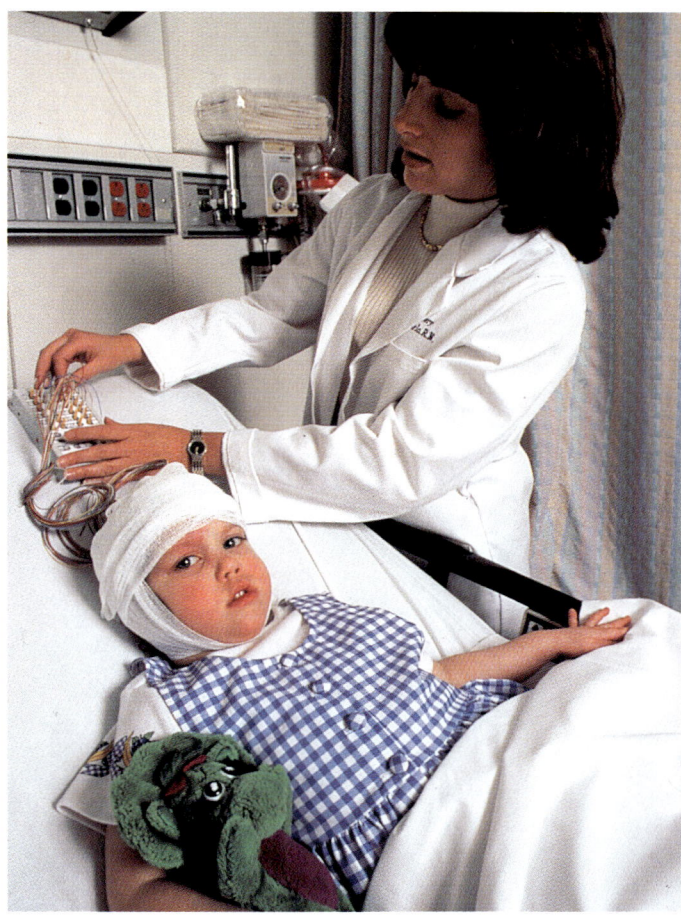

As the Hudson Valley region's only **Level One Trauma Care Center**, WCMC has air and ground transport teams on call 24 hours a day, seven days a week, to respond to emergency medical situations. Two helicopter teams, which are comprised of veteran pilots and certified critical care flight nurses, are based at the medical center and in Orange County. STAT Flight (Stabilization Transport and Treatment) responds in minutes to accident scenes and carries critical interhospital patient transfers throughout the 5,000-square-mile region. Some months have seen as many as 67 flights and, most importantly, the unit received a national safety award for its 1,000 consecutive, accident-free air rescue missions.

"We are the only center in the Hudson Valley region that has medivac helicopters," Stolzenberg said. "This is a critical service, since many accident victims are transported to the medical center by heli-

The Children's Hospital at Westchester County Medical Center cares for more than 20,000 children each year.

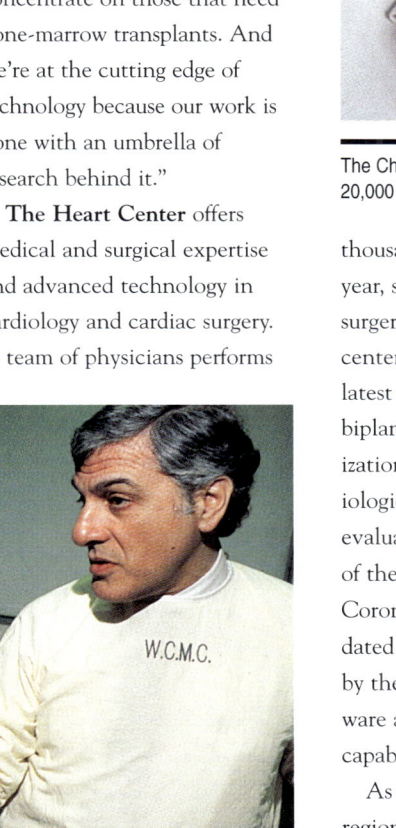

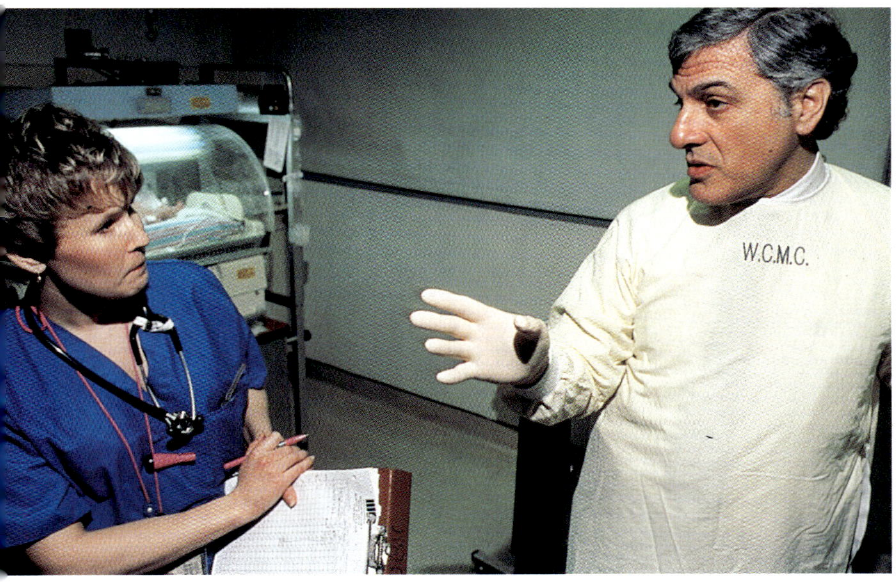

WCMC is home to the only regional neonatal intensive care unit in the Hudson Valley, regularly carrying for babies as small as two pounds.

HEALTH CARE

copter. Also, we use this service to transfer trauma patients and critically ill adults, children, and infants here from other hospitals."

The Trauma Center also houses a 10-bed burn center—the only one between New York City and the Canadian border—which provides services from intensive care to reconstructive surgery and rehabilitation, he said.

The Children's Hospital at WCMC offers care for children from birth through age 21. The center is the only state certified Level III neonatology and pediatric open-heart surgery and cardiac catheterization center in the region, and is equipped with neonatal and pediatric intensive care units and a pediatric "step-down" unit.

The Transplantation Program includes "the largest and leading" kidney transplant program in New York State, Stolzenberg said. He also noted that an adult and pediatric liver transplantation program began in 1996.

The Cancer Center has been designated an "Unrelated Allogeneic Bone Marrow Transplant Center" by the National Marrow Donor Program. The center also provides tertiary level oncology services, and works with the patient and family on quality of life issues. The center is involved in ongoing national cancer research, which is designed to benefit patients in the community and throughout the world, Stolzenberg said.

The Neurosciences at WCMC include a specialized stroke unit, a neuro-muscular program with histochemistry, biochemistry, and immunopathology facilities, and a neuro-oncology section for medical treatment of tumors of the nervous system. A four-bed Epilepsy Center opened in 1996, and the stereotactic radiosurgery program was introduced to manage tumors and vascular malformations and treat functional disorders such as Parkinson's disease.

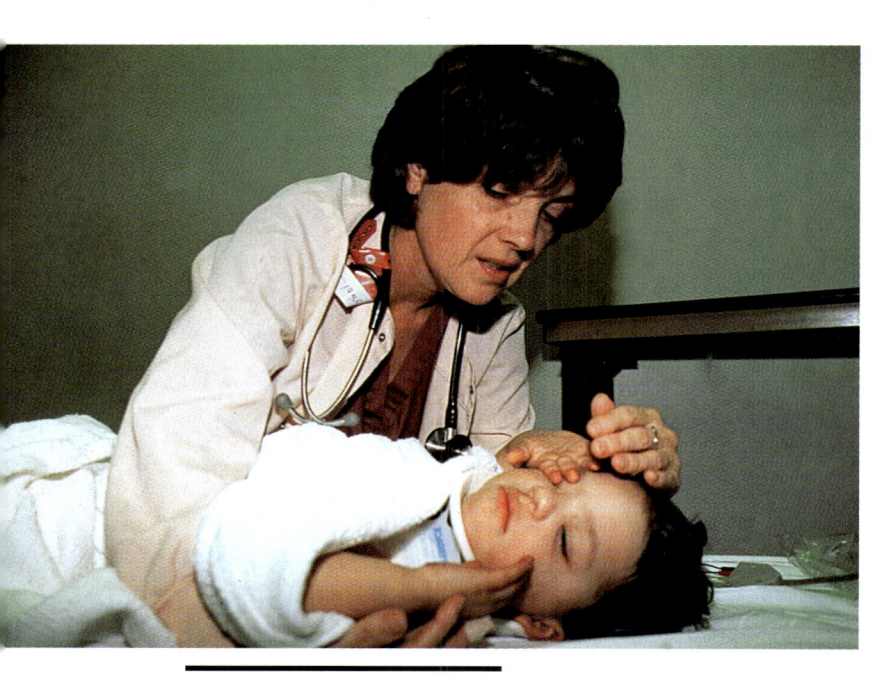

"The Epilepsy Center has all the newest diagnostic equipment and monitoring stations in one area," Stolzenberg said. "We have on staff a team of neurosurgeons, neurologists, pediatric neurologists, social workers, and technicians."

Westchester County Medical Center has grown dramatically since its inception in 1977. When Stolzenberg joined the facility in 1980, it was a 200-bed hospital. Today, the medical center has four major components which provide a total of 1,060 patient beds.

The main hospital contains 530 beds, including the 109-bed Children's Hospital, and occupies 400,000 square feet of space in a seven-story tower. The facility provides acute rehabilitation, an AIDS management program for in- and outpatients, ambulatory care, a burn center, a cancer care center, cardiac services, intensive care and coronary care units, kidney programs, neurosurgical and neurological services, pediatric and adolescent specialties, and perinatal services.

The Behavioral Health Center has 136 beds and provides in- and outpatient services to children, adolescents, and adults. It also has a 20-bed Alcohol Detoxification unit and 15-bed Forensic unit. As part of its designated comprehensive psychiatric emergency program, the Behavioral Health Center at WCMC hosts a Mobile Crisis Intervention Team, which provides crisis services 24 hours a day.

The Westchester Institute for Human Development offers comprehensive outpatient care for those with developmental disabilities. Offered are medical, dental, educational, social, and psychological services.

The Ruth Taylor Geriatric and Rehabilitation Institute, a

Westchester County Medical Center is the tertiary and Level 1 Trauma Center for the 3.6 million people in the seven-county Hudson Valley region in New York, Bergen County, New Jersey, and Fairfield County, Connecticut.

The Children's Hospital at Westchester County Medical Center offers every specialty available, including pediatric cardiology, pediatric neurosurgery, pediatric open heart surgery, and pediatric oncology, as well as a specialized high-risk obstetrical unit.

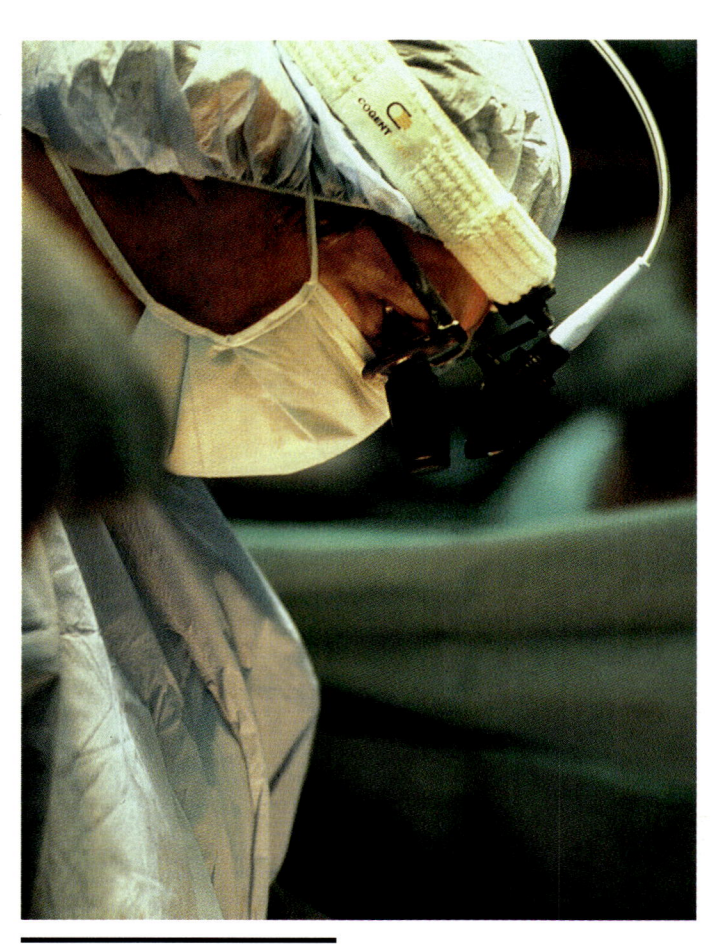

192 / Westchester County: New York's Golden Apple

HEALTH CARE

400-bed long-term extended-care facility, offers a range of medical and rehabilitation services such as special units for assessments, long-term care for AIDS patients, and care for those people suffering from dementia or Alzheimer's disease.

Westchester County Medical Center is affiliated with a number of hospitals in the region, including the following:
- St. Agnes Hospital, White Plains
- St. Johns Riverside, Yonkers
- Sound Shore Medical Center, New Rochelle
- Yonkers General Hospital, Yonkers
- The Kingston Hospital, Kingston
- Benedictine Hospital, Kingston
- St. Vincent's Hospital, New York City

In addition to the hospitals above, WCMC has developed strong bonds with other hospitals in the region for transferring patients in need of the medical center's specialized care. The center has transfer agreements with Northern Westchester Hospital Center, Phelps Memorial Hospital, White Plains Hospital Center, Community Hospital at Dobbs Ferry, Huson Valley Hospital, Mount Vernon Hospital, Nathan Miller Center, Saint Joseph's Medical Cemter, and United Hospital Center.

Also, the medical center's Managed Care Department negotiates and monitors contractual relationships with managed care health care organizations representing thousands of local residents and employees. The center has managed care agreements with over 30 companies, including Blue Cross Healthnet, Oxford, Physicians Health Services, US Healthcare, and Westchester Health Services Network, among others.

In addition to serving the medical needs of the community, the medical center also has a significant impact on Westchester County's economy, Stolzenberg said. He cited the center's 4,000 employees as one example. Westchester County Medical Center is a major employer in its community. In fact, we are the largest single employer in Westchester and the largest hospital in the region."

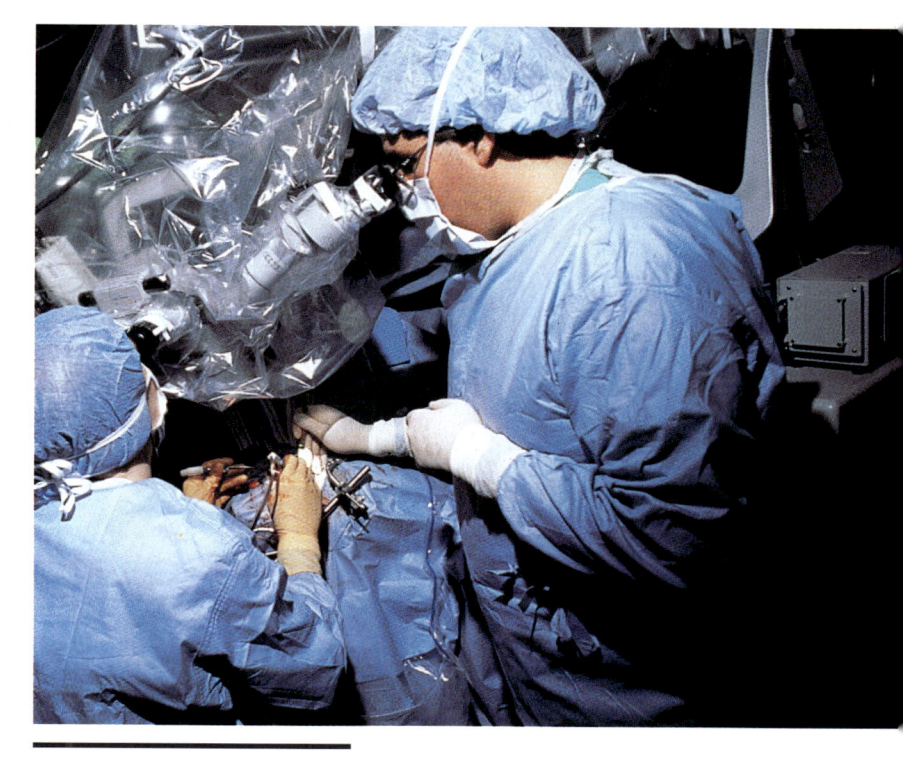

A public hospital, the medical center has a $370-million budget, but only $15 million of that is generated through tax dollars, Stolzenberg said. He noted that the remainder is obtained from standard hospital reimbursements.

While Stolzenberg has witnessed the medical center's substantial growth over the years, he also has seen a number of changes within the health care community as well. "One of the trends now is that New York City hospitals are reaching out into Westchester County," he said. "Also, managed care has been growing steadily. This change is being driven by the economy—companies don't want to pay exorbitant heath care costs, so many are turning toward insurance alternatives."

Fundraising for the new 150-bed freestanding Children's Hospital at WCMC began in 1996. The new hospital will cost $60 million and will encompass 200,000 square feet. It will be the only all-specialty children's hospital in the New York Metro area.

As the health care industry continues to change, Westchester County Medical Center will be at the forefront, and the medical center is well-positioned for the future. Stolzenberg said, "Westchester County Medical Center has been doing extraordinarily well and will continue to do extraordinarily well. Our occupancy has increased and we are seeing the length of stay going down. This means we are doing our jobs more efficiently and effectively. We will continue to be in a very strong position for many years." ◆

State-of-the-art surgical techniques and equipment and the most highly trained medical staff in the region, make Westchester Medical Center the referral hospital of choice for all specialty health care services.

Child Life specialists at the Children's Hospital at Westchester County Medical Center ensure that each child's stay is as close to normal as possible.

Westchester County: New York's Golden Apple / 193

HEALTH CARE

WHITE PLAINS HOSPITAL CENTER

Combining state-of-the-art technology with individualized, compassionate care is the guiding principle of White Plains Hospital Center (WPHC). Since its founding as a voluntary, not-for-profit hospital in 1893, the hospital has continuously expanded its services and physical plant to meet the varied and ever-changing health care needs of the community. Today, the 307-bed institution offers the comfort and convenience of a community hospital as well as the technology and sophistication of a much larger institution.

Throughout its history, White Plains Hospital Center's ability to respond quickly to evolving health care needs has earned it many distinctions. The hospital was the first in the county to establish a coronary care unit, open a fully self-contained ambulatory surgery center, and to add a certified nurse midwife to its medical staff. Most recently, the hospital gained the distinction of being one of the few community hospitals in the country selected by the Yale Cancer Center as a partner for an important cancer research project.

The brand-new Flanzer Pavilion, shown in this architect's rendering, included expanded facilities for emergency medicine, ambulatory surgery, physical medicine and rehabilitation, cardiology, and other hospital services. *Lothrop Associates Rendering.*

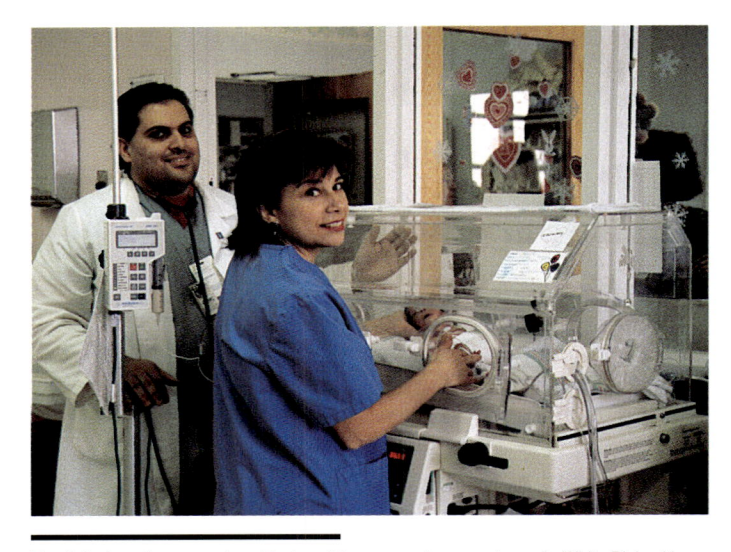

The tiniest newborns, such as Zachary Maurer, receive expert care in White Plains Hospital Center's Level II Special Care Nursery. Zachary is examined by Jesus Jaile-Marti, M.D., chief of neonatology, and Joann Nemeth, R.N. *Photo by Steve Napolitano.*

White Plains Hospital Center's affiliation with the Columbia-Presbyterian Medical Center in Manhattan opens the tertiary care resources of this internationally renowned institution to the residents of central Westchester. This affiliation includes access to the medical center's cardiac catheterization service; additional continuing medical education programs for White Plains Hospital Center physicians, nurses, and other health care professionals; and a relationship for neonatology and pediatric cardiology.

In addition to its broad array of treatment services and programs, WPHC is also a founding member of HealthStar Network, a corporation which will enable participating hospitals to deliver high quality health care services while retaining local control of their organizations. HealthStar Network will allow participating hospitals to negotiate effectively with managed care organizations, develop technologically advanced information systems, and operate more efficiently. As a result of its membership in HealthStar Network, WPHC will successfully address dramatic changes currently occurring in today's health care environment.

Today, with hospital admissions decreasing, patients admitted are frequently more acutely ill and require higher levels of expertise and responsiveness than ever before. At the same time, the need for primary care, outpatient, home care, and outreach services is increasing dramatically. Once again, the White Plains Hospital Center is leading the way in responding to these changes. Its newly constructed Flanzer Pavilion consolidates, relocates, and expands a variety of services in a beautiful building designed especially for convenient access and service. An ongoing renovation and refurbishment program is improving and modernizing existing facilities to ensure the continuity of exemplary patient care in every department.

Designed as a distinctive architectural statement of both the hospital's image and its commitment to the city of White Plains, the 86,000-square-foot Flanzer Pavilion is dedicated to the delivery of the high quality, accessible, cost-efficient care the community expects, with an emphasis on outpatient services. Just off the Pavilion's main lobby is the Maxine and John Bendheim Department of Emergency Medicine, an open, glassed-in area that is user-friendly and features a new layout for trauma treatment as well as rooms for specialized treatment of psychiatric, obstetric, pediatric, and orthopedic patients, and an expanded waiting area. Conveniently located

194 / Westchester County: New York's Golden Apple

HEALTH CARE

next to Emergency Services is the David and Lilly Lieb Family Health Center for primary care.

The Flanzer Pavilion also houses the expanded Norman and Adele Morris Ambulatory Surgery/Endoscopy and Laser Unit, the Harry P. Albert Department of Physical Medicine and Rehabilitation, the William and Sylvia Silberstein Cardiology Center, an expanded Psychiatric Unit, a Pediatric "Swing" Unit that has the capacity to care for adult medical/surgical patients when the pediatric patient census is low, and the Admissions and Testing Center.

White Plains Hospital Center's patient-centered focus has been the springboard for the creation of dynamic programs that address some of today's critical health problems. The hospital's comprehensive cancer program, for example, offers a multidisciplinary approach to the management of the cancer patient. The hospital's program includes state-of-the-art diagnostic radiology equipment for detecting cancer in its earliest, most treatable stages; a spectrum of clinical services that encompasses prevention and screening protocols as well as inpatient and outpatient treatment regimens; and support services that address the complex emotional and psychological needs of patient and family.

The hospital's Breast Imaging Center offers women the most advanced breast care available, including state-of-the-art mammographic and dedicated high-definition ultrasound examinations, as well as computerized stereotactically-guided breast biopsies. MRI of the breast is available for selected cases and full-field whole breast digital mammographic imaging will be available in the near future. WPHC Breast Imaging is one of very few sites in the nation certified to teach an accredited stereotactic breast biopsy course that trains both surgeons and radiologists.

The partnership between White Plains Hospital Center and the Diabetes Treatment Centers of America (DTCA) ensures that Westchester residents with diabetes have access to the latest treatment services for this chronic, debilitating disease. The hospital's diabetes program is one of only 18 in New York State to be approved by the American Diabetes Association.

At the WPHC Diabetes Education and Treatment Center, comprehensive inpatient, outpatient, and clinical expertise are provided by a multidisciplinary team of endocrinologists, a diabetes educator, nurses, physical therapists, and dietitians. The center provides ongoing support groups, classes, and individual counseling for people who are living with this chronic condition.

For its youngest patients, the White Plains Hospital Center is certified for Level Two Neonatal Services. Its six-bed Special Care Nursery offers the most advanced monitoring, respiratory, and nutritional support in addition to radiological and physical therapy services for sick infants and premature newborns arriving as much as two to three months early. A neonatologist is present at every high-risk delivery, and the unit maintains an affiliation with Babies and Children's Hospital at Columbia-Presbyterian Medical Center in Manhattan for infants who need even more specialized care or heart surgery.

The Division of Geriatric Services offers numerous programs and activities to seniors, including a Medication Awareness Program; HealthAccess, a membership program with special benefits for people aged 55 and over; assistance with nursing home placement; a CareGivers Support Group; the Voice of Help, an emergency response device for the home; a Friendly Visitors Program for the homebound; and the very popular MallWalkers Program, which meets three times a week.

To make health care more accessible and affordable for community residents, the hospital joined forces with four other hospitals in Westchester and Putnam Counties to create the Westchester Health Services Network, Inc. This partnership of hospitals and physicians ensures superior care, simplifies contracting, and helps businesses manage their health care costs.

White Plains Hospital Center provides additional services for local businesses through its comprehensive occupational health program. Many services are provided in the workplace, including screening programs, medical examinations, health education seminars, and specially coordinated treatment of injured workers.

The tradition of excellence established by the White Plains Hospital Center in its century of service to the community is a standard for future achievement. With the support of more than 400 dedicated volunteers and the generosity of many wonderful friends, the hospital will lead the way into the next century.

At Divney Consulting in White Plains, Barbara Cassano, RN, White Plains Hospital Center's occupational health coordinator, performs an ergonomic assessment of Lorraine Zuhlke's workstation.

The popular MallWalkers program is only one aspect of White Plains Hospital Center's multifaceted Senior Services Program. Photo by Steve Napolitano.

Westchester County: New York's Golden Apple / 195

HEALTH CARE

UNITED HOSPITAL MEDICAL CENTER

In February, 1889, fourteen concerned women formed the Ladies Hospital Association to serve Port Chester's sick and needy. Over the following months, they held cake sales, fairs, entertainments, a lawn fete, a garden party, and a charity ball to raise funds to establish a hospital. In July, 1889, the village's first hospital opened in two rooms over Scott's Dry Goods Store at the corner of North Main and Willett Avenue with a medical staff of three physicians and one nurse.

From this humble beginning, United Hospital Medical Center has grown into a progressive health care delivery system providing ambulatory care, acute care, long-term skilled nursing care, comprehensive home care services, and hospice care to an area that encompasses Rye, Harrison, Mamaroneck, Larchmont, and New Rochelle to the south; Rye Brook, Purchase, and White Plains to the northwest; and Port Chester and Greenwich, Connecticut, to the northeast. With a total of 311 beds (226 beds for acute care, 17 bassinets, 28 psychiatric beds, and a 40-bed skilled nursing unit), United Hospital delivers integrated health care by developing primary care sites within the community and coordinating patient movement across the continuum of the physician's office, hospital, home, and nursing home, thus meeting the needs of all age groups.

As a voluntary community hospital, United Hospital Medical Center is committed to providing high-quality health care at a competitive price,

Bruce and Coco Lefkowitz of Rye hold newborn quadruplets Coby Tyde, Trent James, Jenna Lynne, and Kyle Anne, who were delivered at United Hospital Medical Center. *Photo by Jules Alexander.*

with sensitivity to patients' needs, in a safe, caring, and compassionate environment. This commitment is backed by its century-long tradition of excellence in patient-focused education and preventative services for the well, and essential medical services and long-term care for the sick and injured.

United's affiliation with the New York Hospital-Cornell Medical Center further enhances its quality of patient care by bringing the outstanding resources of the New York Hospital-Cornell Medical Center to the local community. As a result, United's patients benefit from the highest levels of medicine and technology close to home. In addition, United's affiliated medical and dental staff benefit from frequent continuing medical education courses with world-renowned tertiary medicine physicians and scientists and the opportunity to achieve academic appointments at one of the United States' preeminent teaching, research, and patient care institutions.

Among United's innovative health care efforts is its Family Life Center. This facility is more than just a wonderful place to have a baby—it combines the disciplines of gynecology, obstetrics, and pediatrics into a single program that extends medical, educational, and emotional support to expectant as well as growing families. At the Center expectant parents can take such courses as childbirth preparation, lactation, infant and child safety, prenatal and postpartum exercise, prenatal nutrition, and baby care basics; young children can participate in Sibling Preparation (with their parents) to get ready for the arrival of a brother or sister; and teens can enroll in babysitting classes. Because family life encompasses many ages and stages, the Family Life Center also offers a variety of seminars for parents and grandparents, programs that address the challenges of raising children today, and the latest information on developments in women's health.

The emergency services department at United Hospital

196 / Westchester County: New York's Golden Apple

HEALTH CARE

Medical Center provides skilled medical care to more than 19,000 patients each year, nearly half of whom require hospital admission and sustained treatment. The department's dynamic patient evaluation system enables doctors and nurses to quickly evaluate and treat critically ill and injured patients. Medical and surgical specialists, on call 24 hours a day, provide rapid intervention whenever necessary, with tertiary care resources available through the NYH Care Network. The department, redesigned for patient and family comfort, also offers centralized cardiac monitoring with satellite bedside units to facilitate nursing supervision.

United was the first hospital in the country to offer Enhanced External Counterpulsation (EECP) outside of an academic environment. This new, noninvasive therapy can reduce angina pectoris (chest pain) by increasing blood flow to the heart through a series of 35 one- to two-hour sessions over four to seven weeks, using cycles of pressure to create and enlarge collateral blood vessels. EECP benefits many patients with heart disease by delaying or reducing the need for bypass surgery.

In response to the emerging needs of an aging American population, United Hospital has created a geriatric services program which includes a dedicated 12-bed inpatient unit; outpatient assessment, offering dementia screening and short-term education; referral information; and preventive health programs. All high-risk elderly clients are screened to assess their health needs, and support services are provided to prevent further acute episodes and unnecessary hospitalization.

Uniquely, United offers the Pain Management and Spine Care Center, which is a multidisciplinary approach to treating chronic pain. The center includes some of the most noted doctors in pain management who view chronic pain as a disease, worthy of extensive evaluation and intervention. Patients receive a customized plan of diagnosis and treatment which draws on the most advanced therapies in an outpatient setting.

United Hospital is a premier center for rehabilitative services, including inpatient and outpatient cardiac and pulmonary rehabilitation, physical and occupational therapy, and speech and language pathology. These services help individuals of all ages return to healthier living.

Founded by volunteers, United Hospital Medical Center's existence today as a vital community health resource is a tribute to the ongoing spirit of volunteerism and the sustained generosity of many friends. Today over 600 volunteers give unstintingly of their time (seven days a week, from 8:00 A.M. to 9:00 P.M.), energy, and expertise to 75 services throughout the hospital, as well as home care, hospice, and AIDS care. They have also provided leadership and support for numerous fund-raising parties and events, including the Buick Classic Golf Tournament and Mayfair, an annual community fair that raises funds for special projects and provides involvement to interested groups for interaction with the hospital family. Over several generations, the hospital's Twig Organization has raised millions of dollars for renovations and equipment.

With its strong infrastructure, highly skilled medical and administrative team, and dedicated corps of friends and volunteers, United Hospital Medical Center is well prepared to serve its community and meet the challenges of health care in the twenty-first century. ◆

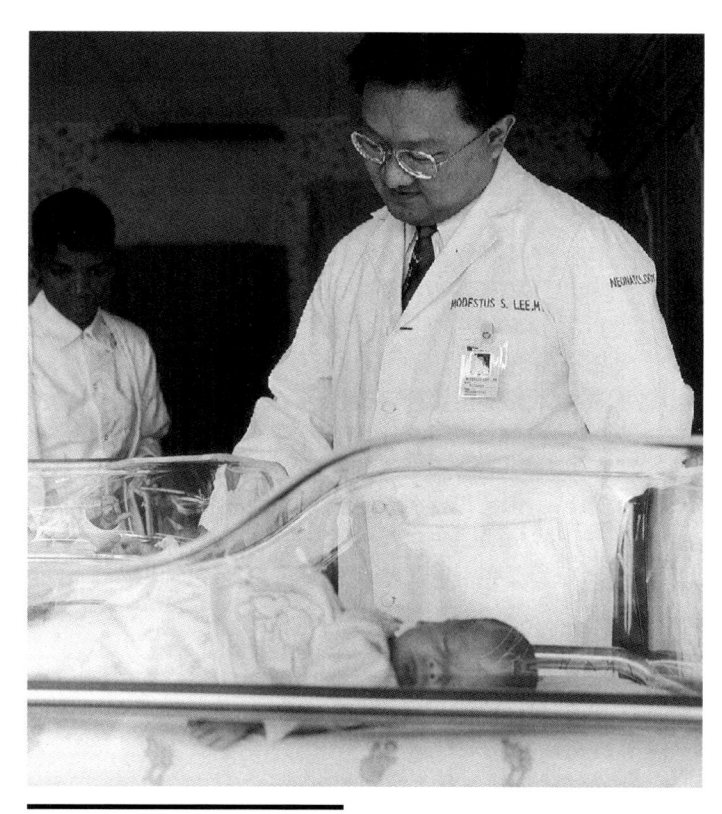

Dr. Modestus Lee, director of neonatology at United Hospital Medical Center, looks in on the quadruplets, who were born prematurely. *Photo by Jules Alexander.*

Volunteer Pat McKernan of Rye conducts arts and crafts activities with Mary Rock *(front)* and Virginia Tortensen *(inside)*. The women are residents in United Hospital's Skilled Nursing Pavilion. *Photo by Jules Alexander.*

HEALTH CARE

SOUND SHORE MEDICAL CENTER OF WESTCHESTER

Sound Shore Medical Center of Westchester, formerly known as New Rochelle Hospital Medical Center, is prepared to meet the challenges of a complex health care industry.

"This industry is very competitive," said John Spicer, president. "But the sophisticated clinical services and affiliations we've developed distinguish this Medical Center from others in the county. We are the largest private teaching hospital in Westchester, a regional Medical Center that provides high quality health care for every member of the family."

Founded in 1892, the Medical Center today includes a 315-bed acute care hospital, a 150-bed extended care pavilion, comprehensive primary and subspecialty outpatient services, one of the largest and busiest emergency departments in the county, and a range of diagnostic services and support groups. Over 70,000 people are served by the Medical Center annually. It employs 1,200 people; 80 percent live in the Sound Shore region. As a major teaching affiliate of New York Medical College, the Medical Center offers residency training programs in the departments of medicine, surgery, anesthesiology, pathology, and pediatrics. The medical staff includes over 500 physicians and dentists, representing 30 clinical specialties.

The Medical Center is also a major affiliate of Westchester County Medical Center and a member of the Westchester Health Services Network.

The Department of Medicine includes a 12-bed medical/surgical intensive care unit, a coronary care unit, renal dialysis treatment unit, a newly renovated and expanded hematology/oncology service, and a diabetic treatment unit, fully accredited and recognized for excellence by the American Diabetes Association. Known for the expert care provided, the divisions of cardiology and gastroenterology treat more patients than any other private hospital in the county.

In addition to inpatient services for adults, the Medical Center has developed a range of programs for seniors. The Geriatric Institute includes a 32-bed inpatient unit staffed by geriatricians and geriatric nurses who care for acutely ill patients over age 70. The Geriatric Clinic offers primary care and specialty services to older patients; satellite clinics in senior housing complexes have also been established. Older people who have experienced memory loss are evaluated and treated in the Dementia Treatment Center.

The Adult Day Health Care Program provides a range of recreational, social, and rehabilitation activities, medical, nursing, and dental care to 30 frail adults. Open weekdays, the program offers a viable alternative to nursing home placement. Meals and transportation are also provided.

The Medical Center also includes a 150-bed extended care facility and works closely with other nursing homes in Westchester.

The Health Access Program provides insurance counseling, health information and education programs, social activities, and other services to people over age 55.

"Southern Westchester has a very large population of older adults," Spicer said. "We are dedicated to meeting the needs of seniors, and have committed significant resources to developing this comprehensive range of both clinical and support services."

Sound Shore Medical Center of Westchester has also devoted major resources to expanding its clinical services for women and children.

Sound Shore Medical Center of Westchester (formerly New Rochelle Hospital Medical Center). The largest private teaching hospital in Westchester County provides comprehensive health care to over 70,000 residents of the Sound Shore region.

HEALTH CARE

The Department of Obstetrics and Gynecology includes a newly renovated patient unit and expanded nursery, where deliveries have increased to over 1,300 annually. The department also features the only Antepartum Testing Laboratory in the county, where women with "high-risk" pregnancies are evaluated and treated by a specialist in maternal/fetal medicine. Ongoing educational programs and support groups are provided for expectant and new mothers.

Women who deliver their babies at Sound Shore Medical Center can be assured that the most sophisticated technology and trained clinicians are available. Staffed by two full-time neonatologists and neonatal nurses, the Level II Nursery serves low birth weight, premature, or newborns with medical problems.

The Department of Pediatrics provides a range of inpatient and outpatient services to infants, children, and adolescents. In conjunction with New York Medical College, the Pediatric and Adolescent Subspecialty Center offers comprehensive diagnostic and outpatient care for youngsters with illnesses ranging from heart disease, cancer, or anemia, to asthma, growth, or learning problems.

The Regional Lead Evaluation and Treatment Center provides services to prevent, diagnose, and treat lead poisoning in children. It serves children and families in seven counties in the Hudson Valley region and also includes a Lead Safe House, a safe housing alternative for families while their homes are undergoing lead abatement.

The lobby of the Suren and Virginia Fesjian Ambulatory Surgery Pavilion at Sound Shore Medical Center of Westchester. Over 6,000 ambulatory or same day surgery procedures are performed annually at this center—a volume of service exceeding that of any private hospital in Westchester County.

"Our Pediatric Training Program is another unique and innovative aspect of the Medical Center," Spicer said. "Pediatric residents are here around the clock daily. Parents can be secure in the knowledge that doctors are always available to care for their children. This range of pediatric services has established the Medical Center as the regional center for pediatric care."

The Department of Surgery includes the divisions of general, laparoscopic, urology, trauma, colon and rectal, and neurosurgery. Surgeons at the Medical Center are recognized as the leaders in the tristate region in providing laparoscopic or minimally invasive surgery, particularly for treating gall bladder disease, endometriosis, and diseases of the uterus. Over 6,000 minimally invasive or same-day surgery procedures are performed annually. "We are at the forefront of laparoscopic surgery," Spicer said. "Our surgeons have performed more laparoscopic procedures here than any other institution in Westchester."

The recently renovated Emergency Department includes three new treatment rooms, an expanded evaluation area, and provides care to 32,000 patients annually. A trauma team provides immediate, often life-saving care to patients who have sustained major injuries or multisystem trauma. A separate evaluation and treatment area, staffed by pediatricians and pediatric nurses, is designated for children.

The most sophisticated diagnostic services are available in the Radiology Department, including diagnostic radiology, nuclear medicine, CT and MRI scans, EEG and EKG, stereotactic breast biopsy, and stress testing.

In addition to the inpatient clinical programs, the Medical Center serves approximately 35,000 patients annually through its outpatient programs. The Home Health Care Agency provides skilled nursing care to homebound patients throughout Westchester, recording over 40,000 visits in 1995.

Scheduled to open in 1997, the Gladys and Murray Goldstein Comprehensive Cancer Center will be a state-of-the-art facility that will offer a full range of diagnostic and treatment services to people with cancer, as well as providing education and support groups. The Center will also house a cancer research and resource library.

"In an era when most hospitals are either reducing or eliminating services, no other hospital in this region can point to such significant growth in clinical services and the development of major new health care initiatives," Spicer said. "Sound Shore Medical Center of Westchester is the health care resource for the Sound Shore region and southern Westchester." ◆

Westchester County: New York's Golden Apple / 199

HEALTH CARE

ST. JOHN'S RIVERSIDE HOSPITAL

St. John's Riverside Hospital in Yonkers prides itself on providing the highest level of care while treating each patient with dignity, respect, and compassion.

"The health care delivery at St. John's is wonderful and unique, and it goes beyond our sophisticated equipment," said Jim Foy, president and CEO. "Through patient surveys, our nurses are always rated 'the best.' They really do care, and they show that care to each patient."

St. John's roots date back to 1869, when a committee of women from St. John's Episcopal Church opened an invalid home to care for the poor. St. John's became the first hospital in Westchester, and later moved to the Grove House to accommodate 30 beds. With the addition of buildings on Ashburton Avenue donated by William and Eva Cochran in 1894, capacity increased to 100 beds, and the Cochran School of Nursing was also established. In 1930 a six-story wing was established on Palisade Avenue, bringing to 237 the number of beds.

St. John's moved to its present 14-story facility on North Broadway in 1963, when it was dedicated as the Andrus Pavilion in honor of its benefactor, the Andrus family.

Today, St. John's is a 273-bed, full-service, nonprofit, acute-care hospital with state-of-the-art medical technology. It has one of the most advanced radiology departments available, and offers progressive services such as cardiac rehabilitation, minimally invasive surgery, a 24-hour emergency care center, a dedicated pediatric unit, and a wound care center. St. John's, the only maternity service provider in Yonkers, has recently completed renovations and now offers modern labor, delivery, and recovery suites and a wide variety of educational programs for expectant parents. Advanced lab testing, physical rehabilitation, and respiratory therapy are also available.

To deliver care more efficiently and effectively, St. John's focuses on "Performance Improvement," in which medical staff members work together to monitor, assess, evaluate, and improve the performance of care. As part of this process, St. John's implemented "Clinical Paths," in which an interdisciplinary team will look at a patient's diagnosis and together examine ways to provide the most cost-effective, quality treatments.

In addition, St. John's sponsors free health screenings and provides health promotion programs, support groups, physician referral, childbirth classes, and community outreach services. For its senior community, St. John's offers a number of programs including the Healthline Transportation Service and Supper for Seniors Program. ◆

A special welcome greeted one of the first arrivals of St. John's new labor, delivery, and recovery suites. St. John's, the only provider of maternity services in Yonkers, recently renovated its maternity unit. Now new moms, dads, and babies receive top-quality, personal attention from board-certified professionals using the latest technology in a warm, comfortable, home-like setting.

SAINT JOSEPH'S MEDICAL CENTER

With innovative and comprehensive programs and services, Saint Joseph's Medical Center in Yonkers is a valuable resource for quality health care in southern Westchester.

Founded by the Sisters of Charity in 1888, Saint Joseph's is a progressive full-service medical center combining advanced technology with a tradition of caring, teaching, and concern.

Saint Joseph's has particular strengths in primary care, geriatrics, mental health, surgery, renal dialysis, cardiology, and cancer care, among others. A sophisticated bone marrow transplant program and affiliation with a nearby linear accelerator make Saint Joseph's a growing center for primary cancer care.

As the result of a major building and modernization program started in 1979, Saint Joseph's includes a 194-bed acute care hospital, a 200-bed nursing home with a specialized Alzheimer's Unit, and a wide range of outpatient programs, including its state-of-the-art Thomas and Agnes Carvel Foundation Family Health Center, busy emergency room, urgent care centers, long-term home health care, geriatric day care, hearing aid dispensary, and Children's Evaluation and Rehabilitation Center. A Birthing Center is scheduled to open in the spring of 1997.

The hospital's 26-bed inpatient psychiatric unit is augmented by several outpatient programs, including court assistance for victims of domestic violence. A pastoral care department and patient representatives are available for needed emotional and spiritual support.

Saint Joseph's has earned a

200 / Westchester County: New York's Golden Apple

HEALTHCARE

reputation for skilled and compassionate health care. Its staff includes more than 250 respected physicians in every medical specialty and an outstanding professional staff.

A teaching hospital, Saint Joseph's is committed to health education with free screenings, an active Speaker's Bureau, publications and participation in community health initiatives in partnership with other agencies, such as schools, churches, and community and civic organizations. Saint Joseph's Family Practice Residency Program, which is the only Family Practice Residency in Westchester, is affiliated with New York Medical College.

Located on South Broadway, just north of the Riverdale border, Saint Joseph's has a long history of serving the needs of Yonkers and its surrounding communities and will continue to adapt to the rapidly changing world of health care to assure its patients both of advanced technology and advanced care. ◆

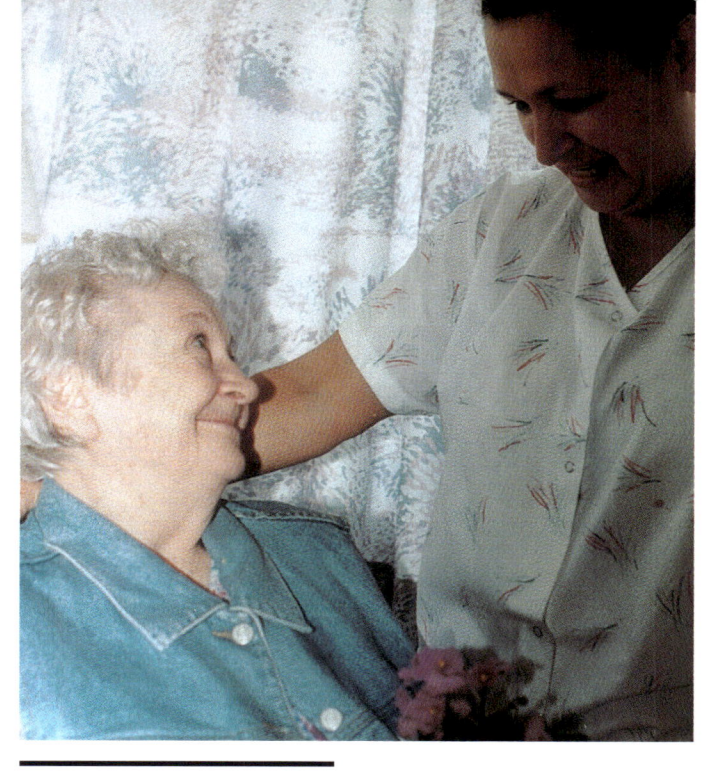

Saint Joseph's leadership in providing a "continuum of care" for the elderly includes a specialized unit for geriatric patients in the hospital, a 200-bed nursing home with a dedicated Alzheimer's Disease unit, Long-Term Home Health Care Program, Geriatric Day Care Program, and a growing number of geriatric specialists on its medical staff.

YONKERS GENERAL HOSPITAL

Since its founding more than a century ago in 1891, Yonkers General Hospital has focused on serving the health care needs of area residents. And while technology and treatment capabilities have changed to meet modern-day demands, the hospital's mission remains the same.

A voluntary, not-for-profit corporation, Yonkers General is a 190-bed, acute-care community health and medical facility with a staff of 700 who provide quality outpatient and inpatient medical and health care without regard to race, creed, color, national origin, or source of payment.

"Yonkers General's staff is committed to addressing the health care needs of the community it serves, and we pride ourselves in providing quality health care for all individuals," said Tibisay A. Guzman, associate administrator & COO for Yonkers General.

Yonkers General has joined with St. John's to expand services and reduce health care costs in Yonkers. The affiliation will insure the viability of both hospitals in this competitive market.

Today, Yonkers General provides a full range of services, including complete 24-hour emergency medical care, comprehensive oncology program, vascular and angioplasty center, complete ambulatory surgical services and respiratory therapy department, an orthognathic surgical unit, corporate employee assistance program/occupational medicine, blood bank/donor program, microsurgical eye unit and laser center, and an A.C.T.I.O.N. (Alcohol and Chemical Treatment in Our Neighborhood) Unit.

In 1995 Yonkers General Hospital opened Park Central Sports Medicine and Therapy Center, located on Central Park Avenue, in order to provide these services at a new and convenient location.

Yonkers General Hospital, celebrating 100 years of dedication to the health care of the community, has spent the past year recognizing the achievements and excellence of its staff. Shown here are respiratory therapists preparing to meet members of the public during Respiratory Therapy Appreciation Week.

Yonkers General places great emphasis on providing primary care and outpatient specialty medical services to adults and their families. The primary care center provides medical care including physical exams and medical assessment, health promotion and disease prevention education, and health-related counseling. The pediatric clinic also offers primary medical care to children including well-baby care, regular examinations, immunizations, and asthma services.

The hospital provides alcohol and substance abuse services, including Westchester's first methadone maintenance program, founded in 1967; inpatient detoxification and rehabilitation unit; alcoholism outpatient clinics in many area communities plus four homeless facilities in Westchester; and an alcohol crisis center. The hospital also offers an outpatient program for mentally ill chemical abusers. ◆

Westchester County: New York's Golden Apple / 201

HEALTH CARE

NORTHERN WESTCHESTER HOSPITAL CENTER

Northern Westchester Hospital Center in Mount Kisco is one of the region's premier health care providers, serving northern Westchester and the surrounding area for more than 80 years. Through investments in people, quality service, technology, and education, NWHC is committed to keeping its community healthy.

As part of its mission to provide quality health care that is accessible for members of the community, NWHC offers special programs for individuals who might not receive care because of financial limitations. In fact, the hospital provides almost $2 million in uncompensated care each year. In addition, NWHC offers a variety of screenings and programs, which detect disease, educate, and promote optimal wellness.

NWHC is also a member of the HealthStar Network, which was developed to address the dramatic changes underway in the current health care environment. HealthStar Network serves as a vehicle for contracting with managed care organizations, developing state-of-the-art information systems and achieving operating efficiencies, and, enables participating hospitals to share resources in a way that will enhance their delivery of high quality health care services.

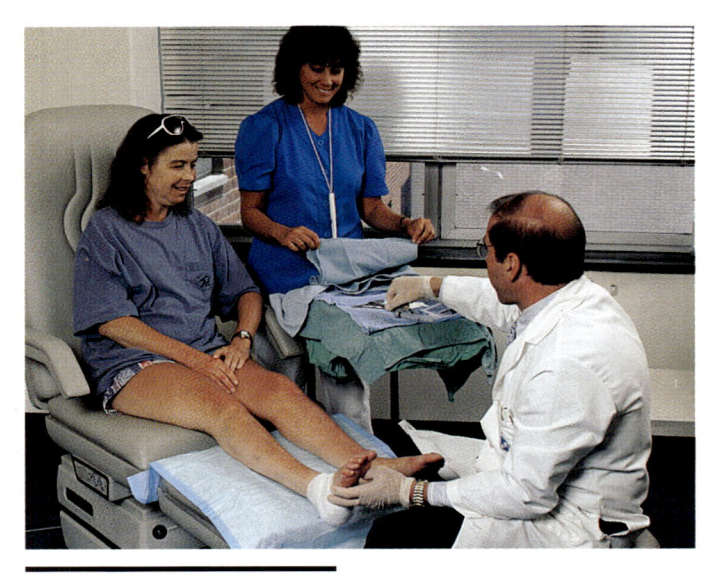

NWHC opened on Stewart Place in 1916. The facility, a converted wooden frame house purchased for $25,000, had 15 beds—12 of which were filled within the first week. In 1920, in response to the community's increasing health care demands, the hospital purchased the former Joseph Moore property at the corner of East Main Street and Moore Avenue—its current site today. Five years later, the hospital opened a 50-bed facility. In the ensuing years, as the community continued to grow, the hospital responded—adding to its number of beds, expanding its facility, and increasing its health care services.

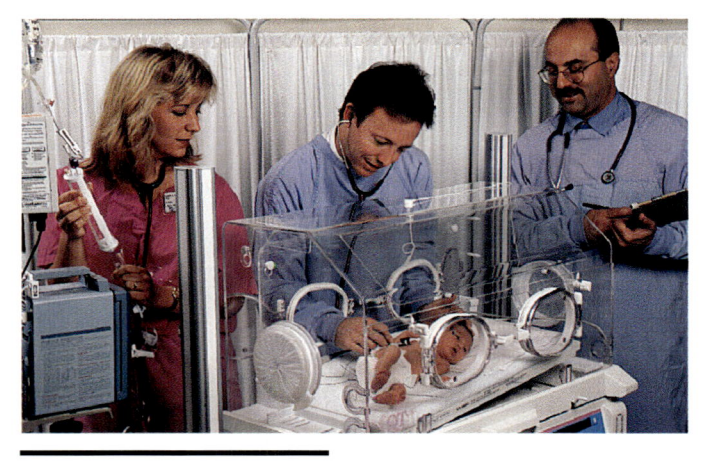

Today, NWHC is a 259-bed facility, with approximately 900 employees and a medical staff of more than 300 physicians practicing primary care and most clinical specialties. The hospital provides a full range of inpatient diagnostic and treatment services in medicine, surgery, obstetrics, pediatrics, and mental health. The hospital also offers comprehensive emergency services and a wide range of outpatient and ambulatory services.

The hospital's medical and surgical capabilities include modern laser and laparoscopic techniques, ambulatory surgery, rehabilitation services, a specialized nuclear cardiology department, plastic and reconstructive surgery, neurosurgery, and orthopedic surgery.

In 1995 NWHC invested $3.2 million to purchase new technology, replace existing equipment, provide computerization, and improve the facility's physical structure, including the addition of a 2,000 square foot Magnetic Resonance Imaging Suite. The new suite offers an MRI unit, the Seimen's Vision, that can perform a variety of applications and produce images of high resolution. In addition, a new Spiral CT Scanner provides faster, clearer images and enables NWHC to offer patients the latest diagnostic medical imaging services. NWHC also offers Interventional Radiology, which uses traditional diagnostic imaging techniques (x-rays, CT Scan, and ultrasound) to perform minimally invasive procedures including angioplasty and biopsies.

NWHC's emergency department is staffed by nurses and physicians experienced in emergency medicine, and treats over 19,000 patients per year. The department provides a host of consulting services, including internal medicine, psychiatry, orthopedics, cardiology, neurology, and pediatrics.

At the Northern Westchester Wound Care Program, patients receive comprehensive medical care and management for chronic wounds, as well as individual counseling and ongoing education from trained professionals.

NWHC's Pulmonary Wellness and Fitness Center is under the medical direction of a board-certified physician and is staffed by registered respiratory specialists who provide a structured six-week program to teach participants how to manage respiratory difficulties and improve their quality of life.

The Northern Westchester Wound Care Program offers comprehensive treatment for chronic, hard-to-heal wounds, and is supported by a multidisciplinary team of physicians and health care specialists.

NWHC's Special Care Nursery provides care to more than 150 premature or sick infants each year. Two full-time neonatologists, along with staff trained in neonatal care, are available 24 hours a day.

HEALTH CARE

Northern Westchester Hospital Center in Mount Kisco has been serving northern Westchester and the surrounding area for more than 80 years.

To support the needs of an increasing number of young, growing families in their service area, NWHC offers a full continuum of maternal/child health programs and services. In 1992 NWHC was the first community hospital in Westchester to open a Neonatal Special Care Nursery. The Special Care Nursery is staffed 24 hours a day by neonatologists to provide immediate care for babies. The Nursery, certified by the State of New York as a 10-bed Level II Neonatal Unit, cares for complications experienced by newborns, particularly those born prematurely or with serious respiratory problems. NWHC's state-of-the-art labor, delivery and recovery rooms allow both mother and father to remain in one room during deliveries. Midwives are also on staff and provide an alternative birthing program. Also available is a Breast-feeding Resource Center, 24-hour Warm Line and various support groups for families.

NWHC also offers an on-site Prenatal Care Program for pregnant women in Westchester and Putnam Counties who might not receive services due to financial limitations. Eligible women receive comprehensive prenatal care from a team of professionals that includes a physician, nurse, social worker, and nutritionist.

For its corporate neighbors, NWHC offers an Occupational Health Services Department that provides businesses a continuum of care for occupational illnesses and injuries, from prevention through disability management and rehabilitation for their employees. The department also provides immunizations, drug tests, physicals, on-the-job-injury exams, wellness and education programs, and Department of Transportation exams.

NWHC also offers a variety of health education and wellness programs, including Lamaze and parenting classes, Totsaver (infant CPR), sibling tours, stress management, CPR, EMT classes, health screenings, diabetes support groups, and senior citizen activities. These programs are offered at the hospital and throughout the community, in the workplace, at schools and senior centers. Through NWHC's Speakers Bureau, health care professionals are available to give lectures on current health issues to local groups, businesses, and organizations. The hospital also participates in health fairs and other programs to create health awareness in the community.

Volunteers play an important role in enhancing the quality of care at NWHC. The Volunteer Corps is comprised of over 400 members of the community whose dedication is seen in virtually every area of the hospital, including transportation, patient visits, rehabilitation services, flower/newspaper/book delivery, and the visitor's desk.

The 300-member Women's Auxiliary organizes various fund-raising activities, including the hospital's annual Crystal Ball gala, which raises approximately $100,000 each year. In addition, the Auxiliary coordinates an annual Fashion Show, the Baby Photo Program, Tours for Tots, and the Gift Shop.

In addition, the Twig Organization has 200 members in 14 branches (individual Twig groups) from various towns in northern Westchester. The Twigs provide handmade items, ranging from patient tray favors for the holidays to stuffed animals and mammography gowns. Proceeds from the Twigs' Thriftree Shop, which sells new and used clothing, furniture, and jewelry, enable the Twigs to contribute approximately $100,000 to the hospital annually. ◆

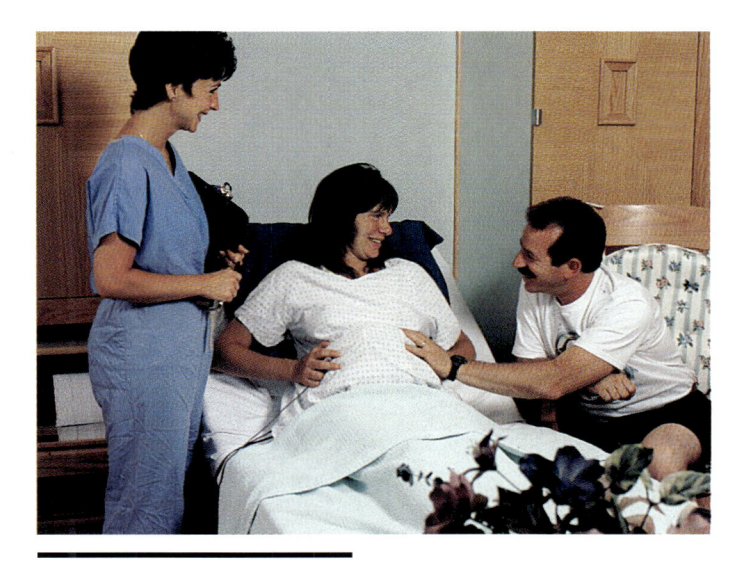

State-of-the-art labor, delivery, and recovery suites (LDRs) allow mother and father to remain in one room during every phase of their child's birth and offer a warm, home-like environment.

HEALTH CARE

THE BETHEL HOMES

The Bethel Homes is proud of providing quality care and stimulating activities for the elderly in a friendly, comfortable, and homelike environment. Its three homes (soon to be four) offer this care for over 500 persons.

"We are licensed by the state and federal government, so our standards don't change. However, how we deliver care sets us apart," said Chief Executive Officer and Executive Director Janet M. Beard. "We support a higher quality of care and provide everyone with the comforts of home."

The facility derived its name from John Wesley's ship, *Bethel*, which brought Swedish immigrants to America. The Bethel Swedish Methodist Episcopal Home for the Aged was authorized by the Swedish Methodist Conference in 1911 and opened in Brooklyn in 1914. In 1920 it was expanded and relocated to Ossining.

In 1959 the Bethel Methodist Home was constructed in Ossining, and in 1972 the Bethel Nursing Home was built. The Bethel Homes provide nursing care and assistance with daily living and coordinate rehabilitation, therapy, and other special care as needed.

Bethel emphasizes recreational activities, Miss Beard said. "This is wonderful therapy. When one of our residents first came to our nursing home after suffering a stroke, she asked: 'What reason do I have to live?'"

"We began working with her and discovered her painting talents. In fact, paintings she made here were exhibited in a big show in Albany. Now she wants to live and be an active member of society. That's our mission—to make the lives of our residents as fulfilling as possible."

The Bethel Springvale Inn is a retirement residence with 158 apartments, enabling active seniors to enjoy affordable, comfortable accommodations in a secure environment with stimulating activities and companionship. The caring staff helps arrange for doctors' visits, medication, and any other individual needs.

Construction is now in progress in Croton-on-Hudson for the Bethel Springvale Nursing Home, a $22-million skilled nursing facility. Adjacent to the Bethel Springvale Inn, the building has 40 private and 80 semiprivate rooms, recreation rooms, a courtyard, garden areas, and the Adult Day Health Care Center.

Bethel's staff of 250 includes physicians, nurse practitioners, nurses, social services, physical, occupational, and recreational therapists, support personnel, and volunteers. "Bethel has a profound economic impact on Westchester," Miss Beard said. "Our weekly payroll alone is over $100,000—most of which goes back into the community."

Bethel also provides outreach services to hundreds of seniors living alone or with their families. The programs include Lifeline, a personal emergency response system; Adult Day Health Care, a program in which specially equipped vans transport registrants from their homes to the Ossining campus during the week; and Long Term Home Health Care, a "nursing home without walls," in which Bethel's staff brings services into the homes of the 150 participating clients.

"One of the most important things we do is 'reach out,'" Miss Beard said. "These programs enable older folks to stay at home and receive the same care as our 'in house' residents. My community involvement design for the future is to expand our outreach services." ◆

Continued contact with family and friends is one of the most important aspects of life to residents, so Bethel encourages frequent visits, phone calls, and letters. Photo by Whitney Lane, 1996

Bethel believes quality of life, dignity, independence, and purpose are essential. Therefore, the Homes provide seniors with a host of stimulating recreational activities. Photo by Whitney Lane, 1996

Although Bethel was founded by and for Methodists, today it is a nonsectarian, nonprofit organization that does not discriminate on the basis of race, creed, color, age, national origin, sex, disability, marital status, blindness, sexual preference, or sponsorship in admission, retention, and care or access to treatment or employment in its programs or activities.

204 / Westchester County: New York's Golden Apple

Photo by Joe Vericker

CHAPTER · FOURTEEN

THE MARKETPLACE

Westchester's hospitality industries vitalize the economic life of the area.

RESIDENCE INN BY MARRIOTT
Page 208

DORAL ARROWWOOD
Page 212

RYE TOWN HILTON
Page 214

Photo by Joe Vericker

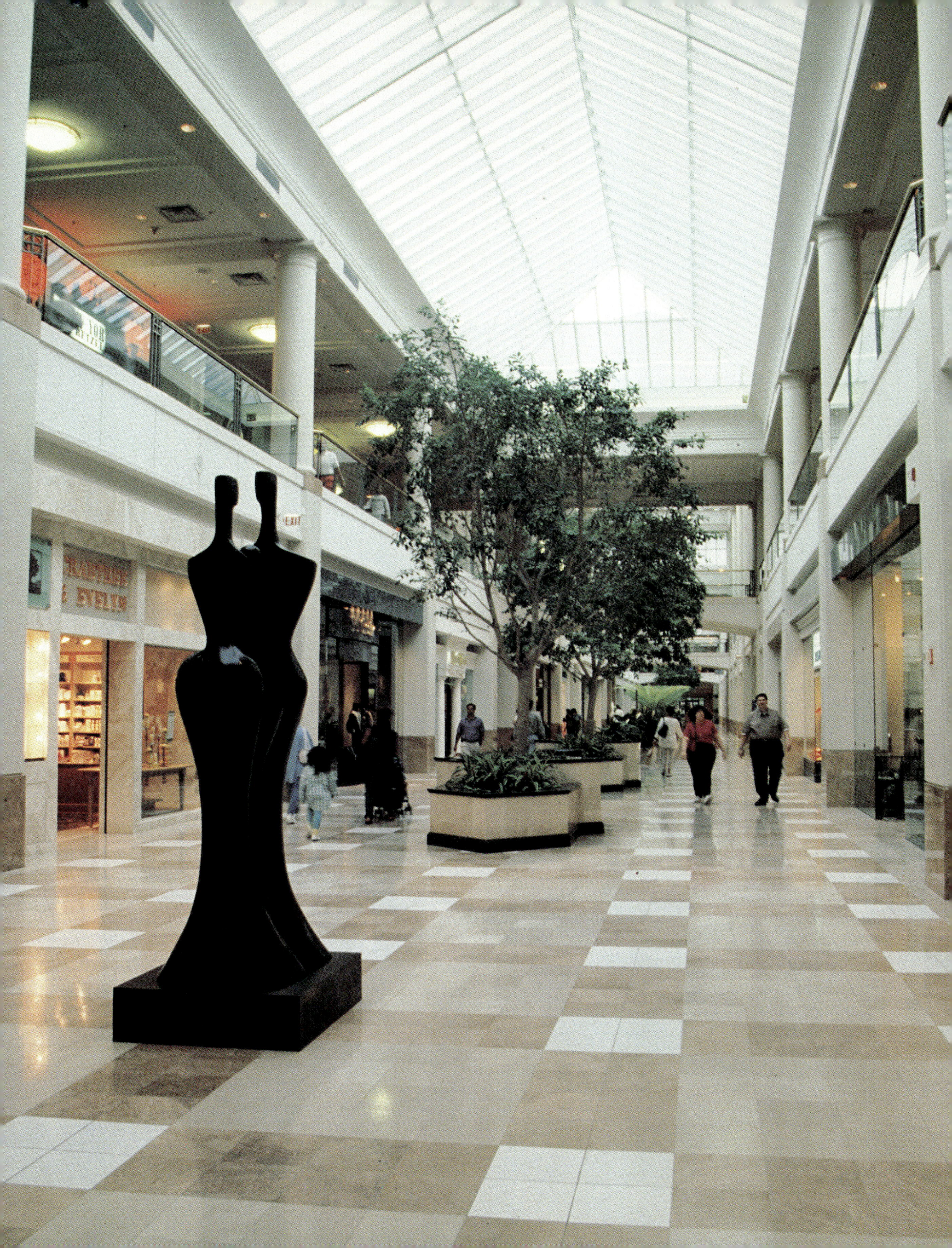

THE MARKETPLACE

RESIDENCE INN BY MARRIOTT

Residence Inn, the Marriott Corporation's newest hotel in Westchester County, officially opened for business on July 15, 1996, at Five Barker Avenue in White Plains, the site of the former La Reserve Hotel. Complementing Marriott's other hotel facilities in the county, Residence Inn offers 125 studio, one- and two-bedroom suites and a unique homelike ambience for extended-stay guests. The addition of an extended-stay hotel to Marriott's roster of county-based lodging products reflects the corporation's mission to meet the needs of every traveler coming to Westchester County.

Residence Inn has the distinction of being the only all-suite hotel in the county. Ranging in size from 700 to 2,200 square feet, each Residence Inn suite more fully resembles an apartment than a typical hotel accommodation. Separate living/dining and sleeping areas, beautifully appointed bathrooms, and fully equipped kitchens provide the comforts of home that encourage guests to settle in, whether they plan to stay a few days, several weeks or months, or much longer. Residence Inn attracts corporate executives relocating to Westchester, businessmen and women needing a temporary home base in the county, families who are remodeling homes or who are between homes, former Westchester homeowners returning for lengthy stays, and individuals simply seeking spacious accommodations as well as warm hospitality.

In keeping with Residence Inn's goal to be a "home away from home" for its guests, furnishings have been selected for their comfort as well as elegance. Every unit has multiple telephones, large-screen cable televisions (with HBO and premium channels), and computer data ports. User-friendly kitchens contain essential appliances, including a dishwasher, and are outfitted with dishes, silverware, glasses, and cooking utensils. For guest convenience, an iron and ironing board are also provided in every suite.

In addition to these exceptional accommodations, Residence Inn provides many hotel amenities as well as a number of very special value-added features that make guests feel truly welcomed and well cared for. Complimentary services include daily housekeeping,

The Westchester Residence Inn by Marriott offers a tranquil "home away from home" in an urban setting.

208 / Westchester County: New York's Golden Apple

THE MARKETPLACE

grocery shopping, and same-day dry cleaning service. Guest facilities include a covered parking garage; a fully equipped coin-operated laundry; and a spacious "family room" complete with fireplace, sofas, piano, television, library of books and video tapes, selection of games for kids of all ages (in a variety of languages) and round-the-clock availability of coffee, tea, and soft drinks. Health-conscious guests can take advantage of the hotel's well-equipped gym (Stairmasters,™ exercise bicycles, treadmills, universal equipment, and free weights). Residence Inn even welcomes family pets.

Complimentary continental breakfast is provided daily. An expansive buffet features assorted muffins, danish, and breads; french toast, waffles, and a variety of cereals; fresh fruit and yogurt; and a selection of juices, coffee, and tea—a perfect way for light or hearty eaters to start the day.

Four weekday evenings from 6:00 to 7:30 P.M., Residence Inn hosts a get-together for its guests. On Mondays, Tuesdays, and Thursdays, a variety of hors d'oeuvres and a selection of wine, beer, and soft drinks are served; Wednesday evenings feature a buffet dinner. These hospitality hours are designed to provide opportunities for hotel guests and staff to meet, get to know one another, and relax at the end of a busy day.

Christopher's Restaurant, adjacent to the hotel, offers moderately priced American-Italian cuisine at lunch and dinner. The restaurant also provides room service to Residence Inn guests. At lunch, Christopher's menu features a variety of sandwiches, salads, and light entrees. In the evening, its menu focuses on grilled chicken, fish, and steak dishes.

Residence Inn has three facilities available for business and social functions. Two small executive boardrooms on the ground floor accommodate between 15 and 40 people for meetings and presentations. On the 16th floor, a 2,200-square-foot Presidential Suite features panoramic views and an exquisite setting for the ultimate in gracious living and for hosting receptions for 50 to 100 people.

Centrally located in White Plains, the Residence Inn is accessible from any direction. It is two blocks from the White Plains train station and just a few minutes from the major

A fully-equipped kitchen in each suite enables guests to prepare meals as they would at home.

Hotel managers get acqauinted with guests at complimentary evening hospitality gatherings.

Westchester County: New York's Golden Apple / 209

THE MARKETPLACE

Daily housekeeping service ensures your arrival to a clean, comfortable home each evening.

highways of lower Westchester County, which provide convenient access to New York City as well as Fairfield County, Connecticut and Rockland County communities. This setting places the Inn within the neighborhood of over 30 *Fortune* 500 companies' headquarters and makes it the hotel of choice for many corporate executives and their families.

The first Residence Inn was built in Wichita, Kansas, in 1975 by Jack DeBoer and opened under the name of "The Residence." This product caught the attention of Robert Brock of the Brock Hotel Corporation, and in 1981, when he purchased the small chain, properties existed at Wichita Downtown, Wichita East, Denver South, and Tulsa, with planned openings for Houston Astrodome and Denver Downtown. By 1984 there were 31 Brock Residence Inn Hotels, and it was apparent that the product had found its niche in the market. With this in mind, Jack DeBoer created the Residence Inn Corporation and formed a joint venture with the Holiday Inn Corporation to purchase Brock Residence Inn from the Residence Inn Company. In 1987 the Marriott Corporation purchased the Residence Inn Company.

Although the Residence Inn product is relatively new to the area, there are over 200 Residence Inn hotels nationwide, located primarily in suburbs of major and smaller cities. Over the past several years, market research has consistently cited Residence Inn as having the highest rate of occupancy and highest level of guest satisfaction in the industry. These achievements reflect Marriott's commitment to the development and maintenance of quality hospitality products.

In addition to its extended-stay Residence Inns, Marriott offers business and leisure travelers a broad range of lodging choices. Marriott Hotels, Resorts, and Suites provide full-service luxury in more than 290 hotels around the world, including seven flagship JW Marriott hotels and over 100 vacation destinations that include 30 spectacular resorts.

Courtyard by Marriott is the hotel designed by business travelers for business travelers. Courtyard surrounds guests with all the conveniences that make business and pleasure travel easy. With over 250 locations worldwide, Courtyard provides the perfect base of operations for weekdays and weekends.

Marriott's answer to economy hotels is its chain of Fairfield Inns. With over 230 locations nationwide, budget-minded travelers enjoy bright, comfortable rooms, complimentary continental breakfast, and a host of thoughtful amenities and services.

Marriott also maintains Conference Centers in seven states and the District of Columbia, and Vacation Club Resorts in popular vacation destinations in the United States and Caribbean. Marriott Conference Centers are dedicated to meetings. Professionally trained conference coordinators, the latest in meeting and audiovisual technology, and the value of a complete meeting package are all combined in retreat locations that are convenient to major metropolitan areas. Each conference center offers a unique setting for group business or team building, and provides an environment that is consistently comfortable and productive.

The luxurious villas of Marriott Vacation Club Resorts accommodate four to ten persons (depending on villa size) in total comfort and offer great vacation values in great resort destinations. Most villas are two-bedroom, two-bath units with a fully equipped kitchen, living room, separate dining area, terrace, master bath whirlpool tub, color television, and video player. Many villas also include a fireplace and individual utility area with washer/dryer.

Within the hospitality and food industry, Marriott is recognized as the leading hotelier in the world. The Marriott Corporation is also renowned for the excellence of its staff training programs. The company's mandatory and ongoing quality assurance training produces employees who are exceptionally knowledgeable and dedicated to impeccable customer service. Moreover, the company's outstanding quality control guarantees that the highest standards of cleanliness are maintained throughout its vast worldwide network of accommodations. All of this serves as a beacon to business and leisure travelers, ensuring that they will choose Marriott time and time again, wherever they go. ◆

Photo by Joe Vericker

THE MARKETPLACE

DORAL ARROWWOOD

Doral Arrowwood maintains a simple philosophy: to provide state-of-the-art meeting facilities and resort amenities in a tranquil, elegant setting. Doral Arrowwood is a 318,000-square-foot resort conference center situated on 114 acres of trees, rolling hills, open meadows, and a four-acre pond, and is surrounded by a nine-hole golf course—the Blue Monster II.

The resort is conveniently located near several major highways and airports, and is 45 minutes from Manhattan and 20 minutes from Stamford, Connecticut. However, Doral Arrowwood's lush property makes guests feel far removed from the hustle and bustle of contemporary urban life.

"Doral Arrowwood specializes in accommodating corporate executives hosting and attending conferences," said Ed Burns, general manager. "We are renowned as a leading conference center by the International Association of Conference Centers. Doral Arrowwood continues to be a trendsetter for other conference facilities."

But he noted that the property also is a popular weekend resort, appealing to a wide variety of guests.

Those visiting Doral Arrowwood may avail themselves of an extensive array of sports and health fitness facilities, including indoor and outdoor heated swimming pools, Jacuzzi,™ racquetball and squash courts, indoor and outdoor tennis courts, massage therapy, and a wide variety of exercise equipment including Lifecycles,™ Stairmasters,™ and treadmills.

For executive travelers, Doral Arrowwood provides all the necessary guest accommodations and conference facilities under one roof. To ensure privacy and productivity, however, the conference facilities are situated in a separate wing under one roof and comprise 36 dedicated meeting rooms. These include a 7,154-square-foot divisible ballroom; a 170-seat state-of-the-art amphitheater; rooms to accommodate small group sessions; continuous coffee and refreshment breaks; an award-winning conference planning department; and a complete audiovisual center.

Other amenities include individual light, sound, and temperature controls; private registration areas; meeting rooms equipped with front and rear projection booths; and a telephone system that features two-line phones enabling three-way calling, simultaneous inbound and outbound voice, data, and fax session, voicemail, and cellular capabilities; not to mention state-of-the-art ISDN telecommunication capabilities.

Doral Arrowwood's comprehensive conference plan includes guest rooms, meals, continuous refreshment breaks, a full-time support team of conference managers, meeting rooms 24 hours per day, meeting supplies, audio and visual equipment, and use of the fitness and recreation facilities.

All meeting rooms are equipped with a range of audio and visual capabilities. An array of screen, projection, audio, control, video, and display systems includes an A/V Center equipped to record meetings and provide audio and visual cassettes within hours. Secretarial and administrative support services are available as well at the business center.

"We are on the cutting edge of technology," Burns said. "And we will continue providing our guests with the best conference facilities."

Doral Arrowwood is a member of the Interactive Conferencing Network, a national video-conferencing network based in select hotels and conference centers nationwide. The network offers a capability of instantaneously conducting interactive meetings at more than 65 sites throughout the country.

Also for executives, Doral Arrowwood offers Project Excel—an outdoor adventure-based program specifically tailored to each group that focuses on team building through problem-solving exercises and challenging ropes course activities. The program combines the elements of trust, risk, communications, and mutual support—all designed to improve individual and group performance.

Whether travelers visit Doral Arrowwood for business or pleasure, the resort offers an array of dining to satisfy everyone's taste.

The main dining room—the Atrium—seats 250 and serves buffets for breakfast and lunch. Dinner, in a relaxed setting, offers a wide variety of a la

The newly renovated Blue Monster II features mounds, moguls, and bunkers that turn every round of golf into a challenge. The Doral Arrowwood course also features a 25-tee driving range and a practice putting green so you can brush up your strokes—and bring down your handicap.

THE MARKETPLACE

If a few laps in Doral Arrowwood's indoor/outdoor pool don't take away the stress of the work week, then try a steam. A sauna. A massage. And what's your reward for working up an appetite? Your choice of four fabulous restaurants, all on the Doral Arrowwood grounds.

carte menu items and is highlighted by the "Saturday Night Candlelight Dinner Dances," and an extraordinary Sunday brunch.

Provare offers an extensive Italian trattoria-style menu which features fresh ingredients, an antipasto bar, and an authentic pizza oven.

For a more relaxed meal, guests may visit the Pub for snacks, burgers, salads, and sandwiches, and enjoy the fireplace and sports bar atmosphere with pool tables, dart boards, game tables, video games, and live sports events on multiple monitors and a large front-projection TV. Weekends offer dancing to music provided by the Pub's DJ.

At Mulligans, an outdoor bar and grill overlooking the ninth hole, guests may choose from salads, sandwiches, and grilled foods during the golf season.

And, for private dining, Doral Arrowwood offers the Teal and Pintail Rooms (seating 16 each), Essex and Sussex Rooms (seating 50 each), the Middlesex Room (seating 75), and the Ballroom (seating up to 500).

Room service also is available 24 hours per day.

Doral Arrowwood's 272 newly renovated guest rooms comprise a separate wing, providing privacy for travelers. Many rooms have balconies or private walk-out patios, and all offer a number of business amenities, including a study area with work desk, two-line telephone with voicemail and fax/modem dataport, a dictionary and thesaurus, and closed-circuit television.

The hotel was built by Citibank in 1983. In 1986 it was purchased by Carol Management Corp. and has since undergone multimillion-dollar renovations. Under the guidance of interior designer Mary T. MacDonald of Macci International Ltd. of East Hampton, all 272 guest rooms have been refurbished. Influenced in part by the culture of the American Indian and early English and Scottish settlers in the area, MacDonald's design provides the rooms with a dramatic new look. Green, maize, dark blue, and red are accompanied by a rich tartan plaid in new bedspreads and accent pillows. Tweed has been used in upholstery for guest room chairs and in the hunter green carpeting, and together with louvered wood paneled headboards and lighting fixtures of painted wrought iron, accentuate the new look.

The lobby, lobby lounge, front desk, and conference services area have been refurbished with new carpeting and furniture as well.

The Blue Monster II— a Robert von Hagge-designed 3,300-yard par 35 golf course— was reopened in June, 1992, following a $3-million renovation. The golf facilities also include a pro shop, a 25-tee driving range, a practice putting green and bunker, locker, and shower facilities. Doral Arrowwood's PGA professionals provide group and individual lessons.

"Doral Arrowwood's significant investments in technology and renovations are confirmation of its commitment to remain a premiere conference facility," Burns said. "Doral Arrowwood will continue to be a leader in the industry by keeping a competitive edge and maintaining a state-of-the-art executive conference center." ◆

How can Doral Arrowwood make your next conference more enjoyable and more productive? With 36 purpose-built meeting rooms, video conferencing, the latest in audiovisual support, and more.

Westchester County: New York's Golden Apple / 213

THE MARKETPLACE

RYE TOWN HILTON

The Rye Town Hilton in Rye Brook offers travelers the best of both worlds—the sophistication of a business-oriented conference center and the elegance of a country inn. Situated on 40 wooded acres, the Hilton's lush gardens and serene atmosphere belie its proximity to New York City.

"We're only 30 minutes from Manhattan, yet people consider us to be in the country," said Susan Marano, Director of Sales. "So companies can easily transport their people out of the busy city into a relaxed atmosphere more conducive to training." And the hotel offers corporate travelers all the means necessary to help them do just that.

The Hilton, which opened April 15, 1973, has 436 guest rooms and 18 suites which offer cable TV, two direct dial telephones with voice mail and call forwarding, on-command videos, personal coffee makers, refreshments centers, irons, ironing boards, hairdryers, computer data ports, radios, and valet laundry services.

Customers may choose from 35 meeting rooms—totaling 33,000 total square feet—to accommodate between 20 to 1,200 people. Each room is soundproof, and most offer terraces and natural lighting. The 9,570-square-foot Westchester Ballroom, 6,550- square-foot Grand Ballroom, and 2,400-square-foot Town of Rye Suite also are available. The hotel offers a complete meeting package (CMP) of one price per person for meals, meeting room, coffee breaks, and audio-visual needs.

The Business Center is professionally staffed and provides complete executive services and business support. It has three workstations complete with computers, with Internet access, and printers. Secretarial services, copiers, and facsimiles are also available. In addition, the hotel has secured an ISDN line which enables video teleconferencing anywhere in the hotel.

The Hilton also has invested in a Windows-based sales network—Insight—which links all its sales offices, Marano said. "This enables us to gain easy access to customer profiles and histories so we know what their preferences are and how to best accommodate their needs. By upgrading technology for our customers and ourselves, we're able to work smarter."

Whether their stay is for business or pleasure, the hotel offers an array of activities to help guests unwind. Travelers can relax by the indoor and outdoor pools, play year-round tennis, work out at the Fitness Center, or enjoy the Jacuzzi™, and saunas.

Also, the concierge will make arrangements for guests to avail themselves of nearby golf, horseback riding, beaches, historical sites, and shopping.

For dining and entertainment, there's Penfield's, four-star dining with American cuisine served in an elegant setting; The Tulip Tree, casual dining for breakfast, a la carte or buffet lunch, grilled dinner specialties, or Sunday brunch; or the Den Lounge, light dining with a connoisseur's selection of microbrews and imported beers, DJ entertainment, local sports, and news. Seasonally, the terrace is open for lunch to serve light, grilled specialties.

Attention to detail and commitment to excellence have paid off for the Hilton. "We're Westchester County's only AAA Four Diamond hotel," Marano said. "We've received this rating, which is based on the quality of our product and our service, for the last seven years." ◆

Guests of the Rye Town Hilton enjoy seasonal dining on the outdoor terrace.

The spacious and elegantly appointed Westchester Ballroom is one of the many amenities available to businesses at the Rye Town Hilton.

Bibliography

Bolton, Robert. *A Guide to New Rochelle and Its Vicinity.* Harrison, New York: Harbor Hill Books, 1976.

Carlson, Mary R. *Retail Trade in Westchester County, 1987-1992.* White Plains, New York: Department of Planning, 1993.

Cervone, Rose A. *Public and Private Partnership: A Formula for Success.* White Plains, New York: Westchester Department of Transportation, 1995.

Cirillo, Joan J. *The Westchester Book.* New York: Stein and Day, 1976.

Cushman, Elizabeth. *Glimpses of Historic Westchester, 1683-1933.* Tarrytown, New York: Village of Tarrytown, 1933.

Griffin, Ernest Freeland. *Westchester County and Its People: A Record.* New York: Lewis Historical Publishing Company, 1946.

Health and Human Services Directory for Westchester County. White Plains, New York: InfoBase Collaborative of Westchester, 1993.

Hufeland, Otto. *Westchester County During the American Revolution, 1775-1783.* Harrison, New York: Harbor Hill Books, 1982.

League of Women Voters. *This Is Scarsdale.* New York: League of Women Voters of New York State, 1984.

Lipkin, Michael L. *2020 Foresight: Population Projections for Westchester to the Year 2020.* White Plains, New York: Department of Planning, 1995.

Lokay, Janet E. *Be A Westchester Wizard: Discover the Magic of the Golden Apple.* White Plains, New York: Office of Tourism Information Center, 1994.

Morrissey, Regina, and Stephen H. Acunto. *Westchester County: The Golden Apple of New York. A Contemporary Portrait.* Chatsworth, California: Windsor Publications, 1990.

Newitt, Jane. *The Future of Westchester County.* Croton-on-Hudson, New York: Hudson Institute, 1979.

Shonnard, Frederic. *History of Westchester County.* 1900. Reprint, Harrison, New York: Harbor Hill Books, 1974.

Shoumatoff, Alex. *Westchester: Portrait of a County.* New York: Coward, McCann and Geoghegan, 1979.

Roeder, Mary Stein. *The Story of Present Day Westchester.* White Plains, New York: Westchester County Publications Committee, 1934.

Westchester County: A Guide to the Collections of Westchester County. Elmsford, New York: Westchester County Historical Society, 1989.

Westchester County and Its People: A Record. New York: Lewis Historical Publishing Company, 1976.

Westchester County Meeting Planner and Travel Guide. Supplement to *Westchester Commerce.* White Plains, New York: Westchester Convention and Visitors Bureau, Ltd., 1995.

Westchester County, New York. Wilmington, Delaware: Suburban Marketing Associates, Inc., 1994.

Westchester County: The Past Hundred Years. Harrison, New York: Westchester County Historical Society, 1984.

Westchester County's Major Employers: Private. White Plains, New York: Westchester County Association, 1982.

Wirth-Vogt, Toni. *Golden Apple Guide to Business and Livability.* White Plains, New York: The County Chamber of Commerce, 1989.

Yonkers Police Department Annual Report. Yonkers, New York: Yonkers Police Department, 1993.

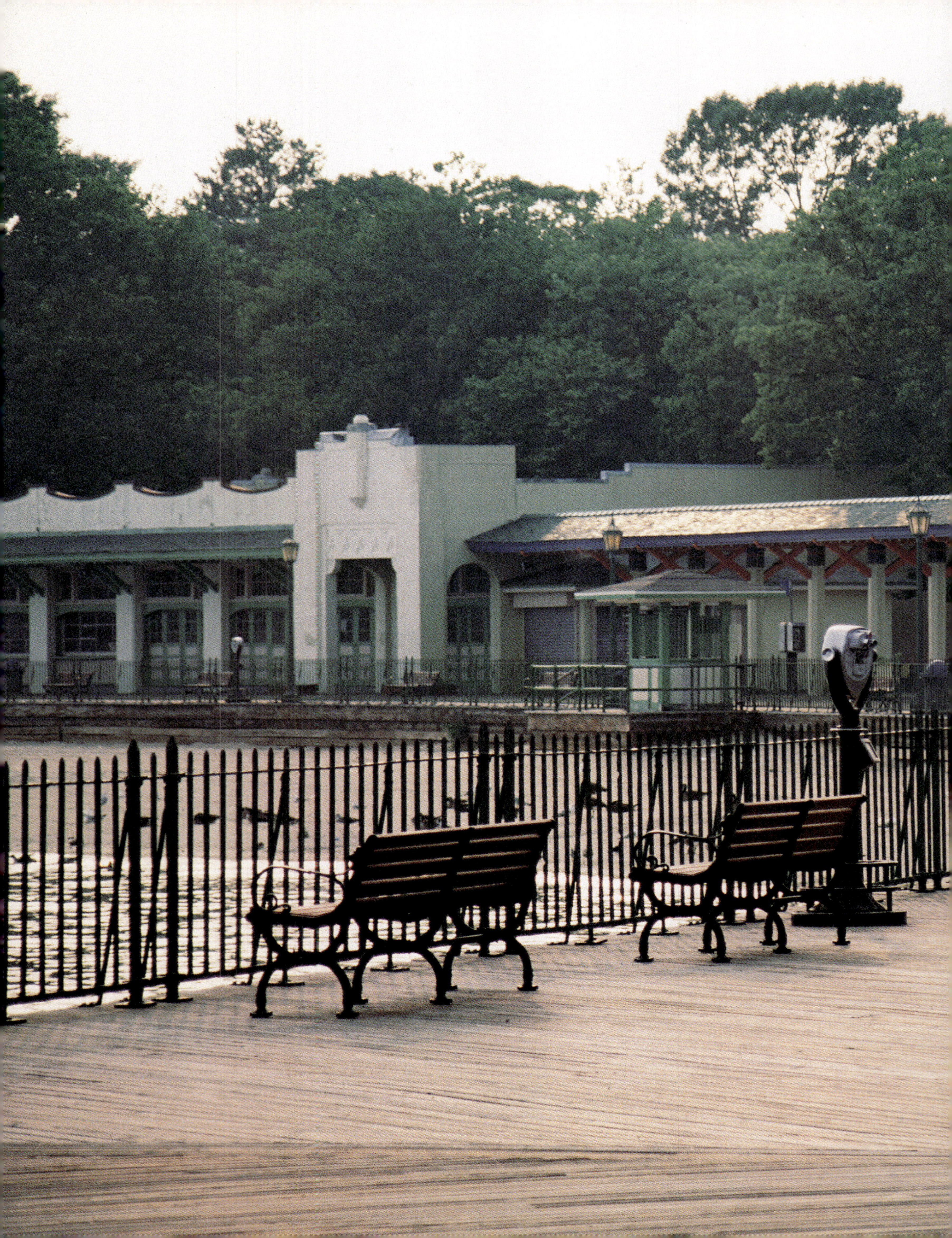

Photo by Joe Vericker

Enterprises Index

Bally, Inc., 154-155

Bayer's Business Group Diagnostics, 157

The Bethel Homes, 204

Bleakley Platt & Schmidt, 164-165

Collins Brothers Moving Corp., 142

The County Chamber of Commerce, Inc., 162-163

Doral Arrowwood, 212-213

Elmsford Sheet Metal Works, Inc., 158

Gannett Suburban Newspapers, 138

Heritage Hills of Westchester, 178-179

Hitachi Metals America, 148-149

IBM Corporation, 156

International Paper, 150-151

Iona College, 174-175

Iona Preparatory School, 183

J.F. Jelenko & Company, 146

Keio Academy of New York, 180-181

MasterCard International Incorporated, 169

The Masters School, 185

Mercy College, 176-177

Monroe College, 186

MTA Metro-North Railroad, 134-135

New York Power Authority, 139

Northern Westchester Hospital Center, 202-203

NYNEX Corporation, 140

Philips Research Briarcliff, 152-153

The Reader's Digest Association, Inc., 132-133

Residence Inn by Marriott, 208-210

Rye Town Hilton, 214

Saint Joseph's Medical Center, 200

Shamberg Marwell Hocherman Davis & Hollis, P.C., 170

Sound Shore Medical Center of Westchester, 198-199

St. John's Riverside Hospital, 200

Tarrytown House Executive Conference Center, 166-167

Tetko Inc, 159

Thacher Proffitt & Wood, 168

Transamerica Leasing, 130-131

United Hospital Medical Center, 196-197

The Ursuline School, 182

The Westchester Business Institute, 184

Westchester County Business Journal, 136-137

Westchester County Medical Center, 190-193

WFAS AM & FM, 141

White Plains Hospital Center, 194-195

Yonkers General Hospital, 201

INDEX

Ahquahung River, 24
airports, 16-18, 41, 67, 98, 101, 104-105
Alexander Smith & Sons, 31
American Demographics, 70
American Public Transit Association, 102-103
American Revolution, 28, 29, 32
Amtrak, 18, 102-103
Andre, John, 28
Andrus Planetarium, 58
Apple Computer, 40
Archbishop Stepinac High School, 74
Armonk, New York, 29, 38
Arnold, Benedict, 28
automobiles, steam-driven, 32

Bailey, Hachaliah, 29
Bally, Inc., 38, 154-155
banks, 45, 56
Battle of White Plains, 28, 53
Bayer's Business Group Diagnostics, 38, 157
Bear Mountain Bridge, 16
Bear Mountain State Park, 16
Bedford, New York, 24, 27, 29
Bee-Line Bus Service, 18, 98, 103
Berkeley College, 81
Bethel Homes, The, 94-95, 204
Birth of a Nation, 32
Bleakley Platt & Schmidt, 164-165
blacks, contributions to early industry, 31
Blessed Sacrament-Saint Gabriel High School, 74
Block, Adrien, 24
Block Island, New York, 24
Blue Mountain Reservation, 64
Blythedale Children's Hospital, 93, 95
Board of Cooperative Educational Services (BOCES), 76-77
Brewster, New York, 30-31
Briarcliff Manor, New York, 40, 65, 80
Bronck, Jonas, 24
Bronx, 16

Bronx River Parkway, 16, 18, 65, 99, 101
Bronx River Valley, 30
Bronxville, New York, 70, 78-79, 87, 101
Buchanan, New York, 32
Buick Open, 118
Burke Rehabilitation Hospital, 92
Burroughs Wellcome and Company, 32

Capitol Theater, 63
Caramoor, 63
carpet-weaving industry, 29
Catskill Mountains, 16
Chagall, Marc, 54
Chevrolet plant, 32
churches, 30, 112
circus, birthplace in America of, 29
City Island, New York, 24
Civil War, 30-31
Cochran School of Nursing, 84
College of New Rochelle, 77
Collins Brothers Moving Corp., 40, 142
Combe, Inc., 40
Common Sense, 28, 54
Community Hospital, 89, 91
commuters, 16, 98, 102
Concordia College, 79
condominiums, 114
conference centers, 52, 66-67
Connecticut, 16, 18, 24, 41, 101
Conrail, 105
Consolidated Edison Company, 45
construction, residential, 19
co-operative apartments, 114
copper mining, 29
County Chamber of Commerce, Inc., The, 46, 67, 162-163
courthouse, White Plains, 28
Cranberry Lake Preserve, 65
Crestwood (Yonkers), 101, 112
Crime in the United States 1993, 17
crime rate, 122

INDEX

Crosby, William, 27

Cross County Parkway, 101

Cross County Shopping Center, 41, 43

Cross River, New York, 56, 65

Cross Westchester Expressway (I-287), 99

Croton Aqueduct, 65

Croton Dam, 30

Croton-on-Hudson, New York, 28, 56, 95

Croton River, 28

Croton Turnpike, 29

Declaration of Independence, 28

Dobbs Ferry, New York, 74, 79, 91

Donald M. Kendall Sculpture Gardens, 50, 58

Doral Arrowwood, 212-213

dropout rate, 73

Dutch, early settlers, 24, 27, 29, 53

Dutch East India Company, 24

Dutchess County, New York, 88

Eastchester, New York, 64, 112-113, 118

education, 17-18, 69-81

E. J. Murray Ice Rink, 65

Elephant Hotel, 29

Elmsford, New York, 62

Elmsford Sheet Metal Works, Inc., 158

Emelin Theater, 63

employers, leading, 17

farming, 24, 27-29

Fisher Body Plant, 32

Fleetwood (Mount Vernon), 101, 112

Fordham University, 81

Fort Lee, 28

Fort Slocum, 32

Fort Washington, 28

freedom of the press, birthplace of concept, 19, 27, 53

freight transport, 105

French-American School of New York, 76

French and Indian War, 27

Fuji Photo USA, 40

fur trade, of early settlers, 24

Galleria, The, 43

Gannett Suburban Newspapers, 40, 138

George Washington's Headquarters, 53

German School, the, 76

Golden's Bridge, 31

golf, 17-19, 41, 52, 63, 65, 118-119

Good Counsel Academy, 74

Gould, Jay, 29, 56

Hackley School, the, 74

Hagan School of Business, 78

Half Moon, 24

Hamilton, Andrew, 27

Harlem Line, (railroad), 101

Harlem Railroad, 29

Harlem River, 24

Harrison, New York, 93, 95, 104

Hartsdale, New York, 26, 74, 101, 120

Harvey School, The, 74

Hastings-on-Hudson, New York, 118

Hawthorne, New York, 79

health care, general, 17, 41, 83, 86

health care, specialized, 84, 92-93

Health Maintenance Organizations (HMOs), 19, 84, 95

Heathcote, Caleb, 27

Heineken USA, 40

Henry Hudson Parkway, 101

Heritage Hills of Westchester, 114, 178-179

highways, 16-17, 41

Hitachi Metals America, 148-149

homes, single-family, 114

hospitals, 18, 32, 83-91, 95

hotels, 19, 30, 52, 66-67

housing, 19, 28-30, 32, 93-95, 110, 112, 114, 122

Hudson, Henry, 24, 101

INDEX

Hudson River, 16-18, 23-24, 28-33, 52, 55-58, 64, 74, 98-99, 101

Hudson River Museum, The, 24, 27-28, 30-33, 58

Hudson Valley Hospital Center, 88

Huguenots, 24-25

Hutchinson River Parkway, 101

IBM Corporation, 17, 32, 36, 38, 40, 84, 156

immigrants, 30

incentive programs, business, 48-49

Indian Point nuclear plant, 46

Indian Resource Center, 56

intermodal transportation center (New Rochelle), 44

International Paper, 40, 150-151

Interstate 87 (New York Thruway), 98-99

Interstate 95 (New England Thruway) 99, 101

Interstate 287 (Cross Westchester Expressway), 99

Interstate 684, 99, 101, 104

Iona College, 77-78, 174-175

Iona Preparatory School, 74-75, 183

Irish immigrants, 30

iron mining, 29, 31

Irving, Washington, 23-24, 29, 55-56

Italian immigrants, 30

Japanese community, 76

Jay, John, 28, 53

Jefferson Valley Mall, 43

Jewish immigrants, 30-31

J.F. Jelenko & Company, 146

John F. Kennedy High School, 74

John Jay Homestead, 28, 53

Katonah, New York, 28, 31, 53, 58, 60, 63, 74

Katonah Museum of Art, 58, 60

Keio Academy of New York, 76, 180-181

Kensico, New York, 29

Kensico Reservoir, 99

Kraft Foods, 38

Kykuit, 13, 52, 56-57

Larchmont, New York, 70, 76, 101, 118

Larchmont Race, 118

La Rochelle, France, 24-25

Lawrence Hospital, 87

Leisler, Jacob, 24-25

Life Savers Corporation, 32

Lighthouse, Inc., The, 93

Long Island, New York, 16, 18, 24, 28, 30-31, 52, 63-65, 81, 98-99, 116, 120

Long Island Sound, 16, 18, 24, 28, 30-31, 52, 63-64, 99, 116, 120

Long Island University, 81

Loral, 40

LPGA/JAL Big Apple Classic

Lyndhurst, 29, 56

Mamaroneck, New York, 24, 28-29, 31, 63, 101, 116

Manhattan, 16, 24, 29, 41, 45, 52, 65, 80, 102-103

Manhattanville College, 80

marble quarries, 30

Maria Regina High School, 74

Marymount College, 71, 80-81

mass transit system, 16, 41

MasterCard International Incorporated, 17, 40, 169

Masters School, The, 74, 185

Matisse, Henri, 54

MBIA, 40

Memorial Sloan-Kettering Cancer Center, 89

Men's U.S. Open, 64

Mercy College, 79, 81, 176-177

Merritt Parkway, 101

Metropolitan Transit Authority, (MTA), 99, 101-102

Mobile Company of America, 32

Mohican tribe, 24

Monroe College, 77, 186

Morris, Lewis, 27

Mountain Lakes Camp, 64

Mount Kisco, New York, 31

Mount Pleasant, New York, 30

Mount Vernon, New York, 27, 32, 44, 53, 64, 71, 86, 101, 112, 123

INDEX

Mount Vernon Hospital, 86

MTA Metro-North Railroad, 18, 99, 101-103, 120, 134-135

Multiple Listing Service, (MLS), 112, 114

Muscoot Farm Park, 63-64

Music Hall, the, 63

National Schools of Excellence, 73

Native Americans, 24, 27

neighborhoods, 112

Neuberger Museum of Art, the, 58, 61

New Castle, New York, 24, 70

New Haven Line, (railroad), 18, 101, 103

New York and Hudson Railroad, 29

New York and Northern Railroad, 30

New York Central, 30-31, 65

New York City, 16, 18, 28-31, 41, 44, 67, 70, 73, 79, 98-99, 101

New York Hospital/Cornell Medical Center, 87

New York Medical College, The, 19, 79, 86, 88

New York Port Authority, 106

New York Power Authority, 45-46, 139

New York Public Library, 30

New York Rangers, 65

New York State Department of Transportation, 98

New York State Electric and Gas, 45

New York State Regents Examinations, 73

New York Telephone, 32

New York Weekly Gazette, 27

New Jersey, 16, 41, 44, 65, 98, 101

New England, 28, 99

New Rochelle, New York, 24-25, 28-29, 31-32, 44, 54, 71, 73-74, 77-78, 85-86, 101-103, 110, 120

New Rochelle Center, 44

Northern Westchester Hospital Center, 89, 202-203

North Salem, New York, 28, 64

North Tarrytown, New York, 52-53, 56-57

NYNEX Corporation, 40, 140

occupational education, 77

Old Dutch Church, 53

Ossining, New York, 29, 95

Otis Elevator Company, 31

Pace University, 79-80

Paramount Center for the Arts, 62-63

parkland, 65, 118

Peekskill, New York, 29, 31, 63-65, 88, 102

Pelham, New York, 24, 29, 32, 101

Pell, Thomas, 24

PepsiCo, Inc., 17, 32, 38, 58, 124

PGA Buick Classic, 64

PGA Championship, 64

Phelps Memorial Hospital Center, 89

Philip Morris International, 17, 38

Philipsburg Manor, 27, 53

Philipse, Frederick, 24, 26-27, 56

Philipse Manor Hall, 24, 56

Philips Research Briarcliff, 152-153

Playland Amusement Park, 63, 122

Playland Ice Casino, 64

Pleasantville, New York, 29, 36, 80

Pocantico Hills, New York, 54, 71

Polytechnic University's Westchester Center, 79

Port Chester, New York, 29, 32-33, 63, 101

P.R. Malloy and Company, Inc., 32

Prodigy, 40

property values, 110

Provincial Congress, 28

Purchase, New York, 24, 38, 50, 58, 61, 63, 76, 80-81

Purchase College, 58, 61, 63, 81

Putnam County, New York, 16, 88, 99, 103

Queen City, 32

rail freight, 105

railroads, 18, 29-32, 56, 65, 98, 101-102

Reader's Digest Association, Inc., The, 17, 36, 132-133

real estate, commercial, 36, 44, 66

real estate, residential, 110-114

recreation, outdoor, 18-19

recreational activities, 17, 113-114

INDEX

rental costs, commercial, 44

Residence Inn by Marriott, 208-210

restaurants, 19, 62, 117

retailing, 19, 41, 43

Ridgeway (White Plains), 112

roadways, 16, 98-101

Rockefeller, John D., 56-57

Rockland County, New York, 16, 88

Rye, New York, 24, 38, 44, 63-64, 67, 74, 95, 99, 101, 122, 126

Rye Beach, 24

Rye Brook, New York, 38

Rye Country Day School, 74

Rye Town Hilton, 214

sailing, 18-19, 118, 120

Saint Joseph's Medical Center, 90-91, 200

Salem, New York, 28-29, 64

Salesian High School, 74

Sanitas Fabric Wall Covering Company, 32

Sarah Lawrence College, 78

Saunders Trades High School, 76

Saw Mill River, 30

Saw Mill River Parkway, 99, 101

Scarborough, New York, 24

Scarsdale, New York, 70, 101

Scarsdale Manor, 27

School of the Holy Child, 74

schools, parochial, 74

schools, public, 18, 29, 71, 73

service economy, 49

Shamberg Marwell Hocherman Davis & Hollis, P.C., 170

shoemaking industry, 29

shopping, 19, 32, 41, 43, 52

silver mines, 29

Siwanoy tribe, 24

skiing, cross-country, 18-19, 65

Sleepy Hollow, 27, 56

Smithsonian, The, 30

Solomon Schecter Day School, 76

Somers, New York, 29, 38, 63-64, 74, 114

Sound Shore Medical Center of Westchester, 86, 198-199

sports, professional, 65

stagecoach travel, 27, 29

St. Agnes Hospital, 88

St. Andrew's (golf course), 118

steamboats, 29

St. John's Riverside Hospital, 84, 86, 90, 200

St. Patrick's Cathedral, 30

St. Paul's Church, 27, 53

St. Paul's Church and Bill of Rights Museum, 53

St. Vincent's Hospital, 93

Student Assessment Tests (SATs), 73

Sound Shore Medical Center of Westchester, 198-199

suburbanization, of county, 32

Sunnyside, 29, 55

SUNY-Westchester Community College, 80

support services, business, 45

Swiss Re, 40

Taconic State Parkway, 99

Tambrands, 40

Tappan Zee Bridge, 16-17, 98-99, 101, 107

Tarrytown, New York, 23, 27-29, 32, 38, 44, 52-53, 55-57, 63, 66, 71, 74, 80, 107

Tarrytown House Executive Conference Center, 44, 66, 166-167

taxes, 47-48

Terry, Paul, 32

Tetko Inc, 40, 159

Texaco, 17, 32, 38

Thacher Proffitt & Wood, 168

theaters, 52, 62-63, 71, 78, 81

Thomas Paine Cottage and Museum, 28, 54

Throg's Neck, New York, 24

timber resources, 27

toll roads, 29

tourism, 67, 77, 80

townhouses, 114

Transamerica Leasing, 40, 130-131

INDEX

transit system, public, 101

transportation, 17-18, 28-29, 32, 35, 44, 49, 66, 97-99, 101-103, 105-106

Tuckahoe, New York, 30, 32, 101

Twin Lakes, the, 64

Uniform Crime Reports, 17

Union Church, The, 54

Unionville, New York, 29

United Hospital Medical Center, 87, 196-197

United States Military Academy, (West Point), 16, 56

Ursuline School, The, 74-75, 182

U.S. Shipbuilding, 32

Valhalla, New York, 19, 79-80, 95

Van Cortlandt, Stephanus, 27

Van Cortlandt Manor, 27, 56

Verplanck's Point, 29

volunteerism, 122, 124

Wallace, Dewitt, and Lila Acheson, 36

Ward Motor Vehicle Company, 32

Ward Pound Ridge Reservation, 65

Washington, D.C., 18, 30, 102, 105

Washington, George, 24, 28, 53

Westchester, The, 43

Westchester Broadway Theater, 62

Westchester Convention & Visitors Bureau, Ltd., 67

Westchester County Airport, 18, 101, 104-105

Westchester County Business Journal, 136-137

Westchester County Department of Parks, 65

Westchester County Department of Public Safety, 122

Westchester County Department of Transportation, 18, 103

Westchester County Industrial Development Agency (WCIDA), 48

Westchester County Medical Center, 19, 83-85, 190-193

Westchester Hotels Association, 66

Westchester Lighting Company, 32

Westchester-Putnam Multiple Listing Service, Inc., 112

West Point, New York, 16, 28, 56

WFAS AM & FM, 141

White Plains, New York, 24, 27-29, 31, 38, 41, 43-44, 46, 53, 65, 70, 74, 76, 80-81, 86, 88, 92-93, 99, 101, 103-104, 112, 123

White Plains Hospital Center, 86, 194-195

Will Rogers Institute, 92

Wilson's Woods Park, 64

workforce, 16-18, 35-36, 41, 43, 76

World War II, 19, 32, 69

yacht clubs, 64

Yonkers, New York, 17, 24, 29-33, 41, 43, 47, 56, 58, 63, 65, 71, 76, 84, 86, 89-91, 99, 102, 112

Yonkers Electric Lighting and Power Company, 32

Yonkers General Hospital, 89, 201

Yonkers Raceway, 63

Yorktown Heights, New York, 43, 124

Yorktown High School, 118

Zenger, John Peter, 27, 53

This book was typeset in Goudy, Zapf Chancery, and Helvetica Narrow at Community Communications, Montgomery, Alabama.